'COPTER

CW00340942

Captain
J.A.T. 'Paddy' JONES

'Copter Pilot

George Mann *of* Maidstone

'COPTER PILOT
by Captain J.A.T. 'Paddy' Jones

© Copyright, Captain J.A.T. 'Paddy' Jones 2007

First published 2007

ISBN 0 7041 0415 6

Captain J.A.T. 'Paddy' Jones
has asserted his right under Section 77 of the
Copyright, Designs and Patents Act 1988
to be identified as the author of this book

Printed and bound on the Island of Malta, G.C.
by Gutenberg Press Ltd
and published by George Mann Books
(a division of Arnefold Publishing)
PO Box 22, Maidstone, Kent, England ME14 1AH

*This book has been long in the making
and I must record my appreciation of the support of those
who have encouraged its appearance in print.*

Particularly

Wendy Chesterman, née Wright
*who, many years ago, when a senior employee on a Borneo oilfield,
used her literary skill to shape the book's early chapters*

Margaret Taylor
a close and patient companion for many years

and

Bridget Cannon née Hosegood
*my physiotherapist in what was then the
Rowley Bristow Orthopaedic Hospital, Pyrford, Surrey, England
whose ministrations largely contributed to giving me back
the partial use of my right arm, so badly wounded
on the 19th of May 1950 in a Terrorist Affray on
a Malayan Rubber Estate.*

*To Pamela Gore Johnston of Ringwood, Hampshire, England
I offer my sincere thanks for the many hours she spent
transferring the original manuscript to disc.*

Contents

Illustrations are to be found between the pages
16—17, 48—49, 144—145
and
176—177

'COPTER PILOT

CHAPTER ONE

In the Beginning

ON THE NIGHT THAT I WAS BORN, FEBRUARY 26 1922, our farmhouse in West Meath was surrounded by a cordon of heavily armed IRA men. My Protestant Irish Father had received death threats from a group of self-styled communists then scouring the countryside desperate for weapons and looking for trouble. Four supporters of this faction worked on our farm. The threat was 'Double the wages or you will die. We know how the Russian revolution started and this will be the same.'

The local IRA Commandant was a childhood friend of my father. "Don't worry," he said. "We will take care of the problem." And so he did. The men were never seen nor heard of again.

There had been an earlier incident in 1918 when my father was still on Active Service in Germany and my formidable grandmother, then seventy-eight, had single-handedly defied a gang of armed ruffians after guns and ammunition. These dangerous times were to set the theme of my life and I am sure that some of my grandmother's genes have helped me survive.

She was a Miss Parkes from Birmingham, born in 1840 who, at the early age of twenty-four, was bluntly told by her doctor that she had to make an immediate choice: either straightway book into a Swiss sanatorium or embark on a long sea voyage. Otherwise consumption would kill her inside a year.

She needed no further prompting and forthwith took a passage on Brunel's famous steamship *Great Britain* to Sydney, in New South Wales where she lived for the next twelve years, carving out a successful career for herself in the large Sydney department store, *Farmers*, which still flourishes today. There, she was firstly assistant manageress of *Gown and Mantle* and then manageress, before returning to England in 1876. Later, while holidaying in Ireland at Mullingar, in the County of West Meath, she met and married my grandfather.

My recollections of Grandma are of a straight-backed old lady

COWARDLY RAID FOR ARMS

OLD LADY'S COURAGEOUS ACTION

Further details are now available regarding the cowardly raid for arms made on the house of Mr. Jones, a Protestant farmer, residing at Ashfield Cottage, Derry-golan, between Kilbeggan and Tullamore, some nights ago. It appears that on Mr. Jones's returning from a visit to a sick friend he was held up outside his garden gate by men who at once covered him with their revolvers. Five masked men then proceeded to the house in which was Mrs. Jones, an old lady of 78 years, and in a peremptory tone demanded Mr. Jones's gun and ammunition. This was firmly refused them. Two of the raiders then went through the house and thoroughly ransacked presses and broke open a wardrobe. While this search was proceeding, one of the intruders kept a revolver close to the face of Mrs. Jones and told the old lady that he would shoot her if she resisted. With commendable courage, Mrs. Jones replied "Shoot away; that's all you can do. It will come back on yourselves and may do good. You are ruining your country as the Bolshevists of Russia are doing. Are you men to enter a woman's house in her 78th year like robbers?"

One of the raiders then returned to the kitchen and threatened to shoot her if the gun was not given up. The gun was subsequently discovered and then they immediately left. Mr. Jones was afterwards permitted to return to his house.

Mr. and Mrs. Jones live alone, their son, Lieutenant Jones, being on active service in Germany. It is stated that the district has been quiet until lately.

The local Press reported the armed raid
on the Jones's family farm in 1918

in black bombazine edged with black lace who used to walk me to the railway bridge at Charfield in Gloucestershire — just one of my several childhood homes — and prop me up on the parapet to see and feel the trains rush by below.

It only seems like yesterday that we heard her oft-spoken comment that allowed no contradiction: 'There is *no* harbour like Sydney harbour!' For she was forever recounting experiences of her stay in Australia and there is little doubt that today, she would be regarded as something of a character, albeit perhaps a rather boring one when launched into her favourite theme.

Nevertheless, it may well be that her beloved Sydney Harbour had something more than a good view to commend it, for although given up by the British doctors at the age of twenty-four she, in fact, lived to the ripe old age of eighty-eight.

Grandfather John Jones was considerably younger than his wife and well-educated by the standards of his day. Perhaps it was this that in later years provided him with a more than usually keen appreciation of a drop of Jamesons — indeed it was admitted that he could even appreciate two drops.

My father had served as a lieutenant in the Royal North Lancashire Regiment and, during the 1914-18 war, had fought for long periods in the trenches in France. My English mother had also played her part as a volunteer lady driver with the British Army Service Corps, ferrying repatriated wounded servicemen in a Crossley Tender or Sunbeam Tourer for urgent treatments between English hospitals.

She was only nineteen when she met my father in Lancashire when he was on leave from the Army of Occupation after the end of the war and both knew at once they were meant for each other. They were married by Special Licence in five days and, as soon as he was demobilised, my father took his bride back to the family farm in Ireland.

But in these troubled times my father soon came to know that his own life and the life of his beloved wife and burgeoning family might well depend on a whim of some ruffian or rebel. He could see what was going on all around, robbings and killings and burnings. He always slept with a loaded revolver under his pillow.

From 1919 to 1922 there could be an unexpected knock at the

13

door and perhaps grandfather or grandmother would answer it to be asked, initially courteously enough, for a revolver, shotgun or ammunition which, it was claimed, was certainly in our possession. Father had, of course, brought a number of souvenirs back from France and it was quite impossible to keep this fact secret.

Truly, the times were tough and the snuffing out of a life of little more importance to some than blowing out a candle to you or to me. And, strangely enough, I was to experience similar circumstances many years later. History was to repeat itself far away from Ireland on an isolated rubber plantation in Malaya, where life was also cheaply held at the time.

Meanwhile back in West Meath, my father struggled on for as long as he could against civil unrest and plummeting Irish prices for farm produce but in 1924 he gave up trying and sold our farm to long time neighbours, the O'Briens, whose descendents continue to send me a Christmas card every year. We moved across the Irish Sea to Charfield in Gloucestershire. There my father purchased a small farm and became involved in training horses for riding and polo and also rode with the Berkeley and Beaufort Hunts. I do recall that my father, in after years, often mentioned that the then Prince of Wales, later the Duke of Windsor, rode with one of these packs and that although he was a poor horseman, he invariably remounted and carried on after a fall!

For me, a long association with horses commenced on this farm and I may have been about five years old when, in his enthusiasm to teach me riding, my father had placed me bareback on a horse with the intention of leading the animal the half-mile or so down the public highway to our farm. In short, the horse got away and galloped down the steep road, with me clinging to its mane and hanging on as best I could with, of course, my father rushing along behind in a vain attempt to catch the horse and its intrepid rider. He was not to catch up before my noble animal had passed through the open farmyard gate and come to a halt at his closed stable door, with his rider quite unhurt and, undoubtedly, very pleased with his achievement!

Training of hunters and polo ponies was not to prove a financially successful venture and after a little over four years we sold up and moved to Bournemouth, where my parents bought a greengrocers business and from where my father developed a successful egg retailing section. I recall that he drove a Morris Oxford car in which, after attendance at the Keswick Private School during the week, I usually accompanied him to Wimborne or one or other of the local towns possessing agricultural markets.

Later we sold up to sail from Southampton in the Cunard liner *Arania* to Halifax, Nova Scotia, Canada and this some time ahead of the Great Depression of 1929. From Halifax we went by steam train the long overland journey to Lakeville, a small village in New Brunswick, fairly close to the United States border and several miles from the larger town of Hartland on the long and wide St John River.

I can clearly remember arriving at our destination. We stepped out of a warm railway carriage into the icy cold of a Canadian winter and were driven in a large horse-drawn sleigh the four miles to our new home. Immediately after our arrival the 'surprise parties' started, with all the neighbours converging upon the house and, uninvited, opening the door and walking straight in, much to the consternation of my mother. Later we discovered that this was the customary way of welcoming new arrivals. It certainly gave my mother a shock.

But we soon adapted ourselves to the new and very different lifestyle and surroundings. Looking back, there is little doubt that I spent many of my happiest days there in the Great Outdoors. Our farm ran to about 150 acres with an additional amount of virgin forest available for clearing. Apart from a few acres of heavy clay, the soil was loamy and easy to till, though it contained more than its fair share of flints and stones. All our ploughing, harrowing and seeding was done with horses and because spring and summer were short, the work had to be done in a hurry immediately the snow cleared and the ground thawed out. We children helped, and most of us could handle a team of horses by the time we were eight or nine years old.

Money was short until the first harvest and my father had to make do with worn-out, second-hand farm equipment. The hay rake shafts, which broke time and time again, were once more made serviceable with crude wooden splints; the dilapidated

15

harnesses which should have been scrapped long before were still mended with wire and string. I am perfectly convinced that even if my father had then had the money to buy new equipment he would nevertheless have carried on with the old.

Loose flints were a real menace at grass-cutting or mowing time and would all too frequently damage the cutting edge of the knife, often to such an extent that the team would have to be stopped while the knife was removed and replaced with another. We had a sort of trip mechanism fitted to our Albion Mower by which it was possible to raise the whole 6ft-long knife a good four inches off the ground when a stone or flint was seen ahead, but of course in thick, lush meadow grass the damage was invariably done before stones or flints were detected and angrily thrown onto a heap.

On those heaps of flint and stone wild gooseberries and blackcurrants grew in profusion and provided many a pot of delicious homemade jam. Strawberries also grew in the fields and strangely enough seemed only to thrive on the poorest land. In the woods wild raspberries abounded and in the peak season it was easy to collect several pails full up to the top with the red berries. We had to watch out for bears since they were also fond of all this fruit and even the smallest or baby bear was still bigger than some of us.

Our farmhouse was two-storeyed, with overlapping planked walls, wood-shingled roof, and windows that were double-paned to keep out the cold and securely mosquito-netted, a protection certainly needed in summer. I have since travelled in many parts of the world but have yet to experience more persistent or viciously painful mosquitoes than the Canadian variety. They attacked in squadrons and seldom failed to hit their target.

The outhouses were also wooden and inter-connected, which was much appreciated when outside temperatures registered below zero. The grain, hay and root crops were stored in one large building and the horses and cattle housed next door. During the winter months, all the water for our stock had to be pumped by hand from a well and carried in buckets, a long and tiring job.

There was one particular outbuilding that deserves special mention — our privy. This was so quaint that we developed a

My Grandmother, Elizabeth Jones (née Parkes)
in the garden of Hillside Farm, Charfield, Gloucestershire
circa 1927
with my late sister, Maureen, (bottom left)
Self with Teddy. (bottom right) and infant brother Bill

My Father
an officer in World War I

My Mother
on a happier occasion

Self, serving as an Officer Cadet
aboard the 14,000 ton
MV Van Der Velde
before the deadly collision in convoy

The Longest Covered Bridge in the World
at Hartland, New Brunswick in Canada
spanning the St John River about three miles from our family farm

The crew of Lancaster U for Uncle after last 'Op'
467 (Australian) Squadron Waddington, 1945
Ground crew, front row; Aircrew, rear
Self, newly commissioned, arms folded, forage cap, second from right

Self in Tail Turret of U for Uncle
halfway through my 30-plus tour of operations
RAF Waddington, 1945

kind of affection for it. It was a companionable two-hole job, fitted with buckets and the walls were papered with the previous year's calendars and old magazines. I remember that *The Saturday Evening Post* always maintained a prominent position, and that it invariably housed a pretty good library. Many a pleasant read was enjoyed by all at different times in this sanctuary. If there was a particularly nasty job to be done, the privy was a good place to retreat to.

But there were snags. In the summer the space beneath the two-holer swarmed with mosquitoes and once my young brother, who had successfully escaped there to avoid doing his share of the milking, got so badly bitten that he was unable to sit down comfortably for several days. And it was even worse in the winter when temperatures were down below zero. Not only did one get frozen tripping along the path, for the privy was not connected with the house in any way, but once inside it was like being in a refrigerator. Few of us then were inclined to loiter, especially as under such conditions most of the reading matter was frozen stiff. Still, generally speaking it compared quite favourably with other such places in the district.

We also had an old granary in which my father kept five-hundred Leghorn hens. He had devised a novel system of keeping the fowls warm and encouraging them to lay throughout the long cold winters. The scheme entailed piling all the cow and horse dung available against the outer walls of the building and stacking tightly packed spruce trees up to the eaves. All this froze hard. There was no smell whatsoever and the building was kept amazingly warm. In the spring the novel 'cosy' was removed and spread on the land as manure and the outside of the building was given a thorough spring clean.

Eggs were always a good proposition and even later when the worldwide economic depression hit us, we could usually sell them for cash in St John. They were crated and sent either by Canadian National Railways from the railhead at Lakeville, or by Canadian Pacific from Hartland, New Brunswick. The latter method was preferable because it was quicker, although entailing a seven-mile buggy drive to Hartland.

In those days this was a small, straggling town on the banks of

17

the St John River which, at this point, was nearly a mile wide and bridged by what is, even today, the longest covered bridge in the world. Built entirely of timber, its roof was intended to prevent any great depth of snow forming and blocking the roadway during the winter months.

The idea was excellent although it did create a further problem. Often barely enough snow drifted onto the bridge to allow sleighs to run smoothly and speed restrictions had to apply. On our side of the river was displayed a large sign which read: 'Traffic to proceed at no faster than a walk,' which meant a slow crossing. So in the winter people often drove over the frozen river and at least twice during our stay in New Brunswick strangers to the district were drowned when, through ignorance, they drove over a weak patch of ice and horse-team, sled and occupants all fell through and perished.

On occasions the bridge itself had been known to collapse in the middle when, as the ice broke up in the spring, large chunks jammed and piled up against the centre sections, crumpling the structure as if it had been matchwood.

The weather played an important part in our lives and the blizzard that once snowed us in for three days was a completely unforgettable experience. It was impossible to see more than a few feet ahead and we were unable to cover the hundred yards to the barn where the stock were housed. Anyone venturing out under such conditions would have quickly lost their sense of direction and certainly died in a most unpleasant manner.

We children looked forward to the spring, bringing with it sunshine, green fields, and an end of the seemingly eternal snow. Between the end of March and the middle of April — or sometimes even later — the thaw set in and gradually the snow blanket disappeared, and everything became a morass of mud and slush making our sleighs and buggy practically useless.

In the early spring our few dozen maple trees were tapped for their syrup. This was done by boring a hole about two inches deep into the trunk with an ordinary brace and bit and then driving in a metal spout. The syrup slowly dripped into a receptacle hung below and was afterwards collected and boiled in a big cauldron until the water content was greatly reduced, and a delicious

18

golden syrup remained. Further boiling would turn it into a solid candy. The syrup, spread on buckwheat pancakes, tasted like something out of this world.

As the season progressed the mud slowly dried out and all kinds of animal re-appeared. The rabbits gradually changed their white winter coats for the more conventional garb of their English cousins. Porcupines and small New Brunswick bears came out of their hibernation. Groundhogs, squirrels and our old odiferous friend, the skunk, could frequently be seen and beavers abounded in the nearby river and in the swamp which bordered the farm. When we saw all these animals about once more, winter was really behind us.

Then quite suddenly, grass and other vegetation sprang up and three or four weeks later, the Canadian summer had started, and this could be as hot as the winter was cold. Such was the heat in high summer that the metal wheel-hoops on the horse-drawn vehicles became loose due to expansion. Then we had to drive into the nearest stream and let the wheels soak in the cold water to put things right. But, generally speaking, summer did not present nearly as many problems as the winter.

Though to me, as a child, our stay in Canada was happy, money problems began to beset my father and mother. In those days potatoes were the main crop in the province and at first the high prices obtained made fortunes for the growers. But soon the worldwide economic depression hit us and prices flopped from seven dollars a barrel down to four dollars and then to as low as five cents. Finally it became almost impossible to sell the crop for any figure. On many occasions I took the horse team with a load of potatoes down to the sheds at the railhead, only to return with little more than two dollars in payment for the lot and it became an everyday sight to see thousands of barrels dumped on the roadside, their contents left to rot.

The years 1930 to 1934 spanned a very tough time for many. In the cities, hundreds of thousands struggled to survive on the breadline, supported by meagre State or local relief. Many took to begging, others became hobos or tramps riding the railcars out into the countryside in search of casual work and, more importantly, food.

19

We saw many of these and helped them as far as we could. But, like every other family around us, we found it difficult to make ends meet. In the cities — incredible as it may sound — many people died of starvation, and although I can never remember going hungry what I do remember is being very cold.

Basic background warmth in our farmhouse centred on the cooking stove and when wood the basic available fuel was scarce, frozen or wet, the stove went out. Then we suffered. But never as much as those who lived in the cities.

Inevitably country people sought some escape from their everyday troubles, and hunting was a favourite pastime. Moose and deer were the usual quarries, but also, to some, hunting of other men's wives was also particularly popular! It was often said that the best way to get rid of an unwanted husband or rival was to go on a shooting expedition with him into New Brunswick Forest, for there any accident could happen. My mother used to relate three incidents quoted in a Woodstock newspaper during this period. The first man to be reported as accidentally shot was mistaken for a bear; about a week later, a second unfortunate victim killed outright was taken to be a moose. The third incident, ridiculous beyond belief, involved a victim allegedly being mistaken for a prairie chicken!

We struggled on in Canada for as long as we could but, eventually, with no visible 'light at the end of the tunnel' my parents decided in 1934 to sell up and take us all back to England. There the family settled on a small farm near Reigate in Surrey and I was packed off to the Hiberian Marine School in Dublin to prepare for an apprenticeship in the British Merchant Marine.

However, I never completed the course for, once again, my parents' farm failed. They couldn't afford the fees and I had to be withdrawn from the school. A living-in job was subsequently found for me on a large sheep and cattle farm on the South Downs, near Eastbourne in Sussex, which is where I was working at the outbreak of war in 1939 which was when, like many others, I saw my chance to move onwards and upwards and seized it. I volunteered for aircrew in the RAF and was accepted for training as a pilot, only to fail a relatively easy maths test at No. 11 Initial Training Wing at Scarborough, following which, because I was officially a citizen of neutral Eire, I was allowed to leave the Service with an Honourable Discharge.

Nothing daunted, I returned to the land of my birth and joined the Irish Army, in which I spent thirty-eight days, on the Curragh Camp in County Kildare abortively trying to arrange a transfer for pilot training in the Irish Army's Air Corps. Brief though it was, this proved to be a most interesting time.

Crashed aircrew and all other combatants — German, British or Allied — who found themselves on the soil of strictly neutral Eire were interned for the duration of hostilities. They were housed on the Curragh and I would see quite a few of them regularly strolling around or, more particularly on Sundays in the Protestant Church on the camp: me on compulsory Church Parade, them on their own initiative but in separate groups, and all in full uniform.

The Irish Army occupied the central pews in the church, separating the two enemy contingents. But a dramatic change occurred once the service was over and erstwhile foes happily fraternised outside.

Back on square-bashing and weapons training once Sundays were over, I was shocked by the paucity of basic equipment the Irish Army possessed at that time. Many of the rifles were ancient, some even dating from the Boer War, and ammunition was in short supply. I knew that the Irish Army would fight heroically to defend the country's independence, but was glad, on this showing, that the possibility of a German invasion of Ireland was completely remote.

I had applied for transfer and now the answer came. Transfer refused without any reason other than that on my discharge document, 'Improperly enlisted' appeared above 'Character and Conduct Very Good'. The only possible conclusion was that my previous brief service in the RAF must somehow have some bearing on the matter.

It was an extraordinary situation. Here I was, thirty-eight days after joining the Irish Army once more a 'free' man, with no money, a few civilian clothes and a pair of old army boots generously donated by the Quartermaster. Acutely aware of my predicament, I knew I had to get a job somehow, somewhere, which is why, in the filthiest weather, I decided to leave Eire and head for Belfast where I reasoned my Marine School background should earn me employment and much needed money afloat.

And, counting the few coins in my pocket which took only seconds, I knew that to cover the hundred and forty miles north to Belfast there'd be no train for me.

I'd have to walk.

CHAPTER TWO

Getting Airborne

THE WEATHER WAS FILTHY, WET AND BITTERLY COLD. My section NCO, Corporal Laughlin MacGlyn, passed the hat round and, despite my protests, pushed five shillings into my hand. It might not seem much but there were no rich men in the Irish Army. It was a lot to my comrades and a fortune to me. It was the kindest of gestures and much appreciated.

MacGlyn later obtained his commission and, for a while served with the Press Department on the Curragh. When he left the Army he followed a career in journalism to become the editor of a womans' magazine in Dublin. He was surprised and delighted when I paid him a visit after the end of the war.

The five shillings my comrades gave me was most welcome for, added to what I'd got in my pocket, it bought me a bed and a breakfast in a soldiers' hostel near the Irish Army Headquarters when I arrived wet and somewhat footsore in Dublin at the end of the first day of my trek to the north. And it also left me with a small surplus of cash to cover the rest of my journey.

Next morning found me on my way again, walking to Drogheda, where I was fortunate enough to obtain free lodging with an Irish Army Unit based in the town and a free breakfast, too — a piece of bread and dripping.

During the third day I was seized with sickness, but struggled on and arrived in Dundalk late that afternoon. Once north of the town, I lay under a haystack and snatched a few hours sleep. The next stage of the journey was to be the most critical, for to cross into the North undetected meant having to avoid military patrols on both sides of the border, then not too far distant. So I decided that the best course of action would be to make a very early start across country avoiding roads and probable checkpoints.

I resumed my trek at about one o'clock in the morning taking me approximately due north, checked against my father's old army marching compass, which he had given me two years before.

Despite fears to the contrary, nothing untoward occurred and, half covered in mud and wet to the skin, just after dawn I found a sheltered hedge and, completely exhausted, fell asleep beneath it.

I woke up much later in the day terribly hungry and suffering badly from stomach pains and diarrhoea. To add to my misery the November drizzle which had plagued me on my journey now turned to heavy rain. A search in a nearby field for something, or anything, to eat resulted in the discovery of some mangels — cattle food — one of which I dug out of the mud, wiped almost clean on a soaked trouser leg, hacked apart with my penknife and ate raw, quenching my thirst from a nearby ditch. I was certainly growing weaker and my stomach pains had got worse, but I was to some extent fortified by the knowledge that the border must have been crossed at some time during the night.

The time had obviously come for an immediate return to a road where, perhaps, with a few discreet enquiries, I could find out where precisely I was and how much further I'd have to trudge to reach Belfast. Consequently not much later I met a farm worker and learned that Newry was only two miles away and I really was well north of the border.

So it happened that exactly five and a half days after leaving the Curragh Camp a very bedraggled Paddy Jones walked into Belfast, looking like a scarecrow and feeling nearly dead with hunger. The last of my money had been spent in Dundalk and I needed more fast, so I didn't delay in finding the Shipping Office in search of a job afloat.

There was a problem, of course, I had no British Identity Card. Fortunately, I still had my RAF discharge documents with me, so in the Shipping Office, when asked for my Identity Card, I managed to persuade the clerk that it had recently been lost and was at that moment in the process of being replaced, meantime here were my RAF papers. No need to have bothered; my luck was out that day and employment was not forthcoming.

That evening I walked out of Belfast and again slept under a haystack. A sandwich kindly donated by a sailor in the Shipping Office staved off the fiercest pangs of hunger and made me feel a little better. This proved to be the last night of sleeping rough, but it was a memorable one.

Awakened at about four o'clock in the morning by a clucking sound which clearly indicated some poultry not far distant, I decided to investigate and walked round the haystack; to find a small henhouse. Feeling still very hungry and thinking that one egg more or less was unlikely to ruin the farmer, I broke into the shed, quickly and quietly searched each nesting box and ultimately found an egg. Just as silently I started to open the door when suddenly a loud sniffing sound came from outside. Covert investigation revealed a very large dog, presumably belonging to the farmer who was unwittingly providing me with an early breakfast.

I stood motionless, hardly daring to breath, and it was at least twenty minutes before the dog moved off, making it safe to leave. The egg was hard-earned but, raw though it was, tasted marvellous!

Early next morning I walked back into Belfast and presented myself at the Recruiting Offices of the Royal Inniskilling Fusilliers, volunteering for duty in an attempt to join the British Army. The Officer looked at my R.A.F. and Eire Army honourable discharges and then eying me up and down said quite rudely, "We don't want *your* sort here!" I retorted that his manner was hardly consistent with the recruiting placard outside. "However," I went on, "being chairborne at such an early age *must* have a frustrating effect. A few months active service might be the answer to your problem." I left the office thinking, from his expression, that my kindly advice was not entirely appreciated.

Later the same morning I managed to obtain employment as a messboy on a large Dutch tanker. But although now in a job, the problem of getting to Bangor where the ship was anchored had still to be solved. I had no money to buy a train ticket to Bangor, I had to be on board by two o'clock and it was then twelve forty-five. The ship was sailing that afternoon.

After some hesitation I swallowed my pride and approached a woman in the office of the Mersey Coal Company — the ship's agents in Belfast — explaining that my funds were insufficient to boy a railway ticket and asking if she could advance me that amount. I can still see her astonished look as she replied, "But the train fare is less that two shillings!" However after a little

25

deliberation the required sum was produced, so all was well.

Just before two o'clock I stepped on board my new home, the Dutch Motor Tanker *Rotterdam*, my thoughts less on the job than on the prospect of having a square meal — the first for almost a week.

We sailed later that afternoon and for the next three days I was very seasick but, once recovered, settled down well and tackled my new duties, which included washing great piles of dishes, scrubbing messrooms, cleaning corridors, and various other chores.

With one exception the crew were all Dutch, though some of them spoke English moderately well. The odd man out was a young Northern Irishman from Belfast, who subsequently became a teacher in London, and it was not long before we became firm friends. He had an apt surname for a Britisher on a Dutch ship. Believe it or not, it was Holland.

It was on the 5th December, 1941, that we left Bangor Bay and we were not many days out when our convoy of about twenty-eight vessels was attacked by submarines, three or four ships being lost. By the time we reached Halifax, Nova Scotia, more ships had been lost and many brave sailors with them. We sailed on from Halifax unaccompanied, the destination being Aruba in the Dutch West Indies, where we were to collect a cargo of aviation fuel. This loaded, we returned to Halifax and again braved the dangers of the North Atlantic crossing.

I made a second voyage on the *Rotterdam* to Galveston, Texas, for repairs in dry dock, returning to England by way of West Africa, sailing across the Atlantic and joining a homeward bound convoy at Freetown, Sierra Leone. It was about this time that our sister ship, the *Amsterdam*, was torpedoed in the West Indies.

Once docked in England I signed off the Rotterdam, having had some hairy adventures ashore and made many good friends afloat, and it was just as well that I did for that ship died shortly after, torpedoed like her sister.

On the *Rotterdam* I had earned rapid promotion so that I could join my next ship as an Able Bodied Seaman. This was the *Theseus*, another Dutchman but a coaster this time, basically hauling Blue Circle cement from Cliffe, in the Thames Estuary, to

Londonderry in Northern Ireland, to be used in the construction of barracks for incoming units of the American Army.

A little later I shipped out on yet a third Dutchman, the 13000 ton freighter *Van der Velde* on the North Atlantic run and now I had the status of *Stuurmans Leerling*, Apprentice Officer, for two crossings of the Atlantic, the last with a cargo of 1200 tons of TNT from the Brooklyn Navy Yard in New York and 500 tons of powdered dried egg in large tins.

We sailed independently up the American east coast and into Halifax, Nova Scotia, where we joined a convoy bound for the UK and set sail without incident. But two or three days out of Halifax, near St. Johns, Newfoundland, I had just come off watch and sagged back on my bunk at midnight when there was a deafening crash and I was abruptly hurled to the floor.

First thought — *torpedo!* It transpired, however, that we had been rammed by a wayward ship in the convoy.

Daylight found us totally alone on a relatively calm sea with a thirty-foot gash in our starboard side aft of the bridge, through which the sea had flooded Number 5 hold where all of the TNT and most of the dried egg was stowed. The copper-sheathed 57 pound wooden boxes of highly volatile explosive were bumping around in the flood in sympathy with the slight lateral roll of the now stationary ship and had begun to break up — a horrific sight. As their contents spilled out to line the bottom of the hold, the empty boxes snagged against the gashed side and then, with the roll, floated out on the sea. The convoy and its naval escort had left us to cope as best we could with a stricken ship, a most dangerous cargo and a trail of bobbing empty TNT boxes.

With a severe list and down by the stern we made slow progress to The Narrows, off St John's. Because of the nature of our cargo the port authorities refused us entrance to the harbour and sent us down the coast to a small fishing village on a rocky inlet called Bay Bulls. Here, St Johns' stevedores made it clear they wouldn't handle our cargo, so we — the deck crew — operated the steam winches and nets and very, very carefully, unshipped it ourselves.

Over the next ten days we loaded boxes of TNT into small, wooden hulled fishing boats, gingerly clearing the hold. The operation completed, I was paid a bonus of two hundred Canadian dollars for operating one of the two steam winches, although I was serving as a junior ship's officer at the time. As an ex-Able Bodied Seaman I had been considered sufficiently well qualified and experienced to handle a potentially very dangerous operation, hence the bonus. I later banked the money in St Johns, where it remained for the rest of the war.

In 1952 I was privileged to receive a decoration — The War Memorial Cross with Clasp — from the Government of the Netherlands in recognition of what we, who were not Dutch nationals, did to save a Dutch ship at Bay Bulls.

Extensive repairs followed and we eventually paid off in Glasgow where I left the sea to rejoin the Royal Air Force as a Sergeant Rear Gunner with Australian Squadron, No. 467, operating Lancasters out of RAF Waddington. I flew twenty-nine missions — plus a voluntary extra three with a crew short of a rear gunner. My twenty-first operation was the Dresden raid of February 13 1945. My logbook records a round trip flight time of 9 hours, 45 minutes. I was commissioned in the same month with the rank of Pilot Officer and, at the end of the war, was accepted for training at the RAF Marine Craft Officer's School at Corswell in Scotland.

Christmas 1945 saw a group of us Trainee Air Sea Rescue Skippers taking a high-speed launch across to Belfast to pick up turkeys for the Mess Christmas Dinner. I passed out with a mark of 87 percent on the navigation paper (more than making up for the failed maths of 1940) and was posted to an Air Sea Rescue Unit at Newlyn in Cornwall, where I became Second Officer on a 112 foot *Fairmile*. The war being well over, my stay in Newlyn proved to be short and I found myself on the way to Hamburg, posted as Transportation Officer to 431 Equipment Depot, dealing chiefly with service stores arriving at the docks.

There, as a relief from the daily grind, I took up gliding as a hobby, flying out of RAF Utersen, and was fortunate enough to gain the assistance of a famous pre-war German glider pilot, Herr Krunefeld. I still retain a pencilled series of his explanatory drawings. He was, I believe, the very first glider pilot to cross the English Channel from the Continent and I think he held the rank of Colonel in the Luftwaffe. A very fine elderly gentleman.

The certificate which declares that I have qualified as a Glider Pilot is signed by Lord Brabazon of Tara of the Royal Aero Club and there is absolutely no doubt that this early success as a glider pilot and the great joy that it gave me was to urge me onward to the flying career which eventually was to follow.

And it also gave the lie to the gratuitous comment scrawled on my original honourable discharge from the RAF — *'Not likely to become an efficient airman pilot.'* More happily, below was appended — *'Character and conduct, Very Good.'*

My first civilian job after demobilisation was as an 'official learner' at the Rustenburg Platinum Mine in South Africa's Transvaal. After about three months of very unpleasant work as an 'underground sampler' I resigned and eventually made my way down to Cape Town where, thanks to my earlier experience at sea, I managed to get work on the Ebenezer Docks as a stevedore foreman supervising native labourers loading ships chiefly outward bound for England.

This was in the autumn of 1948 and, with Christmas only two or three months away, ships' officers were intent on making adequate preparation for the festive season by loading cases of South African brandy as additional cargo under the watchful eyes of absolutely everyone concerned, since this was a tipple also much favoured by the native labour. I have some riotous stories to tell about this time — but not in this book.

It wasn't much later that I decided I would follow the cases of brandy and signed on as an Able Seaman aboard the *SS Pakeha,* a Shaw Saville tramp steamer Liverpool bound where I paid off two days ahead of Christmas and headed for my parents' home in Wexford for the holiday, shortly after which I got a job as Assistant Manager of a large rubber estate in what was then called Malaya. Travelling by ship and by train I reached Sungei Siput, a straggling village which bordered the rubber estate on which I was to work and which also lent its name to the whole of the surrounding area.

Communist-inspired terrorism was rampant in the country at

29

this time. 'The Malayan Emergency' as it was then called, had begun with the murder of a European planter on the nearby Lintang Road and many other European planters and tin miners as well as Malays had been killed in ambush. Even Sir Henry Gurney, a visiting fact-finding Senior Government Official from London, had not escaped.

As a consequence, armoured jeeps and cars became a necessary adjunct to life at tin mines and rubber estates. Most European planters carried firearms and I was soon made an Honorary Inspector of Police empowered to legitimately use my weapon in the apprehension and arrest of terrorist suspects.

It was on the morning of May 29th 1950 that I decided to drive down to the Headquarters of the Kamuning Rubber Estate. The manager and his wife were on leave in Penang and not expected back for a few days and there was paperwork to attend to and some matters I wished to discuss with our elderly Indian accountant. I took a Malayan Auxiliary Police Constable with me, armed with a Lee Enfield rifle but, for once, I was not armed myself. The constable had already received a few driving lessons and, to give him experience, on the outward journey I let him take the wheel. My beloved Alsatian, Sheba, stretched herself out on the back seat of my Morris 10 as we made our way cautiously over the unsurfaced slippery road. It had been raining all night.

In response to the repeated insistence of my lady friend at the time, a Nursing Sister at the main hospital in Ipoh, that I should think about protecting myself, both front doors of my car had been reinforced with steel plate. A narrow steel plate now also covered the lower part of the windscreen and a shaped steel plate the back of the driver's seat. This was industrial quality steel plate, of course. Combat quality heavy armour plate, the good stuff, simply wasn't available. Nevertheless, that steel plate was one of the factors which saved my life, but the principal factor without any doubt, was my lady friend's urgent persistence. She hailed from Ireland, as I did, she later married an English lawyer who was a friend of mine.

We reached the Estate Headquarters without any untoward incident and I busied myself with paperwork and administrative matters until about four thirty in the afternoon. There had been more heavy rain in the interval and, for the journey back to my bungalow, I drove the car with the constable beside me and Sheba on the back seat. As I turned into the narrow, wet and slippery estate track which led up to my bungalow, I was well aware of possible danger. The track sported a series of hairpin bends climbing to a high ridge beyond where I accelerated as the road fell away sharply. The young constable had a round up the spout of his Lee Enfield and we were going fast downhill approaching the last of the hairpins when a single shot rang out from the ridge above and behind us. Then all hell broke loose.

We were hit by a hail of bullets. The guard and my dog, Sheba, died instantly. My right arm was shattered as it gripped the wheel and I lost control of the car. My left shoulder was sliced open and the right-hand front wheel of the Morris was blasted, causing it to slew into the bank above which our assailants were hidden.

Although badly wounded and bleeding heavily, my mind was quite clear and I managed to hook my left forearm into the guard's rifle sling. With my left hand I jerked my driver's door open and then once more slammed it shut. As I'd guessed, this had the effect of drawing another fusillade of fire from the terrorists, but it was a ragged one this time and I prayed it had emptied most — if not all — of their magazines. They'd need a few precious moments to reload.

Bracing myself, I shoved the door open again and jumped out, straight into the sights of one of the terrorists, a Tamil on the bank above. I saw him clearly and he immediately opened fire on me with his Sten gun and I took a bullet in my left leg, but the rest of the burst went wide. Then, still hanging on to the Lee Enfield, lurching, staggering, sliding, I fell into cover behind some big logs on the terrace below the car and from there I got off three or four rounds in the terrorists' general direction. Shortly after that some of the Malay constables stationed at my bungalow arrived, drawn by the sound of gunfire. By this time the terrorist band had probably retreated.

I was steadily losing blood and getting weaker by the minute but one of the constables volunteered to accompany me over the mile or more down to the Ipoh road. He was a brave young man for neither of us knew where the terrorist band had gone to, nor whether or not it might at any moment return. I later recommended that this constable's courage was officially recognised, but as far as I know it never was.

Down on the main road to Ipoh we made several efforts to stop passing vehicles, but none would until I put a bullet across the front of a heavy truck and, once up beside the driver, thrust the muzzle of the Lee Enfield into his side and commanded "Drive!" He got me to the Sungei Siput police station from whence I was taken to the main hospital in Ipoh where my lady friend, on seeing the state I was in, collapsed.

I underwent major surgery. The brachial artery had been severed by a bullet and was repaired by a suture. The associated radial nerve in my right arm had been damaged and a repair was attempted. My left shoulder was a mess and there was a bullet in my left leg just below the knee, which had to be left where it was for about a year. I had blood transfusions and was on morphine for ten days. Initially I was not expected to live.

Later from Singapore I was flown back to Europe by KLM and later became a patient at the Rowley Bristow Orthopaedic Hospital in Surrey. It was touch and go with the right arm but this was saved by the ministrations of a superb physiotherapist, Miss Hosegood. She later married, had a family and was widowed over twenty years ago. More recently we renewed our earlier friendship.

The bullet in my leg was eventually removed in Sydney, Australia, by a military surgeon at which time the Crown Agents for the Colonies awarded me a Permanent Disability Pension of just under £1 a week.

It is worthy of note that this princely sum has remained unchanged over the years, whilst its actual value has steadily lessened. Meanwhile, the pain which drifts down my right arm to fingertips and of which I am conscious as I grip the control stick of my aircraft has, if anything, increased.

I returned to Malaya with a disabled right arm. The company which employed me offered no compensation but instead tried to recover the cost of my return to Malaya. It failed. I was promoted to Senior Assistant on the Temiang Estate outside the town of

Serembang in the state of Negro Sembilan. I took up gliding again and got my fixed-wing PPL at Kuala Lumpur Flying Club after direct RAF tutelage by Flight Lieutenant (later Wing Commander) Robert Church. I was determined my injured right arm would not stop me flying. I became part of the newly formed Malayan Auxiliary Force and built up a considerable number of flying hours in my logbook.

On the morning of July 24th 1951, accompanied by an Indian Estate foreman and two armed Malay Special Constables, I began an inspection of a stand of old rubber trees which was scheduled to be replanted. I was armed with a newly issued ·5 Reising sub machine-gun and the constables with short-barrelled Lee Enfield rifles, standard Lee Enfields which had been specially modified early in the Emergency to be carried and used more easily by Malay Constables who were racially much smaller than their European counterparts.

Particularly, this morning, my inspection was to ensure that Estate labour was applying bagged fertiliser to a recently replanted area and not to the adjacent stand of old rubber trees due to be cleared for the replant. Additionally I was also on the lookout for any 'cut lump' activity.

Rubber trees were 'tapped' every two days for their latex, the milky-white fluid which is used to make rubber. After the tap, a cup-like receptacle attached to each tree collected any dripping latex, which would coagulate in the cup into a soft, round valuable and readily saleable lump. It was this which, moving swiftly from tree to tree, the 'cut lump' thieves stole.

And on this particular morning, on the lookout for them as I was, I suddenly saw the figure of a woman running fast away from us and the rubber trees, towards a muddy, shallow, eminently fordable stream which marked the boundary of our Estate.

Naturally, I thought 'cut lump' and immediately gave chase, trying to head her off from our boundary. The small group of men with me followed. I was panting with effort. Very briefly, I paused to draw breath. And in that moment I glimpsed on the edge of the primary jungle beyond the stream, a brief flash of a khaki uniform and a cap with a red star. At once I knew we had run into an ambush and hissed at the constable who had run up

33

behind me "Larry, larry, orang jehat — run, run, bandits!"

He, not immediately aware of what I had seen, began to argue, but then something made him halt, call out to the others, and run.

And so we all went, through the old rubber trees, running fast, weaving in and out of the stand as the Chinese gang opened fire behind us. I could hear bullets whizzing by as I ran. One hit the heel of my left shoe. It was then I heard the terrifying sound of bugles being blown over on the left and in the trees as some of the Chinese ran almost parallel with us, firing as they ran. Intelligence later suggested that two uniformed gangs were involved said to number approximately fifty bandits in all.

Then, abruptly, the trees gave way to a clearing and a mound of earth, from uprooted rubber, behind which we could dive and shelter and fire back at our pursuers, who then broke off their attack and I led my small party back to my bungalow.

Later, I returned with a European Police Lieutenant and several Malay constables to the scene of the ambush and, oddly, found a large number of bullet casings on the ground. Odd, because both Chinese and Tamil terrorists usually left nothing behind them, scrupulously scooping up casings for future reloading.

Subsequently I discovered that I was named on the Communist Death List and for this, and other reasons, I left for Australia to be trained as a commercial pilot.

Here it should also be mentioned that on the Dutch liner *Orange* en route from the UK to Singapore on my way back to Malaga I had met a charming Dutch girl with the result that we had married in the Registry Office in Serambang. But shortly after the second ambush she left to join her brother, a senior KLM Freight Manager in Sydney, Australia. I never saw her again and the divorce came through after three years. Miekie has since died in Melbourne.

At Bankstown Airport, in Sydney, a test of my competence both in the air and on the ground presented no problems. The medical examination was a different thing. I could not admit to the constant nagging pain in my right arm, nor could the disability pension be mentioned, even if it was only one pound a week. I kept quiet and the medical was passed.

I received my commercial licence on December 4 1952. I was thirty and I was now flying for a living. I became a jobbing pilot around Australia and flew a variety of aircraft: Moths of all sorts, Austers, Dragon Rapides, Miles Geminis and Chipmunks. I flew a light aircraft for a very large sheep farm in the far west of New South Wales and had a host of other contracts, and in June 1953 I accepted an offer from the Royal Aero Club at Bankstown to instruct ab initio pilots, many of whom were later to join the Royal Australian Air Force. By September 1953 I had logged 700 flying hours and was hearing the call of helicopters. These were few and far between in Australia then and all flying training was in Europe, so that was where I went.

Courses were very expensive and I needed a job, so I became a Flying Instructor at Denham Aerodrome. I had been in England for two of three weeks when the BBC invited me to appear on the highly popular weekly programme 'In Town Tonight'. I had taken part in the same programme back in 1951 after returning seriously wounded from Malaya. Now I was scheduled to be interviewed immediately before the famous film star Greer Garson.

When the programme ended the studio audience crowded round her, begging for autographs. She was mobbed. But then, amazingly, I heard her say, 'Yes, yes, in a minute. But first I must talk to Mr Jones' and there she was, pushing her way through the throng to shake my hand and say, 'What an interesting life you have led' and we spoke together — all too briefly. I was stunned.

At Denham, on one occasion I test flew a Chiltern Special (G-AFGH) powered by a water-cooled Cardinal Ford engine. I recall the flight with clarity because the water in the radiator boiled whilst I was in circuit and the engine seized as I completed the run-in to land.

I joined an aerial spraying company in June 1954, initially based at Bourne, near Cambridge, and sprayed forestry over England and Scotland before flying an Auster further afield. Accompanied by another Auster, piloted by Johnnie Johnstone who had flown in the Naval Air Arm, I headed for what was then the Anglo-Egyptian Sudan, a flight of approximately 5200 miles via France, Spain and Egypt. Our job was to spray DDT on

35

Sudan's cotton fields to eradicate the Jasid fly, a pest which —
migrating in from the desert — threatened to wipe out the
thousands of acres of cotton in both the White and the Blue Nile
areas of this vast country in a very short space of time.

Our two small Austers proved of great interest to Sudanese
villagers who, on occasion, were seen spreading out their not
always too white garments on ground next to the crops we were
aiming to spray — presumably to have us get rid of other
uninvited insect visitors for them. We were always happy to
oblige until our contract ended.

Then, on November 8, we left our Austers in storage near
Khartoum and made tracks for France. I was to become a
helicopter pilot.

CHAPTER THREE

'Copter Pilot

IT WAS EARLY MARCH 1955 AND THE LOCATION A famous old grass covered airfield, Issy Les Moulineaux on the outskirts of Paris. In the years preceding the Great War, Issy Les Moulineaux had been famous for many pioneering flights. Well known airmen of that bygone era — Bleriot was one — had taken off from here to set records in the flimsy flying machines of the period. It was now the base for Fenwicks, the official French agents for the American Bell Aircraft Corporation, and one of the two flying training schools sharing the field.

Earlier in the year Bahamas Helicopters, an American organisation, had advertised for experienced commercial fixed wing pilots to convert. I had been interviewed and then placed on a waiting list. Now the company had come up with an offer of employment subject to satisfactory completion of a ten-hour course of flying training on helicopters, at their expense, at a flying school in France, the course to commence in mid-January.

It began just ahead of my 33rd birthday and I took to it like a duck to water. It has been suggested that experience flying light aircraft, such as in crop spraying, makes for an easier transition to flying helicopters than experience piloting airliners, since these more massive aircraft are not generally hand-flown.

There were three British pilots on the course, two being ex-RAF.

Most of the actual flying training at Issy was conducted from the nearby airfield of Guyancourt. It was more suitable for this type of noisy activity than the headquarters field where encroaching houses and offices limited helicopter activity to little more than hasty arrivals and departures.

The aircraft used were American Bell 47s, bubble enclosed carbon copies of the machine featured in the opening scene of the long running TV series M.A.S.H. It was powered by a single 178 horse power six cylinder air-cooled Franklyn engine. The pilot was seated on the left side of this three-place machine but when fitted with dual controls for instructional purposes, it was two place with the flight instructor positioned on the right.

The 'all up weight' (AUW) or total permissible loaded weight of this aircraft was approximately 2300lbs and it possessed a realistic cruising range of about seventy miles in an hour on around twelve US gallons of gasoline.

The flight controls suggested a similarity to those of a conventional aircraft because, when in level flight, the centrally positioned cyclic control stick and the two rudder bars, appeared to serve the same basic functions as the central control column and rudders of its fixed wing cousin. However this likeness was deceptive. The intricate manoeuvres which only a helicopter could perform sometimes called for the simultaneous use of four controls and a high degree of co-ordination. The initial impression of similarity was rapidly dispelled on a student's first training flight.

My knowledge of the French language was minimal and one of the instructor's ability to converse in English was little better. We got by in German which he understood and in which I was almost fluent, due to being stationed for two years in Germany immediately after the war. Apart from this there was no language problems at all at the school because the other instructors and Jean Moine, the chief course instructor, all spoke good English. Jean Moine incidentally, was an exceptional helicopter pilot, who among other feats of derring-do had landed an early under-powered Bell machine more than 16000 feet up on the summit of Mount Blanc, a European record height

Much of my training consisted of flying concentrated, oft repeated, circuits and landings at Guyancourt. Always to be remembered was my flight instructor's constantly intoned: *"Tour repris, tour repris!"* — "Do another circuit."

In February, snow showers became more frequent and visibility was restricted when a mixture of sleety rain and slushy snow stuck to the Perspex bubble enclosing the cabin. Due to the curvature of this windscreen it could not be equipped with functional wipers, but fortunately most of our training took place on, or in the close vicinity of, the airfield and snow was never a serious problem. Occasionally very heavy falls could, and did, temporarily suspend training; when we all retreated to a nearby excellent coffee shop to await an improvement in the weather.

We made many engine-off practice emergency landings from various heights, usually onto the airfield, but sometimes they were ordered without any warning over open country to add realism to engine-off or 'autorotation practice'. We landed in pastures, stubble fields, parks and on one memorable occasion inadvertently arrived on the immaculately barbered putting green of an upper crust golf club.

Helicopters at that time were a novelty. If animals were not affected, farmers and other landowners seldom objected to such visitations. Times have certainly changed.

The purpose of these repetitive exercises was to make the student confident that the helicopter could be landed safely if the engine should ever fail in flight. Happily this was an unlikely contingency, but it can and has happened, even when an aircraft has been maintained in first class order.

The school operated a rotary wing theory course intended to clarify the aerodynamic differences between rotary and fixed wing flight. The main transmission in a helicopter incorporates a freewheel mechanism in principle similar to that found on most bicycles. Should the engine stop in flight; this permits the main rotor blades to continue rotating, as does the wheel of a bicycle, initially in both cases due to inertia.

The helicopter, unlike the bicycle is not supported by a road and will forthwith descend towards the ground. Assuming that the pilot has taken immediate action by pushing down the lever controlling the pitch of the main rotor its continued rotation and a safe landing will be ensured. When the helicopter is very close to the ground, fifty feet or less, the same pitch control lever in the cockpit is slowly raised which, when combined with other control actions, again permits the machine to make a safe landing. The reason for this is that although the engine has failed, the relative upward airflow attributable to any descending aircraft ensures that the direction of flight and speed of descent can be completely controlled by a competent helicopter pilot. As my instructors repeated constantly: "Yer don't falls outer the air."

For example, in nature the seeds of the sycamore falling in a twisting swirling motion have the effect of retarding speed of descent, thus demonstrating in nature all the characteristics of the phenomenon known as autorotation. Many medium priced cars are now equipped with power assisted steering, which greatly reduces the physical effort required to manoeuvre any vehicle into or out of a restricted parking space.

For their part, most early helicopters were not fitted with power assisted flight controls. A notable exception were the larger Sikorsky 55s, eight or ten place machines whose hydraulically assisted controls were a prominent feature, a development now commonplace.

With the arrival of smaller and lighter helicopters, vibration from the heavy and fast rotating main rotors down to the pilot-held cyclic stick posed a serious problem, sometimes being sufficiently severe to affect control of the aircraft particularly when flying in those windy turbulent conditions common in mountainous areas.

To attack this problem, two sets of circular metal friction pads, each half the size of a saucer, were fitted in the control linkage between the rotor head and the cyclic stick. One set assisting with the damping of the lateral movement of the stick, the other with its fore and aft movement. Both were adjusted on the ground to achieve optimum resistance of one plate rubbing against the other and an insertion of grease onto each of the sets helped to create smooth operation in flight.

Unfortunately periods of heavy rain always penetrated the space between the plates because the pads were open to the elements and the grease was eventually forced out. This could cause intermittent seizure of the friction pads, control difficulties and possibly necessitate a landing to regrease and adjust. For some perverse reason the nuts on the separate sets were of differing sizes, so two spanners had to be carried in addition to a grease gun, and they had to be of a special type. More things to remember.

For me there was also a legacy of constant pain in my damaged arm and more specifically, in the wrist, palm and fingers, which

40

the passage of time has not diminished. The continuous and only partially dampened vibrations in the cyclic control stick, perforce held by this hand, temporarily increased the pain and weakness and was to cause much discomfort on this helicopter course.

On completion of morning training, our instructors generally flew us across the countryside to the light aircraft sporting field of Toussus le Noble for lunch in the Flying Club's excellent dining room. We were usually seated with our fellow students and instructors or with army helicopter pilots who came in from local training exercises. Due to the language barrier, conversation could be somewhat restricted, loud and meaningless chatter being interrupted when one of my companions might exclaim in English "You like more wine?" or "You like cognac, Monsieur Jones?"

Sometimes we were joined by the Colonel in Charge of the local Army Garrison together with his wife and two young children, all taking wine with their meal. We 'foreign' pilots took the view that our French counterparts were well used to wine and spirits from an early age and had developed a certain immunity to their normal effects. Bearing this in mind, for our part at this time of day we never attempted to keep up with them.

This welcome luncheon interval was a delightful and relaxing experience after what had often been a stressful and demanding morning. In France lunch could continue for all of two hours. The phone was often left to ring with no attempt to answer it during this, one might say, sacred period.

On 22nd February 1955, and four days ahead of my 33rd birthday, the training school awarded me their graduating certificate which reads:

Certificate d'Aptitude
No. 131
Aux Fonctions de PILOTE d'Helicoptere delivre a
Monsieur John JONES
qui a suivre les cours theoriques et practique de
L'Ecole d'Entrainement FENWICK, sur BELL modele 47G
Issy-les-Molineaux, le 22 Fevrier 1955

This much-prized document was signed by the Chief Pilot Jean

Moine, who said he thought that I was the first pilot of foreign origin to graduate from the school, certainly the first British one and perhaps the first to be issued with such a certificate in France. On this satisfactory note, my course ended and I met my future employer, Knute W Flint. He was an American of middle height, in his early forties, with a crew-cut hairstyle and incisive manner, a very experienced pilot who after distinguished war service in the Pacific with the American forces, pioneered the commercial use of helicopters in various parts of the world. He had driven out to the airfield shortly after the satisfactory completion of my course and now asked me to make a solo circuit. He pulled out an expensive Shaeffer pen, went out on the grass-covered airfield, stuck the pen into the ground and said, "Paddy, make a circuit and land as close to my pen as you can." With a good natured grin he added, "But not on it!"

The landing was achieved but it should be said, the safety of the pen was never in doubt.

As we walked across the grassed field towards the Flight Office he remarked, "You will never be a very good helicopter pilot but you should always be a safe one." He gave no explanation, nor did I ask for one. However, in the crew room after pouring out two coffees he looked at me keenly and nodded "You'll do."

Now, more than sixty years later with a total of well over 17000 hours and still flying whenever I can, this intriguing assessment however arrived at may have reflected both accuracy and foresight. The course completed, the American company which had sponsored my training sent me to Egypt where they had a contract with the Egyptian American Oil Company to provide helicopters for oil exploration in the famed wartime western desert.

My employers were engaged in a string of similar activities in the Far East at this time and were operating large Sikorsky type machines in New Guinea and Borneo. They had their main Egyptian base in the city of Alexandria with hangars and maintenance facilities at the nearby airport. Here the company operated seven Bell 47 helicopters which were generally engaged on seismic activities in remote parts of the vast Western Desert. The 'copter crews, together with the geophysicists, geologists and seismic operators were encamped under canvas at various remote locations. These included the El Alamein Cemetery, Abu Quais and the Qatar Depression, the latter merely a great geographical area of sun scorched shimmering sand several hundred feet below sea level and at times one of the hottest places on earth.

These camps were invariably isolated. The nearest Arab village could be anything up to two hundred miles away and the nearest city, Alexandria, four hundred miles back on the coast. So far as the locations permitted the living conditions were very good but flies in their millions found them congenial too. For various reasons my first two months were spent piloting nothing more interesting than the Company's international four-wheel-drive truck. There were no signs of my being required to fly because the six serviceable helicopters were all manned, and with two in the hangar under extensive repair after crashing in the desert, my labour as a driver and mechanic helper was much appreciated, but I hoped for better things.

Like myself, the operating pilots were inexperienced on helicopters, having only recently qualified and accidents happened frequently. The white desert sand dunes certainly made their contributions to these. Operating helicopters at the very low levels often required could create a white-out of blown sand in which ground and sky merged to make visual height assessment virtually impossible. White-outs from blown snow are likewise common in arctic regions. There was one such accident in the desert near the Siwa Oasis where the pilot escaped unhurt but the Bell helicopter was completely wrecked. I went out in the truck with two of our engineers and took it back to the hangar at Alexandria where all of us, pilots and engineers, worked around the clock to rebuild it. The machine was back in the air within forty-eight hours and as the Chief Pilot was heard to remark, "It's earning again and I can hear the lovely clink of dollars, by golly!"

The Bell 47 is of tubular construction and devoid of stressed skin in its boom-like fuselage. For this convenient reason the welding torch can be used to stitch together broken tail booms and twisted distorted centre sections. Depending on the type of accident, the engine might be deemed serviceable and safe to continue flying. After inspection and repair, the rotor head and main transmission would often go back into the 'rebuild', but the main and tail rotors were always a write-off and had to be replaced.

I worked on two of these marathon projects and it was an amazing experience to see a rolled up heap of what looked like scrap metal arrive at our maintenance base and two or three days later see it flying out transformed. One could query the legality of the rebuild but it would be difficult to fault the finished product.

There were other unique experiences in the maintenance hangar. On one occasion we worked without sleep to get a crashed machine back to a critical seismic job that simply couldn't continue without a helicopter. The aircraft was finally pushed out to be test flown by a pilot with my surname when, as it lifted a few feet off the ground immediately in front of the hangar, it whipped over onto its back and was completely wrecked again. I'm pleased to say the pilot was unhurt. It transpired that the control linkages had been reversed in the reassembly and this had not been discovered by a tired, jaded engineer on the pre-flight inspection. So, back into the hangar it went for more midnight hours until it eventually went out again — another complete rebuild.

The helicopter main rotor blades, which were principally constructed of wood and fitted with a glued-on aluminium sheathed leading edge, were a continual source of trouble under desert conditions. Take-off and landing often sandblasted the rotor blades, which eventually resulted in the protective sheathing being split off the edge of the blade, exposing the wooden core. This condition grounded the helicopter until the rotor blades were replaced. We had the desert truck fitted with an overhead rack which could convey at least two sets of these long heavy blades at a time to any of the distant camps. I made a number of these marathon journeys alone to deliver replacement blades and return with the damaged ones.

Every minute a helicopter was grounded was a loss of revenue. It was very difficult in that time and place to obtain aluminium sheathed factory spares. Consequently a lot of unorthodox repairs were used to keep the machines flying. It was make-do-and-mend,

44

very effective and very ingenious.

One morning Jim, the Chief Pilot, called me over and said, "I've got a hell of an urgent delivery for you."

He told me where — about thirty miles from El Alamein.

"They need a new set of blades. They are on the deck and the seismic crew's going nuts."

"How do I get there?" I said. "All the vehicles are out."

"In this." he said pointing to his brand new Peugeot. There was no roof rack and if there had been it would have not supported the weight of two Bell Helicopter blades. Without a word he picked up a hammer and smashed the windscreen and rear window. The blades were fed through the rear window and out through the windscreen leaving me just enough room to drive.

"Any questions?" he said. "On your way."

The delivery was made and I returned with the damaged blades. Unorthodox, non-certifiable but functional repairs were carried out and the blades were ready for re-issue by noon next day.

Travel in the Western Desert could be hazardous. Thousands of landmines were scattered throughout the region. The Egyptian Army professed to have cleared a track from El Alamein Cemetery to Abu Quais, a distance of about twenty-five miles but returning to camp one day with a set of rotor blades Jim stopped the car and said, "We'll eat here and then you can drive the rest of the way." It was midday and very hot. A minute or so later as we were munching our sandwiches there was a violent explosion accompanied by a great plume of black smoke about five-hundred yards away. "There goes another one," said Jim as a second explosion occurred nearby. There were several more blasts before I took the wheel for the rest of the journey.

Company explosive experts told us that the sands covering the mines were continually shifting with the strong night winds and the exposed mines heated up in the hot sun. Many were defective and the expansion of some critical parts displaced the trembler and detonated the mine. Often a small column of blackish smoke escaping from the mine gave a warning of an impending explosion but it could be five minutes before it occurred.

Once I noticed some Arab women working with pliers, screwdrivers and a rock hammer on a flat circular metal object which, on closer inspection proved to be an anti-tank mine. I asked the interpreter what was going on and he said the 'girls' were hoping to extract explosive for the construction of a bomb to be used for sea fishing.

"How did they learn to strip down mines?" I asked.

"Sir," he told me. "I think you call it try and see."

"You mean trial and error."

His moon face burst into a huge grin, "Yes," he said. "And at first some get killed."

Many relics of the war lay about in the desert. A truck might need only a new set of tyres and some petrol before it could be driven away. The air was so dry that nothing rusted. A helicopter pilot spotted the outline of a motorbike in the sand and landed nearby. He found a BMW machine apparently intact except for the tyres. The mechanics returned with a truck and brought it in. They checked the oil which was OK and the magneto was in perfect condition. They put in a little fuel and it started. It had been out in the desert for at least fourteen years. It was in continual use in the camp after that.

Not all the desert was soft sand. Much of it was hard and flinty and damage to our vehicles was common. Once, when driving alone, my truck ran over a boulder which, unknown to me, pierced the gas tank. The engine suddenly cut out, the fuel gauge didn't work and I would have been in serious trouble if I hadn't had a can of Heinz Beans with me. Half an hour later the hole in the tank had been plugged with strips of rag, well jammed in with crushed pieces of bean tin. Fortunately my truck was carrying two drums of aviation fuel and the rest of the journey was uneventful.

For the whole of the first two months in Egypt there was no flying for me, but the hangar time along side the mechanics had much to commend it. I picked up a lot of practical knowledge which would stand me in good stead later. In my opinion this aspect of flying tuition is generally ignored in otherwise excellent training establishments, where it should be included in the much-loved 'airmanship lectures' to which many schools are addicted.

46

Maintenance supply work along with long dusty trips into the desert had become routine. My navigational ability had greatly improved, permitting me to navigate in featureless terrain if not with impunity certainly with a degree of accuracy undreamt of a few short weeks before. But I was a professional pilot and I wanted to fly. The Chief Pilot agreed with my views and got me on an aircraft to Paris and later Head Office sent me to Brunei to fly helicopters on behalf of the British Malayan Petroleum Company in connection with their search for oil.

CHAPTER FOUR

Borneo

I WAS TO BE BASED AT THE BRUNEI STATE OIL TOWN of Seria and fly for the British Malayan Petroleum Company, though my actual employer, and to which I was contracted, was an American international aviation company called Bahamas Helicopters.

The commercial flight from the UK to Singapore was uneventful and the onward flight with another airline took me to the small island of Labuan, a few miles north of the coast of Brunei State, which had one of the few airports in Borneo at that time capable of accepting international flights. From here an oil company twin-engined Percival Prince took me south-west for about sixty miles to land at the British Malayan grassed airstrip at Seria which paralleled a broad beach bordering the South China Sea.

The airstrip was located at the north end of a twenty-mile well surfaced oil company highway which, at that time, terminated at the seat of Local Government, the small town of Kuala Belait, with side roads off to domestic areas, industrial complexes, markets and bazaars. The outskirts of the town were lit, day and night, with the spectacular flares which burned off unwanted butane gas from the oilfields.

This was the only road in that part of the state. The flight down the coast to Seria had revealed a flat impenetrable jungle inland with, in the far distance, the faint outlines of mountains. The near shore was broken here and there by small muddy creeks but overall, the coastline appeared to consist chiefly of white sandy beaches with rocky outcrops. It was possible at low tide for a 4-by-4 vehicle to reach the state capital, Brunei, without ever leaving the sixty-mile beach, but often hazardous.

The partitioned wooden hut which I was allocated was close to the airfield and the butane flares. It was one of a large group occupied by labourers contracted by a Dutch construction

Myself and a Malay Constable
a few weeks before the
ambush which nearly cost me my life

May 29th 1950

The Bullet-holed back of my car
after the ambush

Its windscreen shattered by terrorists' bullets and leaning drunkenly on a
shredded wheel, the Morris Ten looks done for. But when the spare wheel was fitted
it started instantly and was driven away

My second appearance on BBC TV's
What's My Line

Crop Spraying with a Cesna
in Saskatchewan, Canada

An early oilrig off the coast of Borneo
out in the China Sea. A small
helicopter pad can be seen on the right

The British Malayan Petroleum Airfield
(Anduki Airstrip) at Seria in Borneo
Our helicopter hangar in front. Fixed-wing hangars behind

company. The walls were of attap, a type of native thatch. The boarded floor had holes through which the ground was visible. The roof was partially enclosed by half rotten strips of tarpaulin covering holes in the thatch. In short, it was a dump. The oil company's flying and maintenance crews, generally married, were living in modern well-equipped quarters, as were my colleagues in the helicopter company. Recalling the maxim 'Always insist on the best — it's surprising how often you get it' I promptly expressed my extreme dissatisfaction to the Company Director. "What do you want? The Hilton?" he said. "Yes," I replied. And so, (with a mention that marital status was a self inflicted choice), my residence moved to the well-appointed, air-conditioned company hotel.

The Chief Pilot was an American, Fred Gilbert, a helicopter veteran of the Korean War. Company regulations restricted a new and inexperienced pilot to the carriage of freight for the first seventy flying hours. But pressure of work reduced this and I was flying passengers well ahead of this time. As neither of the two Bell helicopters was equipped with any landing instruments, illumination or navigation lights, officially and from the legal point of view we were not entitled to fly at night other than on a mission of mercy. I went out to collect an injured man from a derrick one night but there was no need for landing lights or instrument illumination for the blazing flares lit up everything like noonday. On another occasion I was taking Spence Wilson, a senior member of staff, from an out-station back to the airfield at Anduki when, for one reason or another we were delayed and got back after dark. The result was we flew up the runway with Spence merrily striking matches so that I could see the instruments, whilst every few moments I had to take my eyes off them and stick my head out of the side of the machine to get a better view of the ground. Needless to say, the Chief Pilot expressed himself forcibly and there were no night flights after that.

Kuala Belait was an overgrown village located beyond the extreme end of the oilfield and near the mouth of the sluggish Belait river. It held the seat of local government plus post office and police station. There was a well-equipped company rowing club and I spent much of my leisure time single sculling on the river. A lovely lady, PA to the MD, compounded the pleasure and we had a close friendship. Later, in England, we became engaged but alas she married another.

There were staff functions on the oilfield, which my lady friend was expected to attend. I usually escorted her to these events to which, as a contracted pilot, I might otherwise not have been invited. Group Captain Douglas Bader was on an official visit to the field. There was an impromptu dance at the MD's house and Bader danced with most if not all the ladies. I noticed that he never sat in a chair but on the arm and it occurred to me that he might have anticipated difficulties with his tin legs if he attempted to rise from the lower level of the seat.

The next morning he paid a courtesy visit to our American contracting company. We saw him arrive over at the control tower escorted by the Shell fixed-wing Chief Pilot. Although the distance from the tower to our hangar was little more than a hundred yards we sent the jeep for him. We watched him wave away the vehicle and walk over to us with his swaying gait, which was surprisingly fast. Fred Gilbert escorted him along the line of American, Dutch and British employees. He greeted each with a very pronounced 'Bahrdahr' as he extended his hand. Later my leg was frequently pulled by some of our American friends with a very good imitation of this greeting.

Most of the flying was mundane, mostly between Brunei and outlying camps carrying mail and passengers to jungle clearings and waiting around much of the day to make the return flight could be monotonous. To relieve the boredom we would fly low along the shoreline looking for crocodiles and sharks. One morning I saw a flurry in the water and dropping down to investigate saw a huge stingray, circular in shape, about fifteen feet in width. It looked like a butterfly with a long whip like tail. Swimming in the sea was understandably not encouraged.

I was puzzled by red circular swirling cloud-like formations in the sea, similar in appearance to the effect of pouring a quantity of pale red ink into a pail of water. A local fisherman enlightened me. The clouds were shoals of shrimp that they netted and spread on the hot sand to dry.

Gigantic trees that could, and did, create landing problems encircled many of the outstations. Where a seismic camp was located on a river bank, it was usually safer and more practical to fly in our float equipped helicopters slowly, following the twists and bends of the river, maintaining the machine at an altitude of a few feet above the water and, on arrival, to hover into the landing pad which was normally constructed near the river bank. Often these camps could be categorised as having 'isolation supreme', although they were always well equipped with domestic appliances including refrigerator, cooling fans and generators. I can remember one guy arriving resplendent in a lightweight tropical suit and leaving a few weeks later resembling a ripe mountain goat.

One day, with a geologist as passenger, I landed at a drilling rig down the coast. Going to the cookhouse for coffee we fell into conversation with a driller who told us the place was overrun with rats that were becoming very cheeky, even coming into the living quarters in daylight. I said, "Get a few cats, that should sort the problem." "Sure," said the driller. "We've tried everything else, but where do we get cats out here?"

There were many stray cats on the Base which had been left to fend for themselves when their owners had returned to the UK or the US. With the able assistance of the odd job man we secured six of the most active cats, one of which appeared to be half Siamese. Next morning we secured them in three large boxes on the outside cargo racks and carrying one passenger we set off on the two-hour flight. All went well until we were about to land when the lid of one of the boxes blew off and the inmates, both ginger toms, leapt off as soon as we landed and disappeared into the bush. The rest were released into the living quarters.

All settled in fine including the escapees who preferred life in camp to that of the jungle. Next time we visited it appeared that the cats had not caught a single rat, nevertheless they had totally vanished from the scene; one of the drillers remarking dryly, "Many will have died of shock!"

Other journeys had a touch of excitement. The terminal stages of flight up to Brunei town, the capital of the State, led over a narrow sea inlet fed by a small muddy creek. Suddenly one of the passengers exclaimed, "Hey what the dickens is that?"

He pointed ahead to where a V-shaped ripple could be seen moving across the surface of the water. On the assumption that this was likely to be a crocodile we dropped down for a closer look. To our amazement it was a very large monkey with a big nose swimming strongly just below the surface. Gaining the bank it scampered away into the bush. It was a Proboscis monkey, common in Sarawak but rare in Brunei. In another drilling camp well into the jungle we heard another monkey story. One of the drillers awoke in the night to the sound of munching. This was intermingled with the shrill piercing noise made by insects called Borneo Beetles. Many camps were infested with them; they were about two and half inches long with gauzy wings. Switching on the flashlight the driller was amazed to see a large monkey sitting on the floor contentedly eating its beetle supper.

Our three small Bell helicopters were generally reliable, but obtaining spare parts could be a problem. In particular, the twin-rubberised belts which rotated to drive the fan cooling the engine frequently broke, making an immediate landing imperative before the engine overheated and stopped. This type of belt had an internal metal core subject to corrosion. And since many of the spares had been bought as Korean War surplus there can be no doubt that they were well on the way to being defective when fitted — something no external inspection could show.

Sometimes, only one of the two side-by-side belts failed, with the continued cooling of the engine being little affected. Unfortunately a partially stripped and flailing belt took the other belt with it more often than not, with a loud bang as they broke away. This was followed by rapidly increasing engine cylinder head temperatures with barely two minutes left to effect a landing before the engine seized. In this connection I had one very close call. My helicopter was en route to a converted navy corvette which was engaged on seismic operations forty-five miles offshore and moving very slowly down the coast. My task was to land on the small stern platform fitted to the ship and bring back a number of boxes containing seismic tracings.

The weather was poor, vision being severely restricted by intensive rainsqualls. About four miles out there was a brief sighting of the vessel and at that moment there was an explosion behind my seat. Both cooling belts had gone. The cylinder head temperature rocketed, the ship had vanished from view, the sea was rough and although I was float equipped, to land on a rough sea was to invite disaster.

I got through to the corvette on the marine frequency to report what had happened and, and in that same instant, visibility momentarily cleared. Less than a minute later the Bell alighted on the platform with only seconds to spare because, as I throttled back the engine, it stopped dead, leaving me stranded at sea.

The engineering section ashore came through with the suggestion that when the engine had cooled sufficiently I should remove one of the two spark plugs from each of the six cylinders and pour a small quantity of oil through the plugholes into them. This accomplished an attempt should then be made to turn over the engine with the electric start motor.

I followed this procedure and was relieved to see that the power unit was turning freely, with no unpleasant noises. The engine was started, run up and thoroughly checked, temperatures and pressures appearing normal and with approval from our operations people, I decided to fly back to Anduki. It was a well-calculated risk and would not have been undertaken had a passenger been involved. There was always the possibility that near 'cooking' the engine might have weakened a critical part and involve me in ditching on the way home. The alternative would have been to have the corvette take me to the small coastal town of Miri and offload the helicopter on to the dock. The ship was leased and this would have proved costly for the oil company which employed our machines on this regular offshore mission. Also, mechanical failure of any kind was not something our company liked to advertise.

I must admit that I experienced a feeling of relief when, after half an hour or more over the South China Sea, the beach appeared below my floats.

We were all very glad when the Korean War Surplus belts were replaced by some with nylon reinforcement. But even these failed occasionally and we made it normal pratice to carry two sets of spare belts and also — because of severe leading — several sets of spare spark plugs.

Sudden loss of power and backfiring necessitated an immediate landing to remove and replace plugs completely fouled. Various additives were mixed with the fuel to no avail. The continuous leading of the plugs was responsible for a number of full and partial engine failures.

The rough running and overheating of the cylinders also often caused failure of critical engine components such as valves, connecting rods and pistons. So it can be stated with confidence that constantly having to replace fan belts and spark plugs on some isolated and frequently windswept beach, resulting in bruised knuckles or burnt fingers certainly dispelled any possibility of monotony!

On September 12, 1956 my flying day had commenced at 6am. There were several stops, including one at an offshore oilrig and I was flying back towards my base at Seria, empty apart from four jerricans of extra fuel strapped to the cargo carriers. I was flying low along the coast looking for turtles to break the monotony when there was a violent explosion behind me accompanied by the pungent smell of burning oil. Then silence, stunned silence, except for turning blades.

Immediate emergency action for an engine-off landing was automatic. I clearly recall seeing the beach coming up at an alarming speed, and bracing myself for imminent impact. A split second later, my floats slithered onto the sand — what a relief! Everything was miraculously intact with no damage to the machine, sitting on the sand a reasonably safe distance from the water.

Inspection revealed one engine cylinder blown off and everything covered in oil which was still sizzling. The nearest village was a twenty-mile walk in hot, humid conditions accompanied by swarms of mosquitoes. The chance of any locals coming my way were nil. The whole sixty miles of beach had the reputation of being haunted.

The VHF radio was virtually useless since it operated on line of sight. Nevertheless I transmitted several distress signals on the chance that a passing aircraft might pick them up, but I had no response and I shut down to conserve the battery. All I could do was stay put and wait for a company aircraft to come looking for me when I failed to return to Seria. I set about collecting driftwood for a signal fire and opened up the emergency kit looking for matches. I found bandages, splints, insect repellent, three sandwiches and several two star flares, but no matches at all.

However I could use one of the flares as a pyrotechnic and light the fire with it. As it would be dark in three hours or so I collected as much driftwood as I could find and in doing so I moved further and further away from the helicopter. Then out of the corner of my eye several wild pigs appeared coming from the jungle to the water to root for crabs. They were big, weighing around 250lbs. Less than thirty yards away some others came out of the jungle looking at me before they wandered down to the sea. They had probably never seen a human being before and did not appear unduly concerned.

But suddenly I was confronted by a large wild boar which in addition to grunting at me was kicking up clouds of powdery sand as it pawed the ground. Knowing better than to try and outrun this apparently enraged animal, I picked up what I hoped was a stout piece of wood and began a slow cautious retreat. The pig kept track keeping up its infernal racket until we were both about ten yards from the helicopter. Then throwing caution to the wind I sprinted the rest of the distance and flung myself headlong into the cockpit.

At that moment the boar charged. I grabbed a half empty jerrican and shouting, threw it at him. He skidded to a stop still grunting and snorting and throwing up large quantities of sand. I sat there wondering what the hell to do next when he suddenly lost interest and trotted off into the jungle.

It was almost dark by this time and I couldn't light the fire fast enough. I threw gasoline over the driftwood, grasped one of the flares and pointing it towards the bonfire, twisted the wire spring. With a violent report a single red star ejected, hit the ground, bounced back through my legs and promptly went out. No second star appeared but there was a disconcerting hissing from the cylinder. So I hurled the whole thing into the middle of the driftwood pile and took to my heels. Instantly there was a whoosh and roar followed by a welcome belch of smoke and flame. I had my beacon.

I was thirsty and made my way to a small stream and scooped up some foul tasting water. Climbing back into the cockpit, I covered myself in insect repellent and prepared to have a nap. The first stars were out and I became acutely conscious of animal and bird noises in the jungle and the sound of the night wind in the trees. It wasn't long before a feeling of extreme loneliness swept over me and I needed to keep a firm grip on my imagination. Finally I dropped into a fitful sleep from which I was suddenly and abruptly awakened by the snarl and whine of an aircraft engine passing low overhead, down the beach and out of earshot.

I tried unsuccessfully to make radio contact. I threw more fuel on the fire and then from far away down the beach came the faint sound of a 'plane. I made another attempt to make radio contact this time was partially successful. The pilot flashed his navigation lights. He was receiving me but I couldn't hear him. The Percival Prince then turned away towards Seria. I ate the last sandwich and settled back in the cabin for a sleep until I was abruptly awakened again by something very strange happening outside. I leapt to my feet, catching my head a resounding crack on the control panel, and by the light of the dying fire, I saw strange ghostly shapes coming out of the sea.

In the next moment Perumal, an Indian medical orderly who was an old acquaintance, had thrust into the cabin anxiously trying to feel my pulse. He fumbled with a packet of sandwiches and a thermos of coffee. "Oh Captain," he said, "we've had an awful trip. Rocks, big rocks everywhere."

He cast a scared glance down the beach. "This place is full of ghosts. They whistle like the breeze in the trees." His voice climbed fearfully. "Then they strangle you." Now feeling a little more confident I said, "Well, I've been lucky."

Although obviously terrified of the haunted beach, Perumal

had steeled himself to bring me assistance. He had come fifteen miles down the coast in a company launch to paddle ashore in the middle of the night, using an inflatable raft and contending with hazards such as submerged rocks, sandbars and floating logs. Chief Pilot Jim Davis had been at the controls of the Percival Prince search aircraft and alongside him in the co-pilot position was Douglas Bader. Subsequently he always referred to me as the 'Pig Man.'

When the main rescue party arrived we got the helicopter through the surf into the sea. Here two power driven canoes were tied on, one alongside each pontoon so that the aircraft could be sailed back to the drilling site at Simalaja and then back to Seria. There engine trouble was diagnosed as a combined valve and connecting rod failure. This make of engine had a legal life of only six hundred hours before complete overhaul with a mandatory inspection at three hundred hours. Few of these engines lasted for very long beyond the first major inspection. This type of failure was common.

Most helicopter pilots consider that of all the mechanical problems they may encounter in their career, the failure of the tail rotor is the most serious. Mercifully few will ever be involved in such a malfunction. Emergency drills have been written into flight manuals to assist in keeping control of the aircraft should a failure of this kind occur. Such instructions should only be read as a guide because they will not always be applicable in practice, as I know from personal experience, having been involved in no less than five such failures.

The relatively small but very fast-revving rotor fitting, at right angles to the main rotor but out on the tail boom of conventional helicopters, is intended to provide a sideways thrust in order to prevent the fuselage corkscrewing in a direction opposite to main rotor motion. In effect, the little tail rotor is an anti-torque device: a force opposing a force. It is acknowledged to be a poor engineering principle, but it works. Obviously a failure can occur and survival may depend on expertise, speed of reaction and luck.

Early on an August morning in 1956, I was flying low along the Miri river on the way back from an offshore vessel where I'd dropped off mail. The empty machine was fitted with pontoons and because of the heat, without either door. Cruising along at 60mph at a little more than one hundred feet above the jungle-fringed river and in smooth air, I was looking forward to breakfast at base only sixty miles away.

Over the middle of the river I noticed that the helicopter was tending to veer very slowly to the right. I applied correction with stick and left rudder and instantly the horizon was spinning around me with the machine losing all forward motion, just corkscrewing down out of the sky into the river. I chopped the power by closing the twist grip throttle and in the same movement entered autorotation. Immediately all spinning stopped and within seconds my floats made contact with the water. The right hand float hit the water first with sufficient force to submerge it. It was obvious that the helicopter was about to describe a dynamic roll and turn over. The machine was now banked steeply to the right with the main rotor blades almost touching the water on that side. The floor of the cabin was awash, covering my ankles.

Without hesitation. I applied full power and through coordination of the flight controls managed to drag the helicopter out of its half submerged attitude and up off the water on to an even keel, where the application of full power caused it to recommence spinning. This stopped as the throttle was closed, with the machine now floating in the middle of the river, apparently undamaged but with the current taking it downstream.

The centrifugal forces involved in the initial spin had been severe enough to throw out the Verey pistol, my camera and several other loose items in the cabin. Now another and potentially more serious problem loomed large. Although the engine had been stopped, the heavy main rotor blades were continuing to freewheel at some speed. As the aircraft was being drawn downstream it was only a question of time before they smashed into the big trees at the water's edge. I jumped onto one of the floats and with the emergency wooden paddle that we carried on all pontoon equipped machines I worked furiously to keep the machine in the middle of the river until the rotors eventually came to rest.

All this time, a small native Iban boat with one elderly man aboard had been keeping pace. He was also paddling but had a small outboard fixed to his boat. I spoke to him in Malay. This old naked, tattooed boatman with a large grin on his face, nodded, obviously comprehended the problem, and tied his boat alongside the pontoon. Not attempting to hide his amusement he drove me down the river to the company wharf at Miri. So arrived a sophisticated twentieth century machine towed in by a grizzled old Iban in a craft which had not changed for centuries.

The engineers found that a support for the tail rotor transmission shaft had broken away allowing a splined shaft to slip out of its housing, so breaking the tail rotor's drive. Sheer inertia had kept it going, albeit slowing down, until I applied rudder which coarsened the blade pitch on this unit. It immediately stopped rotation and induced the violent spin which plunged me towards the river.

A few weeks later I was scheduled to go to an oilrig twenty-five miles from the coast with no passengers just a cargo of mail and canned beer. I took off and climbed to three hundred feet. I was about to make a turn out to sea when I felt vibration and stiffening in both control pedals. The condition becoming severe, I made to put the machine down on the airstrip but then both foot pedals seized solid. The helicopter was now swerving violently from side to side and almost uncontrollable. At one hundred feet above the airstrip there was a loud explosion from the rear followed by a sharp spin to the right. As I fought for control, all I could think was 'Not again!' Still slowly spinning, the helicopter fell into low bushes in the overshoot area and would have rolled over if power had not been applied in time. The damage was one torn float and a break next to an old weld in a longitudinal metal supporting tube. My liquid cargo spread itself over the bushes which some of the locals were later seen searching through in the hope of refreshment.

The cause of the crash was never determined. The relatively heavy tail rotor and gearbox and the tubular extension to which both were attached had broken away causing the foot controls to seize up and the loss of their weight at the furthermost point of the aircraft had also prompted the dangerously nose-down attitude of the machine ahead of impact. But *why* had it happened? No-one knew. Base maintenance was exceptionally good and couldn't be faulted. All one could surmise was that many of the incidents might be traced back to the original source of much of our equipment; the Korean War, and an accompanying doubtful mechanical history.

Some flying incidents had their funny side. I was at a cocktail party in October 1956 when I was introduced to two journalists from a London periodical. They were to be my passengers the next day to photograph life on an oilrig. The man was to cover the story and the young blonde lady was the photographer. Both made it very clear that helicopters were not their preferred mode of transport. I spent the evening trying to convince them that it was a very safe method of getting across thirty miles of sea but the lady was still not convinced. "You have to say all this, Captain Jones, as part of the sales pitch." I had a feeling she had heard about some of my escapades.

We took off next morning to tour the oilfield. The girl with her cameras was placed on the outside of the three-place bench seat. The door on her side had been removed since cameras do not work well through Perspex. She was not happy and confessed to feeling very insecure and I reassuringly said, "No-one had fallen out yet." After a Cook's tour of the oilfield she was more relaxed and chattering over the intercom. We then left for the oilrig. The thirty-five minute flight passed without incident. All this time the male passenger had said nothing. We landed on the platform and they were taken below to talk to the drillers. After an hour or so we took off for the return trip, looking at sharks and giant stingrays on the way.

When we were on the final descent the girl looked at me quite keenly and said, "This has been a fantastic experience for me. I am quite convinced that it is just as safe, if not safer, than riding in a car." Then of course it happened — an appalling explosion from the engine and the smell of very hot oil and exhaust fumes filling the cabin. The engine stopped. An appropriately swift reaction got us down on the grass strip without injury or further damage. I didn't have to suggest that my passengers disembark. The helicopter had hardly slithered to a stop when the blonde was doing the hundred-yard sprint up the runway to the control tower, high-heeled shoes in hand. And it was then her companion uttered the only words he had spoken in the whole flight, "You did a good job getting us down," he said.

We were lucky. Landing a float equipped helicopter in autorotation on a grass or other solid surface calls for skill, sure. But also luck. Luck above all. Luck in abundance. Meeting my passengers in the club later I apologised for the scare adding weakly, "No mechanical contrivance was perfect."

In some parts of Borneo helicopter pilots were making 'firsts' almost every time a machine landed. Quite often it was the first flying machine that the native people had ever seen and they would turn out in their hundreds. The American company which employed me was the first to introduce helicopters and my British Borneo Commercial Pilot's Licence was the first to be issued and is numbered '1'. Borneo was rapidly becoming air minded. There was a feeder service, the oil company's aircraft and also a religious Mission had a single engined aircraft which carried medical supplies, stores and mail to remote outposts and brought in anyone in need of serious medical attention.

Flying was difficult because of the terrain and it was potentially dangerous too when unpredictable weather was added to the equation. At least eighty per cent of the country was covered in thick impenetrable primary jungle where a forced landing would most likely prove fatal. The Mission's aircraft crashed in one such location and, as it had turned over after touching down, the small four-seater was extensively damaged. Fortunately neither the pilot nor the passenger was injured. Native bearers brought in the remains of the aircraft in bits and pieces. I carried a complete wing made fast to the side of my Bell helicopter.

In October an engineer passenger and myself were en route to Brunei and about fifteen miles from the river mouth of the Belingian River. There was an unusual noise from somewhere behind us in the machine and a perceptible slowing of the main rotor accompanied by a swishing noise. Without hesitation I carried out a landing on the river where our pontoons allowed us to water taxi under full control. The swishing sound continued but we had no idea what had happened.

After rounding numerous bends in the river, dodging large

logs, debris and overhanging branches, a small clearing with freshly felled logs appeared. About twenty Ibans emerged from native huts. Because of logs and poles at the water's edge we couldn't taxi up to the shoreline, so the Ibans came out with their canoes and pushed us alongside the rough wooden jetty. It was then discovered that a metal trim tab near the top of the trailing edge of the main rotor had become partially detached from the blade and was acting as an air brake. Since the tip speed of the main rotor was in the region of 500 miles per hour it was fortunate that the distorted tab, involved with such a drag factor, had not caused more serious problems apart from the swishing noise and the tendency of the rotor to slow. My engineer passenger removed the offending tab with a sharp pocketknife saying, "She's right, let's go."

However there was a potential problem. The helicopter had to be towed back into the middle of the river by our Iban friends and released at precisely the right moment. The Bell, floating on water which, unlike solid ground, offered little resistance would slowly rotate in the opposite direction to the main rotors, due to the effect of torque. It was quite usual for a helicopter on floats to make about two and a half turns in this way until the engine built up sufficient thrust to make the small tail rotor spin fast enough to halt this rotation. Meantime the machine would be floating helplessly downstream and, if the engine failed to start, could crash into the trees on either side of the river unless the Ibans could prevent it. Fortunately everything went according to plan and we were waved off by our helpful native friends.

My contract ended in January 1957 and, after two years, it was time to move on. This time to Okanagan Helicopters, the largest helicopter company in Canada.

CHAPTER FIVE

Canada

OKANAGAN HELICOPTERS HAD APPROXIMATELY FORTY machines on strength. Most were Bell 47 models of the type flown in Borneo. There was also a small number of Sikorsky 55's, powered by one nose-installed Pratt and Whitney radial air-cooled engined of six hundred horse power. These ex-Canadian Air Force machines had been flying the western sector of the Mid-Canada Defence Line, but government policy had decided that civilian companies would take over the necessary air support of these isolated but manned Radar Locator Stations.

They had been constructed to give advance warning should the Russians decide to attack and were sited across Canada at some distance north of the United States border. A number of helicopters were being taken over by my employers and I was to fly one of the Sikorskys on this defence line and to be based at Dawson Creek. In 1957 this was a small town in British Columbia located about four hundred air miles north of Vancouver with possibly its only claim to fame being its position at Mile Zero, where the Alaska Highway commenced its tortuous one thousand mile journey north to Alaska and the midnight sun.

However, I was first required to successfully complete the mountain training course at Kamloops, a small town on the western edge of the Rocky Mountain range and, by road, one hundred and sixty miles north-east of Vancouver. Although my flying logbook recorded a total of no less than 1200 hours on helicopters, my mountain experience was limited with regard to rotary-wing equipment. As an experienced glider pilot used to understanding air currents, thermal activity and wind effect on mountain ridges, this was to help on the specialised mountain training course.

My employers operated in the Rocky Mountains of British Columbia, the Yukon Territory and into Alaska and the arctic regions of Northern Canada. The Training School was established to instruct both licensed and student pilots in the methods essential to operate the early and generally underpowered Bell helicopters with an extra modicum of safety. This was often a critical factor when operating at high altitude in a heavily loaded aircraft where, not infrequently, adverse air currents exceeded the ability of the machines to climb through them. The potentially environmentally unfriendly terrain which could be encountered demanded special knowledge of mountain flying techniques, therefore it was company policy that all pilots and, in particular, newly employed ones, should complete this course. The Manager and Chief Pilot of the School, Don Poole, a very experienced middle-aged stockily built Canadian, had been with the company for a number of years.

It was late February and the country in the vicinity of Kamloops was covered in a mantle of deep snow. In the winter months, when working away from the cleared area in front of the hangar, the School exercises usually involved landing on snow. Because the long tubular skid landing gear offered little resistance to soft or crusted snow, with the very real danger of sinking far enough to involve the tail rotor in a ground strike, small flat square shaped pads of wood or metal were attached by brackets near to the aft end of each skid. These had the effect of spreading the weight of the helicopter more evenly particularly to the rear where most weight was concentrated. It was for the want of a better term a type of snowshoe but without the webbed surface, and was often referred to as 'bear paws.'

Great care had to be exercised when taking off from a snow covered frozen surface, particularly if the machine had been parked there overnight. In these circumstances, both skids could be so solidly attached to the frozen ground that in lift-off one might break free slightly ahead of the other.

And so critical was the lateral centre of gravity on conventional helicopters that the ensuing bank as the machine jerked free might be momentarily uncontrollable, resulting in a dynamic roll and a wrecked aircraft.

Over the years this type of incident has been the subject of many official accident reports in Canada. With pre-knowledge it was easily avoided by sliding the machine a few inches forward before lift-off, thus evenly breaking skid contact with the frozen surface.

One evening in the hotel, Don had called by for a drink. We were discussing the various problems associated with winter operations when he commented, "I never cease to be surprised that a simple, safe antidote like this is so often ignored resulting all too often in the loss of a valuable machine and, not infrequently, injury to the occupants."

That evening he also told me of an incident which had occurred with a company Bell helicopter the previous summer. The pilot and his engineer, an 8mm movie camera enthusiast, had been flying to a geological camp somewhere in the Yukon when they spotted a large grizzly bear lumbering along on all fours. This photographic opportunity seemed too good to miss so they moved in to obtain some close-up camera shots. They were flying without the right hand door, which in some circumstances was normal practice, and the engineer was leaning out to obtain clear, unobstructed shots of the fast running bear, now closely ahead.

The ground was sparsely covered with low tufted clumps of dry scrub like stunted bush, offering no obstacle to the animal which went through and over most of it at a gallop, with the helicopter in close pursuit. The ground which had been relatively flat, now abruptly fell away steeply and the animal, moving at full speed, lost its footing near the bottom of the incline to roll over two or three times before regaining its feet. Later the engineer was to say, "This was when that durned old bear got right mad!"

According to the pilot, at this point it stopped in its tracks to turn round and confront its tormentors. Rearing up to a full height of nearly eight feet, it attempted to grasp the landing skids of the helicopter. The 8mm movie camera which had been operating for all of the relatively short chase, continued to turn over as the grizzly faced the now hovering, near ground level, machine with the pilot frantically attempting to 'back off'.

Both occupants were suddenly confronted by Bruno's snarling jaws equipped with long vicious fangs and the bear's outstretched slashing wickedly manicured claws. The enraged beast was obviously intent on destruction, not intending to run another yard, and the boys cleared off hurriedly having acquired a unique photographic record of the event.

The footage was to have an hilarious finale — with the hand held camera still turning over and recording violently gyrating images of the sky, the raging bear revealing a nice set of dentures, the machine's instrument panel and one grim faced pilot determined to 'get the hell out.'

Don told me that this extraordinary film was a star attraction for visitors at the Company Headquarters on Vancouver Airport. Some years later I was to see it and quoting from memory, this amateur and hastily produced record of the real thing was much as Don had told me that night at Kamloops. He of course, knew the participants in this highly dramatic incident, had talked with them at the time and was therefore able to add details which the camera could not show.

The short course included full engine off, or autorotation landings, together with approaches, take-offs and landings in the nearby mountains at between 3500 and 7000 feet above sea level all blanketed with snow. Here, too, using vertical air currents played a major part in the training.

Put simply, the general wind follows the contours of the country and, when coming to a mountain, climbs up one side to descend on the other. If sufficiently strong, the downside wind could be dangerous. The experienced pilot kept clear of it when this was operationally possible. The ascending air current side he could use to obtain 'free lift', like a glider pilot, staying in it in order to achieve the ascent with much reduced engine power.

Ignorance of how to deal with air currents was a potential killer here because the downside in the Rockies often possessed fast downward moving air masses which exceeded in thrust the ascending ability of most helicopters of the period. Extreme, and therefore dangerous, turbulence was a common accompanying factor when manoeuvring high up in the mountains.

One day nearing the end of the course, the Chief Pilot, Don Poole, was demonstrating mountain landing techniques with a loaded machine. We had been flying at about five hundred feet over densely forested country devoid of open spaces for at least twenty miles and the prepared landing site consisted of a flat wooden training platform on a ridge at an elevation of 4,200 feet above mean sea level. With the helicopter on final approach, Don allowed it to gradually sink whilst maintaining a considerable forward speed. We closed to 400 yards, descending to around 100 feet above the trees and, with ever reducing speed, he came in on a flat approach to ease onto the pad in a near perfect landing.

Later, comfortably seated in the crew room, I asked Don, "What if the engine had quit at that very low level on the final landing approach?"

"Well," he answered, "for the last fifteen miles or more we had been flying over dense impenetrable forest. Many of those trees are two hundred feet high. Why does the last hundred yards seem so important when there are no clearings within miles in which to make a successful emergency landing?" I saw the point.

I said, "Such logic cannot be faulted, but I'd sure like to have two engines for this kind of jaunt!" "Don't forget," he observed, "you'd also have two chances of an engine failure."

"Yep," I chuckled, "but not, we would hope, at the same time!"

In early 1957 there were few twin-engined helicopters, and none, operating commercially. So one had to develop a single-engine mentality and when compelled to fly over inhospitable ground as we so frequently encountered, we put our trust in the well-earned reliability of our engine, be it a product of Mr Franklyn, Mr Lycoming or their bigger cousin, Messrs Pratt and Whitney. Nevertheless I kept my powder dry and, whenever possible, routed my flights in after years to include potential emergency sites, even though they might not lie exactly on the required track. Unfortunately the nature of this business usually dictated a completely different course of action on long sea crossings, some of which I was to make in the years ahead.

The mountain areas of Harper and Tod lay a few miles to the north-east and at this time were mainly covered with snow. The district was used on the course for practice take-offs and landings. The main rotors created an artificial blizzard, restricting visibility and making excellently realistic practice conditions before the student was subjected to the real thing in the unforgiving Canadian winter. On completion of the course and before leaving for Vancouver, Don walked across, shook my hand and said, "S'long Paddy, you did well." I have yet to be paid a greater compliment. There is no doubt in my mind that his instruction contributed in no small measure to my ultimate survival as a helicopter pilot.

On 16 March 1957 together with three other pilots, Couch, McNaulty and Smith, we collected three S55 helicopters from the Air Force near Ottawa and started on the two thousand mile flight across Canada to Dawson Creek in British Columbia. I flew mainly as co-pilot with Murray Couch and was checked out on the journey for my captaincy. On this flight we encountered very bad weather, with snowstorms at times reducing visibility to three or four hundred yards. Navigation under these conditions was difficult but much assisted, whenever possible, by following the tracks of the two trans-Canada railroads which linked the major towns and cities. Navigational problems were also made easier by the directional use of the radio compass. As long as some altitude was gained between snow flurries, it was possible to tune into the next town's radio programmes, the needle of the radio compass pointed in the direction of the town.

The weather being generally poor, our three aircraft had often to fly low to maintain essential ground contact and at times the presence of overhead power cables posed a real threat. We had no prior knowledge of the location of their massive supporting towers and the sudden appearance of one or more of them out of the murk immediately ahead could be very frightening. On one occasion travelling low in freezing fog, we had to drop even lower than usual to get under snow-laden sagging cables to avoid certain disaster. Being an agricultural pilot, flying under power and telephone lines had been an everyday experience, but flying at near zero feet in snow flurries, sleet and freezing fog was something else!

Later we were flying over snow-covered countryside with the forests of pine and birch trees blanketed white. A great stillness lay over the scene. The wind had dropped, the clouds had cleared, but it was bitterly cold. The glass had fallen to twenty below zero, though as the helicopter was adequately heated Murray and I suffered no discomfort. We refuelled at Nakina, a small town on the railroad and at other similar small places all the way across this great country: Armstrong, Sioux Lookout, Kenora, Winnipeg, Saskatoon, Edmonton and finally reached our destination: Dawson Creek.

I flew many of the legs along the route and, when co-pilot, took in the ever changing scene. We flew over hundreds of frozen lakes and whole vast areas of dead trees where once a great forest fire had passed that way. We saw many moose, some alone and others in groups which usually trotted away as we approached. On another occasion we saw a group of Indians fishing through holes drilled in the frozen lake. They waved as we passed overhead. Where they lived or had come from was a fascinating puzzle because in all this bleak wilderness there were no habitations at all to be seen — not even a tent.

There was ample time during this trans-Canada flight to see and appreciate all that this immensely big country had to offer because we were always flying at relatively low altitudes and at speeds which seldom exceeded ninety miles an hour.

Our three aircraft had flown through many blizzards and encountered gale force winds often in sub-zero temperatures. The journey had covered sparsely populated areas consisting of mile after mile of dense inhospitable snow drenched forests where an engine failure spelt disaster. Then on across great frozen lakes and ice choked rivers. I was amazed to see cars driving along a solidly frozen river somewhere in Alberta and, pointing this out to Murray, he told me that it was common practice in some sparsely populated areas across Canada. It was easier and more convenient to utilise a 'snow road' on a river than attempt to negotiate local roads made impassable in the depths of winter because adequate snow clearing equipment was not immediately available. The single Pratt and Whitney radial 600 horse power engines with which our helicopters were fitted, had purred contentedly throughout the undertaking and except for minor defects, the long flights were completed without a major hitch.

Although well used to flying single-engined helicopters, flights over solid forestry or large areas of open water were never to my liking. There was a saying in the helicopter fraternity that the engine goes into 'automatic rough' when crossing stretches of water smoothing out again immediately the coast is reached. I guess it's all in the mind!

In 1957 Dawson Creek was a jumble of buildings of various sizes, many of them little better than unpainted wooden shacks. The town, if such it could be termed, boasted a cinema and a bowling alley and the main street possessed several assorted stores, two banks, a post office and, at the crossroads in the town centre, a signpost which proudly informed the sightseer that he or she was standing at Mile Zero on the Alaska Highway.

The Mid-Canada Line camp where we all lived was just outside town. This was the nerve centre for this section of the Line and here technicians and other Line personnel were based before flying in our helicopters to carry out maintenance work or to relieve others already operating advanced electronic equipment on the sites.

The radar sub-stations along the Line were located about thirty miles apart and, in good visibility, the mast of one site could often be seen from another. Each was equipped with a radio beacon onto which we could home with our radio compass should poor visibility make location of the sub-station difficult. For ease of identification all the sites carried numbers. Dawson Creek, the master, being known as 900. My own assignment was to supply aerial transportation to two sites to the west and four to the east. These isolated posts, only approachable from the air, were usually manned on a round-the-year basis by two operators and two or three maintenance people. A high wired security fence marked each perimeter. Refuelling facilities were available on some sites but we normally planned to do the round trip to a sub-station and back without refuelling.

The sites each boasted three long, low, hutted buildings, the materials for the construction of which had been flown in by helicopter or hauled along frozen 'water roads' by caterpillar tractor trains. In each case they were completely dwarfed by a 150 foot geodetically constructed radar scanning mast on top of which were six or eight bowl shaped scanners or receivers.

We took turns with the flying and endeavoured to have one machine on standby in the event of an emergency and the third in the hangar on routine maintenance. However, due to the pressure of work, the system often took a tumble with two helicopters working flat out and a harassed ground staff struggling around the clock to get the third one off inspection and onto the tarmac for the compulsory standby. There was little entertaining being done during off-duty hours, but the camp was comfortable, the food excellent and we had a good library and easy access to town.

Then the thaw commenced and everything was covered in thick half frozen mud. The walk into Dawson was an unpleasant experience and the reward seldom worth the effort there being a woeful lack of suitable female company. In fact no female company of any sort. I soon decided that being sprayed with mud by passing vehicles and slipping and sliding in and out of wheel ruts had little to recommend it. So for much of the remainder of my short stay I remained in camp and amused myself with a generous assortment of books, some of which must have escaped the attentions of the Canadian censors.

Our supply flights were not free of problems relating to weather for, although the thaw had set in and the deep snow which had covered the muskeg was melting away, the temperature was still well below freezing for much of the time. Particularly so at night when the sun had dropped.

The muskeg itself was not altogether level but presented a somewhat uneven appearance. It resembled a mixture of half rotting vegetation mixed with moss and lightly interwoven with a woody fibre. It was impossible to walk on because one sank into it with every step, making each a great physical effort. It also acted as a type of thermal insulation, preventing the sun's rays from reaching the frozen ground beneath. So tenacious was this vegetation that when we attempted to clear an area around the camp using a bulldozer, the blade quickly clogged up, to ride unevenly over its surface. It was with the greatest difficulty that the job was eventually completed.

During the day we frequently flew into wet sleeting rain and localised snow-showers, reducing visibility to less than one

71

hundred yards. In these conditions it would be dangerous to carry on and occasionally an unscheduled landing would be made in a clearing or even on a frozen pond or lake. As we were flying with a wheeled undercarriage as opposed to skids, one had to be very careful when landing away from a prepared surface. The loaded machine weighed 7300 lbs. This represented a fairly high wheel loading and, to land without the risk of a breakthrough, it was best to put down on packed snow or solid ice. When landing on a frozen lake it was very important to check that the ice was thick enough to support the weight of the machine. In the depths of winter this was no problem but in late winter and early spring a day-to-day knowledge of ice conditions in the working area was vital.

Part of our route of patrol was through the celebrated Peace River farming country, much of which was opened to farmers after the Great War. One of the sites was within ten miles of a farm which on the slightest pretext I made sure to visit. The coffee was out of this world and so was the farmer's charming daughter! Early one morning I was perched, as usual at the kitchen table when with a deafening roar, one of the other helicopters passed low overhead, made a circuit and then flew west back towards the base. I realised that my little secret was out and later heard that after I was posted from this area the other pilot knowledgeably took over.

One day doing a routine stores job we flew into what appeared to be a mixture of sleet and rain. About two minutes later the helicopter began to lose height and further application of power did not help. An old abandoned seismic camp appeared ahead. I landed heavily in a clear space next to the remains of a wooden hut. It took every bit of available power to make it in, as by this time it was only just possible to maintain level flight. When the rotors stopped my passenger and I took a look around the machine but the initial inspection failed to show anything wrong. I climbed up to the main rotor head where a glance down one of its three blades revealed a layer of clear ice running its whole length. The other two were in the same state. We had unknowingly flown through an area of freezing rain. The blades had iced up and their aerodynamic shape had altered so the whole rotating mass had lost lift, a situation becoming ever more and more dangerous as more ice was picked up. In another minute the lift being produced by the rotor system might not have equalled the weight of the helicopter with fatal results, for the fuselage had also picked up a quantity of ice and this, of course, added weight to the helicopter at a time when we least wanted it.

Then the weather suddenly changed. The sun came out and slowly our blades de-iced to the point where it was possible to proceed in safety.

Towards the middle of April, a man walked into the flight office to inform me that he was my relief. I was astonished. "You are being transferred to Fort McMurray," he told me. This was the first time I had heard of it and it was bad news. The Operations Manager in Vancouver had assured me that I was to remain at Dawson Creek for some time. It was the least isolated post on the Line and when compared with Site 800 at McMurray could be described as being in the lap of luxury.

I queried these verbal orders and the pilot then informed me that he was being posted to Dawson because he was married and the site had suitable accommodation for couples, so he was bringing his wife. I thought it odd that she had not arrived in the car with him but I accepted the position with poor grace, and departed by Cessna aircraft next morning for Fort McMurray, a small settlement approximately three hundred miles to the east.

On the way across, the Cessna pilot told me that although my relief was married he was awaiting a divorce. I also learned that he had been an old friend of a very senior company official at Vancouver. This was hearsay but it did not improve my feelings.

The ski-equipped Cessna arrived over the camp and circled a few times to announce its presence. The pilot then set course to the east and put down on a frozen lake. He dropped me off casually in the middle of it saying, "S'long, somebody will be along to pick you up." With these kind words he took off, leaving me standing up to the ankles in icy water in the middle of nowhere.

The thaw was now in full swing and although the ice on most of the lakes would permit light ski planes to land for a further two or three weeks, there was always a few inches of melted ice on the surface.

Picking up my bag I trudged through the slush towards an opening in the bush some three hundred yards distant where, with soaking feet, half frozen and dejected, I awaited rescue. It was an hour before I heard the noise of an approaching vehicle and a further twenty minutes before a caterpillar-tracked swamp buggy lumbered into view.

It took over an hour to cover the six miles to camp. The snow packed winter track had melted, exposing surface tree roots, outcrops of rock, and small ridges. On several occasions fallen trees blocked the trail and compelled a diversion. The ride was very rough. The vehicle shook and shivered, clattering, dipping and shuddering along a trail we could barely see. It was the most uncomfortable ride on any vehicle that I have ever encountered.

My new base, Site 800, was twenty air miles from the small town of Fort McMurray. It was a partly constructed campsite on a hill known as Stony Mountain. The crew's living quarters were still only half built, so I bunked with around thirty French Canadian labourers in a large dormitory.

Outside, by comparison with Dawson Creek, the ground was a morass. One slipped and stumbled through half frozen, sticky, slimy mud to the helicopter, to the mess hall, to the sleeping quarters and to everywhere else. There was mud in and on everything.

A dirt track terminated at a railroad halt four miles below the camp. There was no other road to the outside world. Access to the site was either by a weekly rail service from Fort McMurray or by helicopter. McMurray had an airport where, twice a week an airline DC3 landed. We pilots took it in turns to meet this aircraft with one of our helicopters to collect mail, spare parts or company officials from our base in Vancouver.

On one of these trips a colleague and his engineer observed with amusement a very attractive stewardess disembark wearing very high stiletto heels. They watched interestedly as she picked her way carefully down the slatted wooden boardwalk from aircraft to terminal wisely, about halfway, removing her shoes to complete the journey in stockinged feet.

The crew gave her full marks for intelligence and for the elegant picture she presented.

74

By the end of April, the combination of my unfair posting, and the poor living conditions compounded by the nightly orchestral snoring of thirty construction workers was enough. I resigned, not without regret on both sides.

There was no shortage of employment for qualified and experienced helicopter pilots and an independent airline promptly offered me a job flying a Bell 47 in the northern bush at a much improved salary. I accepted.

The job was a seasonal geographical survey in the far north of Canada. I flew, as passenger in a C46, the eleven hundred miles to Dawson City in the Yukon. The flight, which included a number of stops, was over some of the most desolate territory in the country. Although it was late May, much of the landscape was still covered by deep snow, but this was thawing fast and the rivers were in flood and some surrounding forested areas under water.

The pilot I was relieving and his mechanic met me at the primitive airstrip. He left on the Curtis C46 on which I had arrived but before I could even take stock of my surroundings, the Mounted Police had called out every able bodied man to fill sand bags in an attempt to prevent the convergent flood waters of the Klondike and Yukon Rivers from entering the town.

Both rivers were raging torrents. Due to the fast thaw the floods were the most widespread in living memory. We worked through the night and the next morning filling sand bags and dumping them where a breach threatened. The few resident women provided meals and jugs of hot coffee. In late morning word came from the Commissioner of the Yukon ordering me to attempt to rescue five men believed trapped on the McQuestion Bridge over the Stewart River fifty miles from Dawson.

Because of a strong headwind it took me over an hour to reach the bridge, both ends of which had been carried away by the rising water which now threatened to demolish the whole structure. Of the men there was no sign. There were three or four wooden shacks on the riverbank which were already flooded. If the river rose any higher it was likely they would be swept away with the bridge.

There was no sign of movement neither animal nor human, anywhere in this scene of utter desolation, just the swirling, angry waters carrying debris of every description. Having circled the bridge and the roads on either side, I climbed higher for a more general view. A few minutes later, above higher ground two miles along the gravel road and well clear of the river, the lazy trailing smoke of a campfire became visible.

Closer inspection revealed a small dirty-white tent and five men by the fire drinking coffee. The skin of a black bear was stretched out to dry on the ground in front of them.

I landed the helicopter well away from the camp and the fire. Walking over to the group I asked, "Are you all right?" All, except one, were Indians. A tall man, who introduced himself as the foreman, replied, "Sure we're OK. What the heck are you doing here?"

We were interrupted by a very old white man, the camp cook, who shouted, "Wouldya like a kaffee?" He was Louis Burrel, at least eighty-five years of age and renowned as a character who had cooked for generations of bush camps. I accepted the coffee and explained why I had been sent.

With a quiet smile, the foreman said, "We were working on the bridge when the river started to rise. A single-engined aircraft flew over us at low level and we waved and it flew off. When it looked likely that the bridge would flood we left to set up camp here."

"Well," I said, "the pilot must have thought that you were in danger of drowning and that's why I'm here with instructions to fly back with the foreman — that's you." However the Indian laughed, pointed to the distant helicopter and retorted "No way am I going to Dawson in that. Old Louis, our cook, is getting bushed. Take him along."

So the old cook flew back with me to Dawson City saying, "I'm goldarned fed up cookin' for this bunch and anyhow, I need a blankety-blank drink!"

We landed at Dawson outside the one hotel and were met by members of the press and two cameramen up from Whitehorse for the story. Louis jumped out of the helicopter and dived straight into the bar, followed by the press. It must have been the most expensive 'liquid run' on record, and all paid for by the Yukon Government Authorities.

Dawson City was really a ghost town with remnants of the Gold Rush days. The old theatre was just about still standing. Mr Adams, one of the city's old timers, had been a tap-dancing entertainer there back in 1898, and he gave me a guided tour of the building. There were stalls and two balconies from which the shows could be seen. The price of whiskey depended on where the customer was seated. A Bottle cost $35 at street level rising to $70 on the top balcony. His explanation was that it took time for the hostesses to climb two flights of stairs and deliver the drink and time was money in Dawson.

Another version was told to me by an old Irish lady of eighty-five who had been a 'Madam' in Dawson's heyday. "On the top floor" she said, " the girl was expected to stay and chat for a least five minutes. You have to remember that the miner may not have seen or spoken to a girl for ten months or a year and would willingly pay for her time when he came into town tired, but possibly very wealthy."

According to her these were the exceptions because most of the miners left Dawson City as broke as the day they arrived.

I asked her if the girls were strictly respectable or were they 'available'? "Oh," she replied, "These were truly respectable girls. We had a house for the other sort of thing elsewhere. But, of course, these girls had special friends too you know."

The real money in Dawson was made out of groceries, drink, entertainment, tools and mining equipment. At the theatre, drink was paid for with chips purchased at the entrance desk with gold. Mr Adams told me that periodically the floor under this desk was lifted and the soil beneath sifted for gold dust, which it was said, dropped through in minute quantities during weighing and checking. A shaking hand may have helped.

A number of old men from the Gold Rush days lived the year round in Dawson City at an old peoples home and were known as 'The Pioneers'. From them one could hear fantastic stories of an extraordinary period in Canadian history. In these days a Royal Canadian Mounted Police Sergeant and just two Constables kept law and order throughout the whole Yukon Territory. There was little crime and no murders recorded in Dawson during this period.

Orders had arrived during the McQuestion Bridge rescue and the helicopter was urgently required in a very remote and unmapped area to the north to assist in a seismic survey. This location was known as Eagle Plains, thirty miles north of the Arctic Circle and two hundred and ten miles north of Dawson City. It was very mountainous and completely uninhabited country, part of the Ogilvie Mountain range.

We refuelled at Chapman Lake, best described as a very large body of water in the middle of nowhere, from a previously arranged fuel source put in by a Beaver float plane. Our flight had taken eighty minutes, but as the final trip was calculated to take well over two hours — assuming we encountered no problems locating the drilling camp — two extra jerricans of fuel were strapped onto the side panniers to be on the safe side. The refuelling completed, my passengers, an engineer and an oil-drilling superintendent, and I sat down for sandwiches and coffee.

We were discussing the next leg of the flight with the oilman assuring me he knew the drilling area like the back of his hand and no way could we get lost. Having heard similar statements from local experts many times in the past a quiet chuckle was my only response. Suddenly we were all conscious of a 'presence' and there not fifty yards away and silently watching us was a herd of a hundred or more caribou deer. They stood completely motionless in a semi circle around us, not at all frightened but obviously intensely curious.

The oilman whispered, "Watch this, Paddy," and gradually, taking a red coloured handkerchief out of his top pocket very slowly and still sitting, moved it back and forth in front of him.

The animals, with curiosity even more apparent on their intelligent faces, moved closer and, eventually, they were within ten feet of us. They had formed almost a complete circle around us when we all got to our feet and the spell was broken as they galloped away across the flat plain which encompassed the lake.

The remainder of the flight was uneventful. For ease of navigation we followed the Porcupine and East Porcupine Rivers, both running in a northerly direction, to hit the Johnson River, which flowed in from the north-west. We landed at Eagle Plains Camp, sixty-six degrees North. The flight took two hours and fifteen minutes with no problems other than the frightening scenery.

The camp at Eagle Plains was part of the vast Peel Plateau. It consisted of twelve trailer cabins and an operational drilling rig hauled up from Dawson City during the winter on sledges towed by powerful snowmobiles and caterpillar tractors. Because there were no roads or tracks from Dawson City, the operation had been completed by driving on frozen rivers where these coincided with the required route. The normal temperatures of forty or more below zero made this already difficult operation more complicated, requiring internal heating in all the vehicles in order to restart engines after anything more than a thirty minute shutdown. At these low temperatures engine oil freezes, inside an engine or out. It took about a month to cover ground that no white man had ever seen except from an aircraft. Much of this territory was unmapped or, where maps existed, as on my flight, many portions of them were blank.

The country around the camp can best be described as consisting of slightly rolling plains with little obvious growth other than clumps of stunted bushes. This far north, well above the Arctic Circle, the ground was permanently frozen to a considerable depth. The small drill used for a localised experiment was bringing up frozen core from over three hundred feet down and the main drilling rig later reported the presence of permafrost from about seven hundred feet below the surface.

But living conditions in this cabin camp were good. The cabins were screened against mosquitoes and comfortable and we had a very good cook who had been a chef in Vancouver. The old man in charge of camp facilities must have been in his eighties and had been a professional boxer. He was super fit and possessed a full head of snowy white hair. Tom, the helicopter engineer had not been in Canada long. He had come from London where he had driven a taxi but had felt the urge to get out of the rat race. The only fly in the ointment, so to speak, was the mosquito, which attacked in massed squadrons and made life a misery anywhere outside the living quarters.

Work for my helicopter entailed carrying a seismic operator and dropping him off at various pre-selected spots, waiting a few minutes whilst he carried out survey checks then picking him up and repeating the process. Always the main problem was to find a spot clear of muskeg where it was safe to land the skid equipped machine. The surveyor had to be put down close to his pinpointed spot whilst I kept a wary eye out for muskeg which could swallow the machine's skids within seconds and smash the fragile tail rotor as it hit the ground. We usually settled on my choice of the firmest looking piece of nearby ground, even if the surveyor had to sink over his boots to reach his pinpointed spot. Better that than a thirty mile hike back to camp.

We completed this work in five days but due to the nature of the operation a total of only nine hours was flown. Other trips involved longer distances; forty or even sixty miles from camp. The seismic surveyor had his own problem to deal with, particularly the unforeseen depth of frozen ground, which had taken the experts by surprise.

My helicopter's performance gave no serious cause for concern but in May an entry in my logbook reads: 'Johnson Indian Village (deserted) engine backfired over lake.' Examination by the engineer found nothing and it was probably a spark plug partially oiled up — a little scary in the middle of a very large, deep cold lake. Oil was struck here not long after we moved out, the first find in the Arctic regions of Northern Canada, then known as 'Eagle Plains One'.

Late morning on the last day of May we flew back to Dawson via Sid and Chapman Lakes, through Summit Pass. We paused only to refuel from four jerricans secured to the side panniers, not stopping for further fuel at Chapman Lake. With only two people on board the machine was comparatively light and able to carry the fuel required. The only life we saw on the entire four-hour trip were two grizzly bears near Summit Pass and several moose feeding off the bottom of a shallow lake. We landed at Dawson City in the late afternoon and booked into the Pearl Harbour Hotel for a hot bath and a very large whiskey.

80

Early June found us on our way to Granville, an old mining site thirty-five miles south-east of Dawson. The asbestos company had set up a tent camp and had been awaiting our arrival for three days. They were not destined to see the helicopter that day either because, just after take-off, the new and recently installed servo-assisted controls failed in flight and we had to return to Dawson on manual control. Next day with the aircraft again serviceable, we landed at Granville and met the twelve members of the group. Eight of them were geology students doing fieldwork in the university vacation. The party chief was a Canadian Chinese, Randy Lee, with a Master of Science degree. His wife was a medical doctor and later Randy switched from geology to medicine.

We were camped on a piece of sloping ground surrounded by old mine workings. The tents were large enough to sleep four men but Tom, the engineer, and I had one to ourselves. There was also a mess tent, the students taking it in turns to prepare the meals, a set-up leaving much to be desired. But if it had not been for the ubiquitous mosquitoes, life at Granville could have been quite pleasant. One had to wear a head net attached to the hat for some protection against them. Black swarms followed us round the camp.

During the heat of the day they perched on the side of the tent shielded from the sun and caused the white surface to appear black. We took insecticide sprays to the outdoor toilet in a vain hope of protecting our more tender parts. No such luck. They even penetrated the mosquito nets over our sleeping bags at night. We covered our bodies with mosquito repellent, smearing it on all over, but it only seemed to excite them to more frenzied activity. They made life pure unadulterated hell. Strangely enough they were just as bad, if not worse, high up in the mountains when we worked there and one could only really escape their unwelcome attention when flying.

One of the undergraduate group described himself as a professional student. The others hinted that he was not altogether with it. He had failed three university courses in the last ten years and one evening I asked him why he persisted, and wouldn't he be better off finding another career.

"I know what they think," he said, "but it's this way. My Ma lives in Hollywood. She used to be an actress, been married four times; My Pa was her first." He paused. "Fact is, Paddy, when I was eighteen she looked more like a big sister than my Ma. One day she says to me: "Frank, honey, I think its time you went and got yourself some education. Go pick yourself a school as long as its not in California, and I'll pay all your expenses."

He continued, "I figured she just didn't want me around home. I kind of embarrassed her, if you see what I mean." "Yes," I said, "I get the picture. But how come you are still at University?" He grinned, "As long as I stays, Ma pays!"

He took good care to fail each course whereupon he transferred to another, his Mother being perfectly happy to pay his fees and living expenses provided he stayed out of the way.

Each day's work consisted of taking out eight men — two going on every flight — and, in addition, two rock hammers. The men took knapsacks to carry samples, emergency rations for three days and, dependent on the area being sampled, a rifle for protection against bears.

The helicopter was also equipped with a rifle which was carried in a rack attached to the outside of the fuselage. It was what was known as an 'over and under', having a ·22 barrel on top and a ·410 underneath. The latter fired solid slug like a chunk of lead which, at close quarters, was capable of tearing any bear wide open.

I was never called to use it in self-defence.

Grizzly bears were fairly common, particularly in the mountain regions to the north of Dawson City. Unlike their cousins the black bear, they would often attack without provocation and for this reason were considered to be extremely dangerous.

We operated and landed at altitudes around 5000 feet. The men were usually dropped on a selected mountain within a forty mile radius of the camp and picked up at a pre-arranged spot the same evening.

The terrain was not too difficult; although fairly high, it was made up more of rolling hills rather than mountains. It was usually possible to find a creek bed or a sand bar to land on or, in the mountains, most ridges were usually clear enough to permit landings and takeoffs.

The previous pilot had mentioned that it was taking far too long to engage the centrifugal type main rotor clutch on this helicopter and Tom, the engineer, concurred. Both suggested the unit be changed. Checking this out, clutch engagements were frequently taking over three minutes. This was not normal, but the Chief Engineer in response to a phone call said, "Nothing to worry about, Paddy. Once engaged there is no fear of it slipping in flight." Many years of experience since those early days in Canada has instilled in me a firm conviction, that if anything at all is not operating fairly close to its design specification, it's safer by far to ground an aircraft, have the problem resolved and the remedy applied and to ignore any advice to the contrary.

The 11th June was a windy day, some of the frequent gusts exceeding forty miles an hour. One of the student geologists wanted to carry out work in the vicinity of Australia Mountain not too far away from camp. Before taking off it was obvious that, due to the wind conditions, it was going to be difficult to land at the spot required. We experienced considerable turbulence whilst circling the landing point and I mentally decided it was unsafe to attempt a landing there. I flew across to a small clearing about a mile away and told the geologist I could put him down there and I was sorry for inconveniencing him with such a very long walk. He promptly objected, saying, "Hell, its over a mile and with this sort of going it will take me more than an hour to walk over."

This was true and I was forced to agree, but pointed out the danger of attempting a closer landing. He became somewhat annoyed and said, "If it's not possible to land nearer than this I think it best that we return to camp." This put me — new to them and to this type of work — in a difficult position. It was important from my company's point of view that these geologists received the best possible service, anticipating further work at a later date. Circling the original spot once more and mentally debating the possibility of getting down safely where he wanted, I committed the helicopter to an approach.

The wind was now strong and gusty. These conditions made the task more difficult and increased the danger. The selected landing area was about fifty yards ahead and we were fifty feet up, moving forward very slowly into wind when, without warning, the machine began to drop. Everything then happened very quickly.

The descent became rapid and moments later we struck the ground, but not too hard. The main rotor hit a small tree, broke off and the remnants hit the tail boom. The helicopter now rolled over on its right side throwing the three of us together. Part of the main rotor was still rotating and its steel insert core slashed through the Perspex canopy missing us by inches. The tail tubular guard and part of that rotor flashed past, finishing up in front of the machine.

We clambered out of the wreck, shaken but none the worse for the experience. The geologist expressing the hope that he would not be blamed in any way responsible for the accident. My sense of humour was at a low ebb, but I did manage a sickly grin and said, "Heck no, whatever makes you think that?"

We set off on foot making very slow progress because of the rough country. I carried the rifle as a precaution, but apart from two large reasonably harmless black bears, which we left well alone, it was not needed.

Late that night, hungry and dispirited, we walked into camp. Our clothes were torn, feet soaking wet and we had been bitten all over by mosquitoes and black flies.

Three days later a new machine and pilot took over the operation and I was recalled to Vancouver for another job near Prince George, British Columbia. The official report concluded that downdraft conditions were responsible for the accident, it being widely accepted that we should not have been flying at all that day. 'At the time it seemed likely that the pilot had experienced a sudden momentary stoppage of wind, such as is occasionally the case in the wake of a severe gust, a condition not unusual in mountainous terrain.'

The Company stated that the clutch, when examined after the accident, was found to be normal but in view of their earlier reaction to the observations of two pilots and an experienced engineer, their statement cut no ice, and did nothing to allay my suspicions. I flew out the next morning.

I never went back.

On the morning of 3rd July I flew in a single-engined floatplane from Prince George in British Columbia to Delkuz Lake in the Rocky Mountains. Delkuz Lake was used for the general operation of floatplanes. It was just under a mile long, heart shaped, four thousand feet above mean sea level and the surface reflection made it look sea green. The pilot I was replacing gave me a brief outline of the work and left for Prince George.

The Base Camp was a mile from the lake and uphill all the way. Camp transport was a horse-drawn wagon which had been left behind when the copper mines had closed in the thirties. Tom, the driver, and his two Clydesdales, Paddy and Barney, had walked two hundred miles from Prince George at the end of the winter along frozen rivers and game tracks.

The sleeping cabin was infested with Pack Rats. They were larger and cleaner than their better-known cousins but they could not resist other people's possessions. Socks, gloves, vests disappeared overnight and we later found them packed into a large crack behind an old corn bin. After that everything had to be stowed away every night. We slept on the upper floor of the cabin in sleeping bags with mosquito nets slung from the rafters.

Most of the geology crew were university students. All but one, who was from the American Deep South, were Canadians. There was a small group of Indians camped by the river. These men cut wood and laboured on the diamond-drilling rig. The drillers had their own camp. There were twelve of them including Pierre, an ancient French-Canadian cook, who was very temperamental. It was Pierre's habit to go to bed in his tent dressed in long white nightshirt and cap, with a pile of jam sandwiches on the packing case beside him and an Ellery Queen thriller to read.

He was terrified of black bears and one night a bear must have got wind of the jam sandwiches and padded over to the tent to investigate. His very sensitive nose led him right up to the side of the tent where he reared up on his hind legs with his forepaws pressing against the canvas. Pierre deeply engrossed in the crime novel suddenly became aware of a loud snuffling, but before he could leap out of bed the weight of the bear collapsed the tent and the animal fell across the cook. With a deep-throated snarl from one end and, from the other what Pierre later described as 'a very rude noise', the bear found its feet and continued its progress across the tent and through the canvas on the other side, smashing the Tilley lamp on the way. The whole camp awakened by the din, rushed across to help the old man.

Pierre was understandably very upset and complained to the camp boss, "When goldarned bear try to get in bed with me, time I go!" The poor man, in a highly excitable state, dressed in a dusty old black suit and an equally ancient homburg, and carrying a battered Gladstone bag left on the Beaver transport the next morning never to be seen again.

The general maintenance of the Bell 47G had been entrusted to a very young and inexperienced apprentice mechanic from New Brunswick called Merle Stoddard. He had spent a very short time in the Vancouver base prior to flying out with my predecessor. Nevertheless, inexperienced, unlicensed and labouring under difficult field conditions, his work was first class. Canadian maintenance regulations required the attendance of a licensed aviation mechanic at all the mandatory engineering checks regulated by the number of hours flown. All smaller operating companies were short of licensed engineering staff and corners were cut. But not on any machine I was flying. Not if I could help it.

After a total of 200 hours mountain flying time we flew back to Kamloops at the end of the contract.

Base camp was over 4000 feet above mean sea level with much of the work involving landings at over 6000 feet, flying with an engine which was neither turbo nor supercharged.

Early in July an engineer arrived from Vancouver and told us that one of the Bell helicopters had sustained tail rotor damage and was down in the bush fourteen miles south of Dease Lake. This was a narrow strip of water, twenty miles long, in the mountains 230 miles north-west of us. In the mail was a large envelope containing instructions to fly the engineer to the helicopter and enclosing maps for the trip. The all-up load for our flight through the Rockies was beyond normal limits. We were carrying the engineer, his tool kit, plus a complete tail rotor assembley and two full fuel tanks of thirty-six US gallons together

86

with a survival kit including a rifle and six jerricans of reserve fuel. There were no refuelling facilities en route.

In effect, the jerricans of reserve fuel extended our normal safe period of flight, which was two-and-a-half hours on full tanks, to four-and-a-half hours. This should just about enable us to reach our destination and get back to base provided nothing went wrong, such as a strong head wind halving the speed with which we covered the ground. It was going to be tricky. We certainly couldn't add to our load with the weight of more reserve fuel. In an emergency situation we just had to take a calculated risk.

The combination of the heavily loaded helicopter and thinner air at 4000 feet made it a struggle to get airborne and I experienced considerable difficulty in gaining enough height to clear the mountains. As time passed and fuel was burnt off, the weight situation became easier, and our conversation less stressed. We found we had a tail wind and were making a ground speed of 75 miles per hour. Unless the weather changed very rapidly we now had more than enough fuel to complete the trip.

We put down on a sand bar in Chappells Creek and topped up the tanks and an hour later we were at Gold Fish Lake having negotiated a 6500 foot mountain pass in very rugged country. During this last leg the engine had begun to miss, so we decided to put down at the Lake and change all the plugs. Several of them were leaded-up, two completely choked.

As we finished the job George, the engineer, turned to me and said, "Hey fella, seems to me you've done this before!" With a grin I replied, "Yes, George — once or twice."

It is always a scary feeling to hear a single-engined machine malfunctioning, especially over terrain where it might be impossible to put the aircraft down safely in an emergency.

As the damaged helicopter at Dease Lake had been grounded for five or six days, a few of the prospecting camps in the mountains were running short of supplies. We ran a few trips with food and brought out an injured man who had been hurt when inspecting an old mine shaft. The weather deteriorated and kept us at Dease Lake until the morning of the 18th. The other helicopter was made serviceable and able to continue supplying the camps.

Until we could make the return flight to base, we lived in log cabins on the south side of this very long narrow lake connected by a rough track to Telegraph Creek, a small settlement about fifty-five miles to the south-west. Hunting and fishing people stayed at Dease Lake during the summer and fall.

A local man in his late fifties owned a number of floatplanes which brought tourists, hunters, prospectors and fishermen in for the season. He kept their camps supplied and moved them out again in the fall. He also acted as a guide for moose hunters. It was uncharitably suggested that he fed the moose in the winter in order to have them easy to find later.

The geological company occupied two or three of these log cabins and were supplied by the floatplanes. The now serviceable helicopter was owned and run by the airline to which we were attached. This situation was most displeasing to the local floatplane owner and when we arrived a full-scale war of nerves was being waged.

For the two previous nights he had procured dustbin lids and with these and two friends (one of whom was a police officer on leave) he had marched round the camp keeping the geologists awake by banging the lids together, persisting until about five o'clock in the morning.

My first night saw no great improvement because the floatplane owner had now armed himself with a pistol and the vacationing police officer had a high-powered magnum rifle. The noise these made was accompanied with singing and shouting and the crash of breaking beer bottles as they were flung aside. Before we flew out and back to our base, he came across and, shaking my hand, said, "S'long Paddy, no hard feelings — it's all about those bastards you fly for."

The weather cleared and we flew back to Delkuz Lake, greatly troubled by smoke haze originating from a forest fire near Fairbanks almost a thousand miles away. Visibility was reduced to less than two miles and made map reading difficult. These conditions persisted for several days with visibility down to less than a quarter of a mile forcing the helicopters to be grounded until the smog cleared.

The daily pattern followed a familiar round: ferrying geologists and mining experts to local mountain ridges and old mine workings. Not a lot of flying but a lot of waiting around, sometimes all day parked on the edge of a lake or river fishing for trout. This is some of the best fishing in Canada if one can become accustomed to being systematically bitten by black flies and mosquitoes.

As every lift-off from the camp involved a starting altitude of 4000 feet with a fully loaded helicopter, taking off could be difficult, especially on a hot windless day. Occasionally the machine was overloaded to the point where it would not hover. One day we had to sit on a 6500 foot ledge waiting for an approaching cloud to obscure the sun, thereby reducing the local temperature sufficiently to slightly decrease the density altitude and permit a lift-off, but only just.

In early September, Margaret Bourke White, at that time a very well-known *Life Magazine* photographer, landed on the lake in a Beaver. I flew her onto the summit of a local mountain, Ingenaka Cone. She wanted to photograph geologists at work. A student with a luxurious beard was chosen to be the 'geologist' chipping away with gusto at a piece of quartz. She stayed overnight regaling us with her adventures. On one occasion she was filming a simulated helicopter crash and rescue off the coast of Los Angeles from another helicopter when suddenly the engine cut out and the machine dropped like a stone into the sea. She managed to scramble out but not before being taken down some twenty or thirty feet under water. Bobbing to the surface she was rescued, ironically by the 'crashing helicopter' the magazine had employed her to film.

On the final day of the contract, I was bringing out the last two men from a mountain lake ten miles from base. It was very windy, but we needed all personnel out so we could leave for home the next day. Some of the students were already overdue for a return to University. First I had to cross a ridge at 5700 feet before descending into a deep valley containing a lake fringed by large trees on the waters edge. A landing platform had been built over a piece of swamp at the north end, where the boys were waiting for me.

All went well until the machine hit an updraft on the

downward side of the ridge and started to go up very fast indeed. This was 'mountain technique' flying at its best. The vertical ascent increased at an alarming rate and an immediate reduction of power made no appreciable difference. I looked up and saw a large lenticular cloud, still some few hundred feet above, but closing rapidly. I twisted off all power and went into full autorotation in an attempt to slow the vertical ascent with some effect. But to my amazement the machine was still climbing. Then suddenly it started to drop the 3000 feet to the lake below, now well and truly in the grip of downdraft and virtual free fall.

Full power was applied in an attempt to climb out but the machine continued its mad descent. Worse, turbulence was building up. The lake grew larger and larger and as a crash now seemed unavoidable, I braced myself for the inevitable. At that moment there was the most appalling thunderclap from the main rotor system and my descent stopped. The downdraft must have levelled out at this point, about 200 feet above the water, as an updraft on the other side of the lake took effect. Badly shaken, I hovered the Bell to the platform.

Both geologists, blissfully unaware of the drama, hopped in with, " Let's go, Paddy." "Not me," I said. "If this wind doesn't quit we are here for the night." Fortunately conditions improved later and we flew back to camp. There has been no worse experience nor any other incident in a long and varied flying career that even remotely compares with this frightening episode.

The season's work completed, we left that night for Findlay Forks, the first leg of the flight south. The next morning the helicopter was covered in ice. River fog had moved in overnight and dropped the temperature and so we spent a miserable hour de-icing before flying on to Prince George at 5000 feet above the fog layer. Then it was on south to Williams Lake and Kamloops. My logbook records ground speed of 125mph on this leg with a gale force following wind which must have been approaching the normal cruising speed of the Bell. Two days later in London I obtained a contract to fly a Bell in Northern Rhodesia.

CHAPTER SIX

Seismics and Skywriting

CAPTAIN JIMMY YUELL, DIRECTOR OF IRVING BELL Helicopter Sales, met my incoming plane at Lusaka. He was a helicopter pilot of some renown and the Dutch had given him a medal for his rescue work in their terrible post-war floods. Before the war he had flown for Imperial Airways when air travel was only for the rich and famous.

It was known that a lady, swathed in mink, had stepped out of her Rolls Royce at Croydon to fly to Paris. Having found that the next flight was at 3pm, she then asked the name of the pilot.

"Captain Smith, ma'am," she was told.

"And when is Captain Yuell flying again?"

The clerk replied, "At 10am tomorrow." Back came the order, "Book me on that and be sure to tell Captain Yuell I am on board."

How things have changed!

In Rhodesia we had three American Bell 47G2 helicopters, all fitted with the more powerful Lycoming 260 horse power engines, together with standard power assisted-flight controls. The aircraft were owned by a large commercial company in Sweden who, in association with the British company, Autair Helicopters, for whom I flew on this contract, were also supplying spares and Swedish engineers for this mineral search.

The Chief Engineer, Karl Carlson, then spoke little English, but when we met later in India he was fluent. He was invariably dressed in spotless white overalls. As an engineer, he was methodical and thorough. He would insist on climbing up onto the helicopter after each landing back at camp, every moving part being minutely examined before he cleared me for take-off. His was preventative maintenance as it should be and a welcome change to what could be labelled as 'legally sufficient maintenance' on the two previous Canadian operations.

When Karl said, "You can go, Paddy, I tink all OK." I positively knew that it was.

Our camp was at Chingome. Mission Search Africa, controlled by Rio Tinto, used the helicopter for the next six days to convey geologists engaged in traverse work. Jimmy and I took turns to fly the Bell. We set up a camp at Kafue, about fifty miles west of the site, which now constitutes the Kariba Dam. Jimmy and his wife, then on leave, departed to England, and I was left as sole pilot. The accommodation was rough and our food was out of tins because the young geologists there were trying to save money on their living allowances.

Operations were not difficult, and although it was bush country there were a number of natural clearings. The altitude was over 4000 feet and taking off with a loaded helicopter presented the usual problems. Landing the geologists was generally an easy enough task but getting them out again could be difficult, even with the more powerful Lycoming engine. Sometimes on a hot windless afternoon it was only possible to take out one man, land in a large clearing to drop him off and go back for the other man, then take-off from the larger area with both.

In November we took the machine to Kalulushi, the headquarters of the largest copper mine in Northern Rhodesia. We then flew as passengers in a light plane to Kasempa Airstrip, about one hundred and sixty miles WSW where we met the out-going helicopter pilot and flew his machine SE-HAQ back to the camp at Mufumbwe, approximately seventy-five miles west in a vast wilderness of broken bush.

Camp conditions at Kafue had been rough but this new set-up was awful. We lived under canvas on the edge of the 'damba'. This was the local name for the thousands of snakelike clearings, some many miles long, which separate the solid bush of the surrounding country. From the air a sort of patchwork effect is produced, and these vividly green irregular strips cutting through the dark bush form a crisscross pattern which showed up remarkably well on an aerial photograph. All map reading was carried out from damba to damba, utilising superimposed aerial photographs to construct a conventional map.

The terrain was almost flat but covered with swampy patches which often disguised a small stream running the length of the damba. During my stay we had problems with torrential rains.

92

Not only did they restrict operations but they also damaged the rotor blades. These were made of wood covered with fibreglass, of British manufacture and not up to American standards. The fibreglass covering tended to lift, bubble and crack in the very hot weather experienced in tropical climates and the rains, when they came, got through the cracks and into the wood, its weight throwing the rotors off balance.

It is of course vital that each blade of a rotor assembly strikes the air at the same angle and equally obvious that if one blade is heavier than another the angle of strike, which determine the rotor's balance and the helicopter's lateral flight, will all be disturbed.

Before a Bell's rotor blades are attached to a helicopter they are first balanced against each other on a special yoke, and so critical is this procedure that it is always carried out in a draught-free room. Should the blades not balance, tiny weights are secured to the tip of the lighter blade until equilibrium is achieved.

These days, of course, the problem of rain penetration of rotor blades is rarely encountered. Most modern blades are either made of metal or non-absorbent synthetic material. They still do need balancing, however.

The heavy rains at Chingome made living under rotting canvas something of ordeal and we were constantly wet. As Karl said, "At home in Sweden sometime very cold, but the wet here much colder."

The helicopters were used to sample indigenous clearings located at various places in the bush. I dropped in on such a clearing while the geologist got out and took several soil samples which would go to Kululushi for chemical analysis. The absence of vegetation in these natural clearings sometimes indicated the presence of copper. We had the occasional problem with my helicopter and once had to use a hand starter because the battery was flat. This was merely a starting handle of the kind used on cars before the self-starter and which fitted into a slot on the left side of the engine. Very few Bell 47s had to be started this way, just the older machines, later discontinued.

Towards the end of November we moved camp twice. The last move was close to the Angolan border. This site was a long way from Kalulushi and as the only light aircraft strip was at least fifty miles distant it was decided to construct our own strip with whatever equipment we had to hand and I was nominated for the job.

The damba was big with a stretch in front of our camp more than enough to land an airliner. Unfortunately it was not as smooth as if appeared at first glance and levelling it was going to require a lot of effort and ingenuity. With thirty or more native helpers, I picked a big, strong looking fellow as 'boss boy' and set to work eliminating enormous anthills and using these to fill all the holes and depressions.

We broke them at their bases and loaded them on the back of a truck. Three days' work completed the filling process and the next stage, flattening the man-high long grass, commenced. We ran our vehicles up and down to help level the ground and the natives worked with spades and hoes to eradicate the more obvious defects. In six days the work was completed and, with justifiable pride, Karl and I drove down the thousand yards of airstrip at top speed in the Landrover with no problem at all.

The contracted Cessna aircraft arrived, flew 200 feet above the landing ground for its full length, then headed back east in the direction of Kalulushi. The same day a radio message informed us that the pilot had decided to abort because the surface was far too rough. The ride in the Landrover at around sixty miles an hour was remarkably smooth and the surface was excellent for any type of light aircraft, even a Dakota. It was certainly better than many of the Australian outback strips I had landed on in the past. So much for all our efforts. There certainly are pilots and pilots.

I left Rhodesia in time for Christmas in England with my fiancée and her family and left for India early in January. We were contracted to Standard Vacuum to assist with seismic surveys in Bengal. We were operating out of Dum Dum Airport, Calcutta.

The twenty mile drive from Dum Dum Airport into Calcutta was a depressing experience. The road was cluttered with ox carts. Cows wandered at will from one side of the road to the other and beggars of both sexes and all ages, some hideously deformed or maimed, pushed their hands through the windows of the taxi at every intersection or ran alongside asking for money. The filth and squalor on every side was beyond description. Cow dung, fruit peelings and paper lay on the road in heaps. When the taxi drew up at the hotel it was instantly surrounded by beggars, many of them children in rags and obviously half starved.

The three Bell 47s were only partially assembled, having arrived by freighter from Sweden. There were two other pilots, one English, Jacko, and one new Australian, Jan, who was also an engineer. The helicopters were to be used by Geophysical Services International (GSI) carrying out a seismic search in the hopes of locating oil in Bengal Province.

Jacko and I flew the first two helicopters out to the operational area at Labpur, a two-hour flight over paddy fields to join up with the American geologists in a very well organised camp. The helicopters had to be guarded because of the insatiable curiosity of thousands of Indian locals who came from miles around to see the machines and remove souvenirs. It was useless to request that they 'look but don't touch'. These people would push, pull and tug at anything within reach. Two tail rotor control cables were broken this way a week later.

Our work was generally out in the open country and it was frequently necessary for operational reasons to land and shut off the engine. It was the same routine every time, hundreds of locals tearing across the paddy fields from all directions. If the rotor blades were still turning they might maintain a distance from the helicopter of little more than the arc of the blades. When the rotation ceased, in they came. Some of the them with children on their shoulders and all frantically excited, shouting across the fields to others still on the way to join them.

A Swedish engineer arrived very late one night from a seismic camp in the Sudan. In the dark he was allocated a tent. He jumped into bed but let out a yell that roused the whole camp. Hopping about, holding his big toe, he insisted he had been bitten by a snake. An Indian medical orderly arrived to dress the foot while braver members of the assembly gingerly attempted to find the snake. Suddenly a flash of something furry jumped out from between the sheets and shot out of the tent opening. 'Goosie' the camp mongoose had located a bed without a mosquito net tucked in around it and had promptly climbed in and gone to sleep.

Tigers were occasionally seen on country roads at night and one weekend when we were stood down, we went into Calcutta for some nightlife. As we waited in the bar for the dining room to open an excited Jan raced in. Although his English was good under normal circumstances, when he was excited there could be a problem. He said, "A big bloody tiger try kill me on road." Having now got everybody's attention he blurted out the rest of his tale. "Right be ze jeep end nahly get in!" he insisted. There was a long silence and one of the boys asked, "Jan, how big was the tiger?" Back came the answer, 'Ze tail one side of ze road and his bloody head on ze oder!" It was gently pointed out to him that the road was a dual carriageway.

The seismic project involved boring deep holes in the sun-baked ground, ramming home an explosive charge and detonating it. The seismic echoes were then recorded on a graph in a specially equipped American 4 x 4 truck. Indian labourers bored these holes using manually operated hand drills which needed water for lubrication. This often had to be hauled a considerable distance from a stock reservoir of stored rain water, a scooped-out hole in the ground which every village possessed.

The water was invariably filthy, smelling strongly of urine, but there was no other source. So I evolved a safe, simple system for the helicopter to carry and deliver it.

We could sit six full metal buckets each side on the two external cargo panniers and fast hover-fly at ten feet above the ground from dam to seismic point. On the return trips the empty buckets were pushed inside one another and secured to the panniers with rope through their handles. The Indian labourers spilt more water lifting full buckets off the pannier than we lost in transit, so they had to be given a crash course in doing the job safely and swiftly.

One machine carried the water and, as each hole was completed, moved the other drill and occasionally the Indian labourers the few hundred yards to the next location. As it was usual to drill four or five holes at each location there was more

96

than sufficient work for both aircraft. The third machine, when it arrived, was used as standby.

The seismic line stretched across the flat country for many miles, but here and there a river or swamp intervened. Then although it was, strictly speaking, illegal we frequently carried two labourers on each pannier with two more in the cabin and in this way quickly transferred all the drilling crews across a large swamp or river. The Indian boys were usually very light, nevertheless, with six up they constituted a fair load.

The machines took turn and turn about to pick up explosives, but I insisted, for safety, that the sensitive fulminate of mercury detonators be carried outside the helicopter and on a flight quite separate from the seismic explosives. The detonators required very little vibration to set them off. They were packed in special boxes where each two inch long tube lay in its own padded groove, thereby eliminating the possibility of friction setting off an explosion.

On January 16, Jacko crashed his machine on take-off. It was a complete wreck and he was lucky to walk away uninjured. He was not able to describe what caused the crash but he thought that the 'short type' throttle fitted on his machine had some bearing on it. I sent him back to Dum Dum with instructions to pick up the spare helicopter and bring it back to camp.

I also felt that type of throttle was responsible for the crash. The twist grip throttle on Jacko's machine had been the same as those fitted to my own machine and the spare with one very important difference: the range of movement from fully closed to fully open on Jacko's twist grip had been about two thirds that of the others. It produced the same amount of power when fully open because all the engines were the same, but due to its 'short type' restricted circular movement, it was much more sensitive in operation.

Jacko had had very little experience with this type of throttle and it was possible that on taking off fully loaded he applied too much power and then attempted to remedy this by immediately twisting the grip the other way and, conceivably, overdoing it.

I figured it best to get him back flying rather than having him kick his heels in Calcutta worrying about the accident. But I was

97

overruled by the London office which insisted that he return to the UK by airliner and suggested a replacement for him.

I had gone to India as overall manager of this seismic survey, based in a Calcutta office, but I had been diverted to oversee individual operations in the field until they were up and running effectively. Meantime, a young man had been detached from the British Helicopter Company to stand in for me in Calcutta until I could return to my office there. It was an awkward arrangement and I soon found out that the young man was taking advantage of it: making important decisions without my authority. It was he who had engineered Jacko's withdrawal.

London had already named a suggested replacement pilot, only to have me refuse him on the grounds of his advanced age for this kind of high pressure flying. I pointed out that one hundred and forty to one hundred and sixty landings a day were not unusual and that each of our two helicopters would be flying over one hundred and twenty hours a month. They eventually agreed with me and, for the moment, Jan and I carried on whilst efforts were made to replace the crashed aircraft, in order to fulfil the terms of the contract with the American Oil Company.

However, by the end of March I had come to the conclusion that my position as overall manager was in name only and that the offer of the position had been bait, to use my experience, know-how and track record to secure an American Oil Company's seismic survey contract. So I resigned. Significantly, the young man who had so kindly been 'minding shop' for me in Calcutta took over as overall manager on the day I flew out.

One day shortly after returning to London I took a phone call from Bill Armstrong, director of the British company which had employed me in India. "According to our records," he said, "you are fixed-wing rated. Come to the office, I may have something to interest you." There his first words were, "Paddy, what do you know about skywriting?" To which the only reply could be, "Not much."

I did add that I had roomed with a pilot in Sydney who flew an old Avro bi-plane carrying out this type of work over the city on clear cloudless days. Bill explained he had an associate with two Harvards and was looking for a pilot to fly the second machine.

I accepted the job and immediately flew to Dusseldorf to obtain the necessary German licence validation and an endorsement on the German registered single-engined, two-seater, low-wing Harvard. Tommy Thompson, a WWII fighter pilot phoned me from Frankfurt to say that as there were no dual controls in either of the Harvards due to specially installed smoke oil drums in their rear cockpits, no dual instruction was possible. So I got the Flight Manual and Pilot's Notes from the office and talked to the German engineer who showed me where everything that mattered was fitted and how it worked. Then I sat in the cockpit for over an hour checking and re-checking the layout. My only Harvard experience had been some years earlier when I'd made three short test flights with the CO of the Malayan Auxiliary Air Force Wing at Kuala Lumpur and had not forgotten his warning. "Paddy, if this thing drops a wing just as you're landing, as they do, never try to correct with the control stick — always kick harder on the opposite rudder."

The engine was started, run up and magnetos checked. Everything felt fine and taxi clearance was requested from the tower. This was granted by the controller. A little throttle and this large radial-engined monoplane was moving forward slowly towards the runway entrance. I then detected that the machine was veering very slowly to the right. Application of left rudder and a quick burst of power had no effect. The next moment it had run off the taxi track and onto the grass. I stopped, sat back and attempted to figure out the reason for this strange behaviour. The problem was resolved by the controller who, in very quiet German said, "Captain, if you unlock the tail wheel, everything will be OK."

He then told me where to locate the device. In fact the pilot's notes made no mention at all of a tailwheel lock nor had the engineer thought to tell me about it.

The flight which followed was uneventful, but all the way around the circuit my subconscious gnawed at how this German controller came to know this small detail about an ex-enemy aircraft. After a near perfect three point landing the Harvard was taxied back to the hangar and I went up to the tower to give notice of another flight later in the afternoon. But even before stepping in through the open door, the controller said, with a laugh, "Captain, I know what you are going to ask and the answer is that pilots in the German Air Force, of which I was one, often flew the AT6 because many were left behind in France, even before you evacuated at Dunkirk."

This interesting man then told me that he had flown fighters from the Pas de Calais area and was frequently involved in sweeps over the Channel and later flew night fighters. I laughed and said, "Well, maybe we have already met. I was a rear gunner on Lancaster bombers and most of my missions were at night."

I took off again the same afternoon to practice stall and spin recovery and I tried out a loop and a barrel roll, and then I made several circuits and landings before returning to dispersal. I felt reasonably satisfied with my performance, as it was over two years since I had flown fixed-wing.

The skywriting technique had to be both simple and accurate. Tommy ran me through the principles on the ground, writing the word to be 'put up' in capitals on a large piece of cardboard. The compass heading for each segment of each letter to be written was marked in and the time in seconds from 'smoke on to smoke off' also shown. Each letter of a word appeared as a block capital, and the whole word was completed by the two aircraft working together. No aerobatics were involved. A high degree of accuracy was required and precision flying of a high order was necessary because many of the letters were, of course, curved — 'C' and 'O' for example. The turns to produce such letters had to be exactly correct in order to construct a word containing the same sized letters. Also these had to be in a straight line to look professional when viewed from the ground. We used a gyrocompass and stopwatch. The gyro was essential but with practice it was possible to dispense with the stopwatch. It should be noted that the only type of gyrocompass we had toppled at anything over 60 degrees of bank. This was not helpful when we were involved in very steep banking manoeuvres.

The skywriting was done at altitudes of between 10000 and 15500 feet and wholly dependant on where we could locate an area of level, comparatively smooth air for the letters to last without dispersing too quickly. When I had made a few practice 'smoke runs' with Tommy flying close and talking me through on the company frequency, a reasonable degree of proficiency was achieved and we were ready to go.

We wore parachutes because of the fire risk involved in the process of making the smoke. There was always the possibility the equipment might malfunction and set the aircraft alight. The smoke generating installation was simple. There was a fifty gallon tank filled with very thin lubricating oil in the rear cockpit, coupled — through a valve — to a cylinder of compressed air and an asbestos-covered exhaust pipe from the engine which extended down the fuselage to about a metre from the tailplane. A lever in the cockpit released compressed air into the oiltank from whence, under a pressure of approximately ten pounds a square inch, oil squirted into the very hot exhaust pipe to produce a thick band of dense white smoke.

We used to write the letter 'C' together, one aircraft smoking from the top of the letter to meet the other which had, at the same time, begun from the bottom. The idea was to meet in the centre of the curve with one machine passing just over the other and missing collision by three or four metres. Anything more than this gap would not allow the two separate lines of smoke to join correctly.

When I did this the first time it was arranged that my machine would maintain a steady altitude. Tommy was to 'zoom over the top' at the last moment. I saw his aircraft closing rapidly and kept heading straight for him at the same altitude. We were in radio contact all the time but there was no reason to call as everything looked fine. Less than ten seconds later he was very close but showed no signs of climbing. I was just on the point of slamming the stick forward to dive clear when he flashed over my canopy. The radio crackled and I heard Tommy yell, "Thought you were going over the top, mate." I was too frightened to reply.

Most of our work was over Holland, skywriting a brand of cigarettes. In April we went to Toussus Le Noble, near Paris, where I had done some of my helicopter training. The prices at the airfield restaurant had risen dramatically so we found an

101

estaminet used by local workers in their distinctive blue overalls. The food was good and got cheaper each day as the proprietor got to know us better.

In skywriting, cloud coverage is a major problem. We spent many days waiting for a clear sky. We had a contract to advertise wine and the producers wanted the ad in the air when most people were out in the sun at mid-day or when work was finished in the evening. The name of the wine was a long word — nine letters — and it took us until the end of April to get enough clear days to complete the contract.

At the end of April we wrote twice over Paris and then left for Holland and cigarettes again. Amsterdam, Utrecht, Rotterdam, The Hague, Leiden, Haarlem and numerous northern Holland towns all received our attention. In June there was to be an Electrical Trades Conference in Brighton and we were contracted by a British company specialising in oil-filled radiators. I set off from Dusseldorf heading for Croydon Airport. Tommy was to follow the next day. The Harvard was equipped with a magnetic compass and a VHF radio transmitter/receiver which was only good for line of sight conditions and, if one had to fly at low levels, was basically useless.

My plan was to fly west to Antwerp, then Ostend, following the coast to Calais, then across the Channel to Dover and up to Croydon, but the weather dictated otherwise. At 2000 feet east of Antwerp the cloud base gradually lowered to little more than 800 feet in light rain. This condition worsened, necessitating a more northerly heading, which took me to the borders of Holland.

The cloud base continued to drop and was soon little better than 500 feet. Following the border, I passed south of Flushing and attempted to maintain a westerly direction. I was now over the sea. Then, miraculously, the Goodwin Sands Lightship loomed out of the murk and gave me a position fix. Next Margate appeared on the left and I tried to contact Manston Airport and revise my flight plan. Manston did not reply, probably due to the low altitude. Abeam Southend and down to 200 feet, I tried radio contact again but without result.

Airspeed was now down to one hundred and twenty knots in fog and drizzle. A landing was getting urgent and Southend seemed a reasonable idea. I strained to see low level cables, which with the advantage of previous fixed-wing crop spraying in the area, I knew crossed the river in at least two places. Then suddenly, without any prior indication, the sun came through ahead breaking up the overcast and low cloud. I saw Tilbury abeam and my position was about twenty miles down river from London. Relief flooded through me.

With the weather now rapidly improving I decided to stay with the Thames, rather than attempt the shorter overland route to Croydon. Maintaining low altitude to keep clear of the radar at London Airport I continued along the river to Tower Bridge. I carried out a smart left turn onto a southerly heading, passing the Crystal Palace tower and then, with Croydon clearly in sight, called the tower. No reply. I now began to think my radio was out. I made a straight in approach to the long runway which had a slight depression half way down. I remember this because the aircraft was suddenly airborne again, having already touched down a hundred or so yards before this slight surface fault.

I taxied on to the tarmac near the main building with a huge sigh of relief, promising myself a large double Scotch at the earliest possible moment; I was somewhat puzzled by the lack of activity. There was the remaining business of closing my flight plan and questions would undoubtedly be asked about my lack of radio communication as I had entered the London Control Zone.

The tower was definitely unoccupied but I found that the radio hut was open with a duty operator. "Hello," I said, "I've just landed and wish to check in and close my flight plan." He looked at me oddly and said, "The airport has been closed since eighteen hundred hours. Do you wish to contact London Airport? But we can close your flight plan from here and show your late arrival as due to weather." "Sounds good. Go right ahead and do just that," I said. To my intense relief nothing more was heard.

Tommy arrived the next day and both aircraft flew down to Brighton and, as the grass strip at Shoreham was the only one near the town, we landed there. The next three days were spent writing over Brighton. The weather was gloriously clear with not a cloud in the sky.

We flew up to London on the following Tuesday and wrote a

number of sky ads over the metropolis. This sortie resulted in understandable adverse criticism from the Press, eager to disparage a competitor for advertising revenue by saying that an increased number of car accidents were directly due to the presence of our aircraft. The drivers, they claimed, were almost certainly gawping skywards when the accidents occurred.

The authorities in England later banned this type of advertising on the debatable grounds that the obviously impermanent aerial sign actually constituted a much more permanent 'hoarding' within the meaning of the Act and should therefore be subjected to the same legal restrictions as roadside hoardings or advertising signs. Another case of bureaucracy gone mad or the legal implications not being adequately pursued.

That was my last Harvard job, but Tommy went back to Germany. He went up on his own one day, feeling a little seedy from the night before, to write a soap powder advert over Hamburg. He inadvertently put two 'S's in the word but the soap company loved it, as they were kept busy all day, when hundreds of people who had noticed the mistake phoned in.

My next job was flying an old Norwegian registered Bell on potato spraying in Essex. This job should have killed me. In early August 1958 I was on my last spraying job near Sudbury. I had already done a number of runs on the ten-acre field which had three 11000 volt high tension wires strung diagonally across it. All the runs had been under them with sufficient room to clear. One end of this field was bordered by very high yew trees, the other by a hedge in the corner next to the road and a large farm building with two monster oak trees. The wires disappeared into this corner on a converging course with the hedge and the oak trees.

I came down almost vertically over the yews into the field and headed the helicopter parallel to the previous run with the intention of going under the wires, then pulling up over the oaks and farm building. To my horror, just as the helicopter was about to go under the wires, it was instantly obvious that is was impossible to do this and miss a collision head-on with the larger of the two trees.

My reaction was instinctive.

Yanking back on the control stick, I pulled the helicopter up and through the wires, shearing all three. There was a brilliant flash and a sulphurous smell and then I was fighting a madly bucking machine, its badly damaged main rotor blades barely keeping me in the air. I landed without injury in a nearby field, where we removed what was left of the rotors.

The end of August found me in East Africa flying for the Portuguese Government in support of an independent survey of Mozambique. My machine was a Canadian registered Bell, fitted with the bigger engine. Len was my first class English engineer.

Initially we were based at Tete on the banks of the Zambezi and the temperature was well over 100 degrees Fahrenheit as Len and I walked around the machine making a general inspection. The so-called hotel we had been booked into was extremely primitive. Little attempt was made to do anything about the swarms of flies. Every room was infested and the dingy dining room was no exception. The two nights we spent there, bathed in perspiration, and being bitten incessantly by mosquitoes, under mosquito nets gaping with holes, were unforgettable.

Len and I left Tete for a tent camp at Bene in the vicinity of a dilapidated old brick building set in the bush. Here dwelt an extraordinary character called Pedro who described himself as a 'white hunter' and lived there with his wife and young child. He sold elephant meat to the government for native consumption, this being doled out to our 'boys' and others employed on the survey. The ivory was disposed of at the port of Beira.

His wife prepared meals for Len and myself. She was unable to speak one word of English and it took us some time to make her understand what we would like to eat. Their diet differed considerably from ours and we were forced to compromise by eating eggs and chicken cooked in the European way. The other fifteen members of the survey, all of them Portuguese, ate in camp, their food prepared by a Negro cook. Pedro always produced a local red wine for our own evening meal, very welcome after a long, hard day.

The Portuguese Mission to Mozambique was created to

determine the economic and agricultural possibilities of opening up the land on either side of the Zambezi river. This was flat and undoubtedly fertile, but without organised irrigation it currently grew nothing but stunted bush, which could exist on a minimum amount of moisture. There were several groups involved in the project and our own main task was to fly surveyors to each source of the numerous rivers which emptied into the Zambesi from the north. We landed the two men on a sandbar or other convenient spot where barometric and temperature readings at each source were taken, and then flew them to the next point where the process was repeated.

Invariably there were problems landing near the headwaters of the confluent rivers and it was often impossible to land at the exact spot marked on the aerial photograph. Most of these minor rivers were little better than narrow streams covered by overhanging jungle growth. The headwater areas in mountainous terrain were often subject to violent air currents. More than normal caution was called for when attempting to land the helicopter in a river canyon or a narrow valley where it could be difficult to anticipate both wind conditions and degree of turbulence. All these rivers had rapids and many of them were devoid of sandbars.

On rare occasions it was possible to land the skid-equipped helicopter on a large projecting slab of solid rock with the white crested tumbling waters rushing by on either side, or on a bare piece of shingle, with the tail rotor sticking out over the fast flowing current. A logbook entry on August 29 notes 'Tons of crocodiles!'

Circling an area I would try to locate a landing place close to the river source and, shutting off the engine, the three of us would wade through the water and around rocks to reach the spot marked on the photographs, all the time keeping a weather eye open for crocodiles and snakes.

Early in September we moved camp to the Furancungo Government Station on a plateau 4000 feet up. From a tourist point of view the fifty-five minute flight was hard to beat anywhere in the world. We had a panoramic vista of beautiful mountains, jungle-covered country of deep gorges and great

106

ravines. It was all truly magnificent but there was nowhere to land if our engine failed. Furancungo was just a name on a map with a few scattered buildings including a police post. The 4000 foot elevation which made for a much cooler climate and also better accommodation was a relief, but the food was inedible. We ate in a makeshift store. Our first — and last — meal here was a greasy mixture of chopped anonymous meat so strongly spiced that the smell was too much for us. We decided to revert, if possible, to the old diet of chicken and eggs and walked through to the rear of the shack to fix a change of menu with the owner. He wasn't there but what we saw of his kitchen was enough. It was indescribably filthy. Dirty unwashed utensils were scattered everywhere, flies crawled and buzzed about an uncooked slab of unmistakable meat. Len yelped, "Cripes, he's been feeding us bloody elephant."

The head man of our unit, a Portuguese engineer, Senor Capuche, managed to arrange more palatable meals, although they did not represent a marked advance on chicken and eggs. The Senor called on us every evening to discuss the next day's flying. He came from Lisbon but spent considerable time every year in Beira and Lourenco Marques.

The high altitude and mountainous terrain made our job very difficult. Many of the river sources were in virtually inaccessible places where it was impossible to land. We had a number of close shaves because of this. The helicopter generally flew with both cabin doors removed because it was cooler but more importantly it allowed the passenger on the right side to lean out during the last few seconds before touchdown to make sure that the tail rotor was clear of any dangerous obstruction.

On one occasion I had managed to land on two small rocks in a boulder strewn section of fast flowing rapids. I had hesitated a moment before reducing power and throttling back to an idling engine when, abruptly, the tail dropped as the landing skids partially slipped off their perch with a resounding crack. I shut down the engine and waited for the free wheeling main and tail rotors to stop.

To my intense relief the tail assembly hadn't been damaged, but it had settled between two large boulders on the edge of the rapids and the rotor was critically close to the fast flowing water. The situation was quite serious as any damage to the tail rotor in an attempted take-off could, and almost certainly would, mean staying where we were until help arrived. Since there was no other helicopter in the country this could involve a very long and hungry wait or, worst scenario, a dangerous attempt to walk back to camp.

We looked at the boulders, which seemed to be solidly embedded in the river, but the three of us managed to roll one clear. The other would not budge, so working under my instructions the two surveyors got under the tubular boom extension to which the tail rotor was fitted and managed to lift it a couple of inches higher while I forced slabs of rock underneath the landing skids. The tail rotor was now clear of the water and we took off with care. Very relieved, we flew back to camp.

The local people would often burn off areas of bush to clear and later cultivate them. Len and I walked down the road one evening to watch this activity. As well as the amazing amount of flame and smoke we saw numerous snakes slithering across the road into the unburned bush on the other side. That cut the evening walkabouts down.

By early September Len and I had finished our part of the work on the contract and the few available engine hours left on the helicopter necessitated an engine change. So we decided to do this ourselves and got the use of an old building that belonged to the Police Department to do it in.

It seemed to be packed with old farm equipment covered in layers of dust. We stacked as much as possible around the walls to make room for the helicopter, leaving two very large sealed crates which still needed moving. The first we managed to shift without too much trouble, but we broke the second crate open trying to lever it free of the floor. To our amazement it contained a Maxim machine-gun still wrapped in greased paper and perfectly preserved.

The other crate proved to have the same content. These early and basic machine-guns were made well before the turn of the 20th century and some saw action in the Boer War in South Africa. How they came to be crated and still very serviceable in this part of East Africa remains a mystery. We contacted the Police Commandant but he was as puzzled as we were, and had no idea they were there.

In the next ten days Len and I lifted out the old 'copter engine and replaced it with a new one. We also did a complete airframe overhaul while we had the chance.

At the beginning of October I handed over to the relief pilot and left for Queensland, Australia.

CHAPTER SEVEN

Australian Interlude

ARRIVING AT TOWNSVILLE, NORTH QUEENSLAND I transferred to a local airline DC3 and flew to Richmond, a cattle town on the Townsville — Mount Isa railway where my helicopter and the mechanic were waiting and we took off for Challott Plains, a one million acre cattle ranch in the middle of nowhere.

A twelve-man survey team had set up camp under canvas. This was to be a survey to plot boreholes for water and irrigation. Much of Queensland was dotted with large isolated cattle and sheep stations and the region's poor, sporadic rainfall was alleviated to some extent by creating artesian wells. A windmill would drive a pump to raise the water up the borehole into a large pool, something like a village duck pond and known in Australia as a dam.

We were employed by the Australian Army, (which at that time did not have its own helicopters), to identify and annotate new boreholes on our maps with new tracks, buildings and boundary fences. Recent aerial photographs were consulted ahead of each flight and these were compared to the existing survey maps. Any discrepancy was then investigated. The aerial photographs did not always reveal new boreholes, which made it necessary to collect up-to-the-minute data from the station owners.

Many cattle stations were very isolated. The house was often a low rambling single storey building of wood, brick and corrugated iron. It would probably have a verandah and a lawn out front. If the station was near a settlement it might have mains electricity, but most generated their own power to serve the refrigerator and other domestic appliances. Many had only oil lamps and cooked on wood-burning stoves.

The Army Captain and his Sergeant were well qualified for this type of survey and it was very pleasant to drop in on a homestead where the family would be pleased to see a new face.

The sight of our helicopter attracted children like bees to a honeypot, particularly the young ones, for often the older children were away at school in Townsville, Richmond or Brisbane. In addition to the Flying Doctor there was a 'school of the airwaves' which, combined with a correspondence course, gave home-based children the rudiments of a good education.

It was now mid-October and only the start of the Australian summer but the temperature at noon was already high, at over 100 degrees Fahrenheit.

Flying along a large dried up riverbed one day we rounded the bend to see a large body of water swarming with crocodiles. The Sergeant said, "They're all fresh water crocs, protected by law. They are supposed to be harmless to humans. If they weren't protected the locals would kill them all and sell the skins." Dingoes scurried away at our approach. Local Government paid the sheep farmers a bounty to kill them. They had the nature of foxes which, not content with taking a chicken to eat, would slaughter every hen in the coop just for the fun.

Heat, flies and dust were constant companions on this job and often at the day's end there was no way to relax and no proper food and drink. Most of the time we fed the best we could straight out of the tin.

Julia Creek was a small cattle town two hundred and fifty miles south-west of Townsville with a dusty main street, a few well-stocked stores and pubs. Every Saturday night the owners and hired hands drank the place dry. Paid off hands could be seen in various stages of inebriation any time of the day or night, getting rid of perhaps six months' pay before returning to the job for just one more stint when the money ran out. There were hotels in Julia Creek and the engineer and I booked in for eight days.

In 1958 most hotels stopped serving drink to all other than residents at 6pm. The temperature inside the dining room was never less than eighty. As usual I was flying in open neck khaki drill shirt and pants, a type of uniform common to many pilots and very practical and comfortable in the hot temperatures. I took my place in the dining room and was approached by an immigrant Italian waiter who said, "Out, out — no tie you no eat!" The Manager arrived and said, "No problem mate, follow me." On a

111

rack in the rear of the dining room were at least fifty ties. "Take your pick," he said, and I did. One got the impression that in the dining room, one's birthday suit would have been perfectly acceptable just as long as a tie was worn with it. Another common sight in towns all over the country were parked vehicles outside the pubs around 5pm, the drivers being inside at the bar for what was affectionately known as the '5 o'clock swill'. Ladies were not permitted in pubs, so many were left in cars until 6pm when the driver returned after the bar closed.

The contract terminated in early November with engine problems. Maintenance had left much to be desired. I had to leave the helicopter at Julia Creek and, against my advice, it was trained back to Brisbane. During the trip it was badly damaged by shunting and rough handling. When the engine was removed for inspection a very minor problem was identified which, with proper maintenance, should have been remedied in the field. A good example of the work of an inexperienced mechanic.

The next move was to Hobart on the island of Tasmania. This city on the south-east side of the island, and is approached from the sea through a large bay, an area of indescribable beauty. At the time I am writing about it was not the capital of Tasmania — an honour which went to Launceston. Hobart became the capital later. It was, and is the biggest city on the island, with a very impressive harbour. Mount Washington looms over it with much of the residential district built down, and away from, its base.

In early November, the mechanic and I drove up to a small place called Mole Creek near Burnie, on the north side of the island and took over a Bell G model with a smaller engine. I had mentioned to the company the inadvisability of operating this under-powered type for hydro-electric operations involving some landings at around 5000 feet, odd when they were flying the more powerful model at sea level. They refused to change the aircraft employing the strange argument that the other pilot needed the more powerful machine because he was very inexperienced.

When they were reminded that the smaller 260 horse power engine was de-rated and only safe to use on full power above an altitude of 5000 feet, where over-boosting the engine could lead to engine failure, they did not want to know.

112

Bad weather prevented working in the mountains until mid-November, when the foreman of the construction team proved to be a 'pusher'. He and I immediately crossed swords as to how much extra cargo the helicopter would carry onto Clumner Peak in addition to two passengers. The wind was turbulent and the take-off area restricted by large trees.

Pointing this out to the foreman he snarled, "The last bloke could do it." So we got airborne. My decision to take-off was an error of judgement in an attempt to satisfy our 'valued client'. Up we went and struggled up a steep, high-rising gorge fringed on both sides by 80 foot trees and over terrain where it would have been impossible to land in the event of an emergency. With full power the machine was barely able to maintain altitude and at this stage a return to camp would have been the correct, if unpopular, procedure. After ten minutes in the air in turbulent conditions we caught a strong up-draught and another five minutes found us in a position to make an approach for landing.

The wind was now very strong and gusty. Light snow was falling and on the final approach the machine ran out of power and dropped vertically from eighty feet on to the rocky uneven ground and slid forward about ten yards. The main and tail rotors suffered severe damage and something came through the canopy and sliced a piece out of my left ear and the scar is still there. Otherwise unhurt, we climbed out and found ourselves almost on the edge of a 300 foot drop. Another few feet and we would have gone over the side into oblivion.

Frozen to the marrow, we clambered down the side of the mountain, falling and slithering on the half frozen ground. Two hours later we reached the bottom, but the way was blocked by a swamp. Walking for much of the time knee-deep in slime, we eventually got on to a track and made our way back to the camp. My ear had been bleeding all of the way so I found a doctor and had three stitches inserted.

The damaged helicopter was lifted out by another machine and rebuilt back at base in Sydney. I stayed in a Hobart hotel awaiting the replacement machine. My leg muscles had suffered as the result of the steep downhill trudge. It was two weeks before it was possible for me to walk properly.

The next contract was for Rio Tinto on the west coast based in the old mining town of Zeehan. To get there, my mechanic and I negotiated a hundred and twenty miles of rutted, potholed, rock strewn, unpaved track in my Holden car. The last sixty miles into the copper-mining Queenstown had the roots of the great trees which lined the way, pushing up through the surface of an already uneven track. Heavy rain from the previous day had caused the small mountain streams to flood and at one point we were forced to stop in order to remove two large boulders washed down from a steep cutting. On this journey we saw three cars with broken axles and several with smashed windscreens. The final section into Queenstown was very steep and riddled with hairpin bends, revealing spectacular drops of two hundred feet or more. In winter several miles of the section between Hobart and Queenstown would be blocked by snow. The short drive from Queenstown to Zeehan was a pleasure by comparison.

Zeehan was not unlike Dawson City in the Yukon, home to the same kind of wooden buildings, derelict huts and the abandoned mine workings of a past era. This small old mining town was a tourist attraction in the summer, the two hotels doing a roaring trade dispensing beer to thirsty mainland Australians. Nearby, but on the coast, was Strahan, a small fishing town famous for its crayfish. The previous pilot had left the Bell 47G2 helicopter in the yard at the back of the hotel. From this cleared space we flew to the various locations required by our contractors, Rio Tinto, for a copper survey. The area was extremely rugged and much if it was covered by monster 120 foot trees, with enormously thick trunks. Finding a place to land was often a major problem. Clearings were few and far between and it was frequently necessary to cut out our own, but the difficulty was to find a spot to drop off the men to do it.

Sometimes it was possible to find a mountain stream where the foliage was low and clear enough to permit a power-hover with one landing skid perched precariously on a rock poking up out of the water, but there was no room for any error and the woodsmen had to be well drilled by me on how to alight quickly and cleanly. They only ever used axes and handsaws but many of them won renown in international tree felling contests. When a rough

114

clearing had been made the next task was for the men to create a landing platform from trimmed trunks, pulled together to form a rough square. I remember on one occasion attempting to hold the machine steady over the river while a very slow woodsman disembarked. I can still hear myself screaming at the top of my voice "For God's sake get off!"

The slightest error could spell disaster. A puff of wind at the wrong time or a clumsy disembarkation could involve a sudden shift in the lateral centre of gravity resulting in a rolled up mess of scrap metal and human body parts at the bottom of a waterfall. Much of the work was at high altitude and the more powerful engine of this particular machine undoubtedly got us out of potentially dangerous situations so that the work was completed to the customer's satisfaction and also my own.

The mechanic knew little, or nothing, about the particular problems unique to rotary-wing aircraft. He had worked as an NCO on large engine overhauls in an RAF maintenance unit in England, but was not licensed on helicopters in Australia, since obviously he had not worked on helicopters in the RAF.

Returning from an early morning flight I could hear the engine barely discernably missing, clearing for a few minutes then missing again. The engineer looked the machine over and said, "Are you sure you're not imagining things? I've pulled two spark plugs and they are perfectly clean." Remembering some of the Borneo problems I told him the fault might not lie with the spark plugs, to which he replied, "Its not the engine, I heard it when you landed not ten minutes ago and it sounded sweet."

Licensed or not, he was my officially appointed engineer and I had to listen.

The engine carried on missing on the next flight with increased intensity but still intermittently. The mechanic, now openly sceptical, refused to carry out a very simple compression check on it, standing on his dignity with, "I'm not licensed to do that." I was now running out of patience and I retorted, "Give me the compression check gauge and I'll do the bloody job myself."

With a few sarcastic comments he was persuaded to carry out the test and, to his evident delight, all the cylinder pressures seemed OK. The satisfactory result did little to allay my worries because I knew from experience that a badly burned engine valve or distorted stem seldom shows up consistently.

The next flight was early afternoon with Matt, the camp chief, dressed as Father Christmas. Our destination was the village school three hundred yards away. We were to describe a large circle and come in to land on the school playground. We were almost 200 feet over a swamp and still climbing when there was an enormous bang from behind and then silence. The engine had stopped. I slammed the machine into autorotation and, missing large trees by inches, slid into the swamp. We were not hurt and covered in vile, sticky, slimy mud we walked back to the take off point to find the engineer. He was nowhere to be seen. We walked down to the pub and found him drinking with the students.

He looked surprised; "What are you doing here?" he asked. I replied, "What the hell are you doing here? Why didn't you stay by the pad until we had cleared the area?"

It was obvious to us that he had left the yard during the normal run-up checks and had not even waited to see the take off. I continued, "We swallowed a valve and only by the Grace of God are we here in one piece. I want you on the bus out of here tonight."

A pilot has to be very good, very lucky or both to get down OK when the engine stops in a climb at 200 feet on full power. Father Christmas and I were very, very lucky.

It was the New Year before the new engine arrived and we were operational again. I took some leave and went to visit friends in Hobart and I was invited to a dance held in honour of a visiting naval vessel attended by the great and the good of city. I was dancing with the wife of a very senior government official and desperately trying to make conversation. We exchanged comments and then she said, "Is this your first visit to Hobart, Captain Jones?" "No," I said, "I made two flights down here in a flying boat some years back." "Ah yes," she said, "A lovely era, gone now." Another long silence, then I had a flash of inspiration. "Of course, Hobart is the home of Errol Flynn isn't it?" She stopped dead and very icily said, "We don't talk about HIM down here!" End of conversation, end of dance.

116

We did some work for the Mount Lyle Cooper Company in Queenstown. The previous pilot, who normally flew for an airline, had acquired a rotary-wing licence. He had only fifty hours on helicopters and was flying the machine during his three weeks annual leave from the airline. He left the hotel after breakfast and walked over to the machine, did the outside checks and climbed in behind the controls. He started the engine and did the pre take-off checks and a minute or so later pulled up the collective pitch lever to take off. There was a whirring sound followed by a sharp whip-like crack as the main rotors took off across the lake without the helicopter. He climbed out, carefully removed his spotless flying gloves, turned to the engineer and in a slow drawl said, "That is the last time I shall ever fly a helicopter." He left for Melbourne the same day.

During January we moved several camps with all their gear from one area to another, including a diamond-drilling unit the weight of which came to over twelve thousand pounds. It involved us in three hours of flying with a large number of take-offs and landings.

One day the machine was loaded with stores for a bush camp in the Cradle Mountain area. To clear the mountains en route we had to climb to well above 5000 feet. Below us was rugged country. As we reached altitude, we hit a section of very rough air which caused momentary control difficulties. The turbulence was severe. An extra strong thump diverted my attention for a second to the main rotor and in that moment a large eagle plummeted down. Instinctively I swerved violently to the right and the giant bird dived past, only missing the rotors by an uncomfortably close margin.

Shaken by this close encounter I banked the helicopter to the left in an attempt to obtain a 'visual' on the bird. This action may have saved my life because another eagle, almost certainly its mate, flashed past me on the right. An impact with either would have shattered the relatively flimsy wooden blades with disastrous results. The next time we made that trip we could see two eagles circling above us and it was only then we realised that they were attacking us as because we had flown too close to the nest.

I used part of my time in Hobart to keep up my hours on fixed-wing aircraft and I see that my logbook records several flights from Cambridge airfield with young ladies from the Victoria League as passengers. A very pleasant way to spend time! Tasmania was one of the most beautiful places I had ever visited. Even that intrepid sailor Joshua Slocum, who sailed round the world single handed at the end of the nineteenth century, said that the island was the one port of call where he could have lived for the rest of his days.

By the end of February 1959 the contract was finished and I was on my way back to Canada.

In May I joined a large helicopter company based at Dorval Airport, Montreal, who were associates of the company I had worked for in Africa and India. They had a mining contract with a mineral exploration company. So I was flying a Bell 47 from the camp at James Bay, an inlet on the south end of Hudson Bay. My very experienced engineer, Rus Shand, was from Manitoba. We loaded spare parts, personal gear and extra fuel near St Eugene, Ontario. When the company issued us with winter parkas I knew I was home!

It was the end of May and we had a journey of six hundred miles to do. We headed north for a four-hour flight to Senneterre. We landed en route, refuelled from the jerricans and pressed on to the floatplane base near the town. Here we made a short stop to top up tanks before flying along the railway line to Macamic Lake, where we stopped for the night. Still following the 'iron compass' of the railway, we crossed back into Ontario, landing at Cochrane, after flying the last twenty miles in a blinding snowstorm.

We followed the railway wherever possible, always a good insurance policy in the event of engine failure in remote areas. To do this we picked up the Abitibi River where the line first crossed it, and due to the now appalling flying conditions, we were forced to fly low over the river all the way into Moosonee, the railway's terminal point. The total flight from Montreal to James Bay had taken nearly ten hours.

Moosinee boasted a railway station, a log cabin type boarding house, an Ontario Provincial Police Post, two or three stores, a

118

Post Office, a landing space and office for floatplane passengers, a few dwelling houses and very little else. Across a narrow neck of water was the Hudson Bay Trading Post Moose Factory. The post was administered by a factor or manager, hence the Moose 'Factory'.

The flying base operated a number of Beaver and Norseman floatplanes and a couple of Catalina flying boats known as Cansos in Canada. Many of the Bay employees had come from Scotland as apprentices to this famous Company, spending years learning the business in an isolated Trading Post, a few becoming Factors in larger Trading Posts. There was a well-staffed hospital to cater for the Indians, trappers and hunters. The Indians were a Federal rather than Provincial responsibility and their affairs were administered by the Royal Canadian Mounted Police. The bad weather continued for three days and kept us on the ground. Two geologists and another eight men arrived by rail making us a party of twenty. Later in the season a diamond drilling crew increased this number by ten.

We got airborne at the end of May. A flying boat took stores and some of the party to Beaver Lake. It took us two and half hours to reach Eastmain to refuel from a forty-four gallon drum of aviation spirit. Pumping out that drum was a most miserable experience.

We had no heater on board the Bell. In Montreal The Ops Manager had said, "Heater? You don't need a heater — it's nearly June!" It *was* June and we were still flying in snow. My clothing was totally inadequate for these arctic conditions. My log entry for June 13 reads: 'Anomaly Lake. Snowing. Freezing rain all day. Blade ice in flight. Two attempts to bring in parties — both abandoned due weather.'

I got so cold I contracted a type of 'flu and ended up in the Moose Factory hospital after suffering from a swollen throat for weeks.

It took another hour and a half flying time from Eastmain to the camp at Beaver Lake. We saw no human life on the entire trip, but there was a great deal of animal activity. Passing over a small lake we were amazed to see a tree trunk moving across the water apparently under its own power. Closer inspection revealed

119

a whole colony of beavers pushing it along. They all dived as the helicopter approached but when we pulled away they surfaced and headed back to the tree.

The helicopter was fitted with pontoons: rubberised floats each built with four separate water tight compartments and a sort of canvas scuff pad firmly stuck to the bottom to permit landings on thick spiky and lumpy muskeg without any chance of being punctured. Considerable care had to be taken with these inflated floats as any damage to one or other of their four separate compartments would result in that section's deflation, requiring a difficult and not always satisfactory repair.

Much of my waiting time was spent in trying to construct safe landing sites. Most of the lakes were densely fringed with light bushes and small trees so that often I had to land on the water some way out, wait for the rotors to stop, then paddle ashore. The boys always carried an axe and after finishing their work would prepare a landing site for the return flight in the evening, an important and urgent job. For when starting up on water, a helicopter will turn around several times until attaining enough tail rotor revs to be brought under full control. This is due to engine torque effect and lack of surface friction. If a wind is blowing across a lake and into shore the Perspex bubble and mass of the helicopter could act as a sail, and smash the machine back against the shore. It is not difficult to imagine what happens then.

Trees were cut to make frame tents: hut shaped frames covered by canvas. We had bunkhouses, a cookhouse and store tents. After two sleepless nights listening to the snoring of several geologists, I removed myself to the helicopter spares tent and slept there for the summer.

We had to move canoes from one camp to another by helicopter. This involved strapping one canoe on the right cargo pannier and its outboard motor on the left, in order to balance the weight and ensure stability in flight. Although the cargo versions of the canoes could carry large and awkward loads, they were comparatively slow and would sometimes take two weeks to move heavy drilling equipment to a required site. Consequently, for such loads, the Catalina was used instead. On this occasion, it

120

had brought in heavy drilling equipment, but could only get so far up a river inlet, leaving a good five miles of swampy muskeg to be crossed on foot with the load. Rus and I had no doubt that we could lift the bulk of it but we had no underslung slings for the heavy drill motors. First we flew in all the drill rods and camp equipment plus the drilling crew which was comparatively easy but kept us busy for a couple of days. Next was the turn of the drill motors. Stripped down to little more than the block each weighed close on six hundred and eighty pounds. This was loaded on the right cargo pannier opposite my piloting position on the left. So another two hundred pounds was required on the left cargo pannier which with my own weight balanced the helicopter and made it safe to fly. But the total all-up weight remained a problem. An eight hundred and eighty pound load was way over what the Bell was rated to lift and strictly illegal.

To reduce the all-up weight we removed the doors, the aft stabiliser and fin, the heavy starter battery, everything in the cabin including cushions, spare plugs, tool box, first aid kit and fore extinguisher. We drained the fuel tanks and then carefully measured out seven gallons which, I calculated was slightly more than the fuel required to cover eighteen miles with an overloaded helicopter. This was poured back into the tanks. The load was checked for security and we were ready for the attempt.

I ran the operating revs up to 320 per minute, brought up the collective stick and continued to apply power. The Bell came off very sluggishly and it was held in a hover for two or three seconds, then gently placed back on the ground. Rus was standing by with a one-gallon can of fuel fitted with a spout and, as I nodded he poured this into the fuel tank to compensate for the loss of fuel in the run up and hover. Critical. I lifted off again and moved slowly forward onto the lake maintaining a foot or so over the surface. For the moment it was impossible to gain any more height.

It is normal operating practice in all helicopters, particularly when heavily loaded, to gradually increase speed at the expense of height until, at about eighteen miles an hour a sort of phenomenon occurs where the forward motion kicks in extra lift. This could be called trading height for lift. Technically it is called transitional lift. I now started to gain height but the machine felt like a brick fitted with sparrow wings. The load was landed at the drilling site where with a great sigh of relief the engine was shut off and the gallant Bell, refuelled from cans, was ready for use again. Years later Rus claimed that this was a 'lift' record for such a helicopter. No civil aviation authority in the world would countenance this crazy trip, but we got away with it.

Such marginal jobs were few but other than obtaining, at a very considerable cost, a more powerful helicopter, this was the only practical way for a one-off effort. And the risk to life and limb applied only to the pilot!

The mining company was interested in locating asbestos and copper; also any worthwhile metals including, but not especially, gold. This, because its relatively low selling price, pegged by the US government since before the Second World War and the high cost of mining it, made it unattractive unless discovered in the form of high grade ore or as an alluvial deposit. Several finds were registered but of nothing worth mining on a commercial scale.

Twice a week I flew the chief geologist up to see the prospectors. One such place was close to a swamp. As we got out of the machine we were attacked by millions of biting black flies. By comparison the mosquito momentarily seemed harmless. How the prospectors lived with these things is beyond me. One of the French-Canadian prospectors, Croteau, was nearly sixty. He and his partner Luke were going to a location one hundred and sixty miles from Beaver Lake. Because of the very changeable weather and the fact that the helicopter had no radio we had to exercise great caution. We had to be sure that we could run two trips on the same day. Luck was with us and the following day we moved them and their camp and the day after that we moved his canoe. The whole area was swamp and the lake unnamed, so we called it Croteau Lake.

Although generally liquor restrictions applied to the camp, none applied to the helicopter crew and two bottles of Scotch came in on the Catalina each month. It also brought in helicopter fuel in its ample wing tanks from which it was pumped out manually into 44 gallon gas drums. The engineer who did the pumping was usually a beer drinker but after his efforts he assisted in the consumption of a bottle of Scotch. I can still hear his voice: 'I hate whisky. I'll be glad when I've had enough of it!'

The only mechanical failure we had was a failed clutch on take-off but with no consequential damage. Towards the end of September the camp closed down. The first winter snows had fallen and flocks of Canada geese were flying south. We had no intention of being snowed in or iced up so Rus and I left on September 29th in snow showers.

That night we had our first civilised bath for four months.

CHAPTER EIGHT

The Sheikhdom

OCTOBER FOUND ME LIVING AND TEACHING AT A SMALL flying club on the outskirts of London frequented by film people.

In November I got a call from Captain Allen Green of Bristow Helicopters. He said he had heard through the grapevine that I was an available experienced freelance Sikorsky pilot and he was offering me an immediate short term contract to fly a new Westland Whirlwind helicopter which was a British manufactured Sikorsky 55 built under licence, out to Kuwait and to stay on there for about three months to train and check out the sheikhdom's pilots.

This delivery flight was very urgent. Westland had not delivered the aircraft on time and the Sheikh was becoming impatient. Hopefully it might be possible to smooth ruffled feathers by a fast delivery well ahead of Christmas.

A month earlier, two helicopters of the same type had been flown to Kuwait but they were together, escorted by a DC3 support aeroplane with engineers aboard, and a comprehensive selection of spare parts, to remedy any possible breakdown on the very long trip. Which was a different proposition entirely to the flight I was being asked to undertake, with only a flight engineer who had never been trained to pilot a helicopter sitting by my side.

It was a generous and challenging offer. I was checked out by the Chief Helicopter Test Pilot, John Fay, at Yeovil. The machine had Bren gun mounts, the weapons would be fitted in Kuwait. It was intended for patrol work along the border with Iraq. There were many formalities to be completed. En route fuelling facilities had to be arranged and permissions to overfly certain territories obtained. Long-range tanks were fitted to accommodate lengthy stretches over the Mediterranean, the flight from Rhodes to Cyrus being of serious concern. The tanks would give us five hundred miles but for such a long stage we could not guarantee absolute safety.

Engine oil consumption was another consideration. The oil reservoir tank was modified to extend its range, for the length of the total flight would be nearer four thousand miles than the charted three thousand five hundred.

Much of this would be over long stretches of water and, if the weather was poor, sections of the route would have to be flown at low level. We had a radio compass but its efficiency was governed by the altitude of the helicopter and, to a lesser extent, the weather. So Eric, the engineer and chief map holder would at all times need to try to maintain sight of the ground or water over which we were passing. In fact, the pair of us would be flying by the seat of our pants.

The route was to be Southampton — Cherbourg — Lyons then down the Rhone Valley and across to Nice — and over the Ligurian Sea to Corsica then Rome — Naples and across the high country to Brindisi — Corfu, through the Greek Islands to Athens and Rhodes, across two hundred and fifty miles of sea to Cyprus, and on to Beirut then down the pipeline to Baghdad and on to Kuwait. The Baghdad to Kuwait bit had to involve overflying Syrian territory to enter Iraq and the Syrians and the Iraquis refused the visas. The Iraqui consul in London suggested unofficially that I proceed without the visa and fly to 'T One', the oil company pipeline station inside Iraq and close to the border with Syria. He added, "It's true there's a spot of trouble there at the moment, but it's only a local disturbance and will have stabilised by the time you get there."

We left for Cherbourg on December 15 and thought we would play it off the cuff when we got to the Middle East.

Overnight the weather deteriorated and the planned onward flight to Lyons was deemed inadvisable and we diverted to go via Toussus Le Noble where I had done my original training. Even here, where I knew the lie of the land, we were forced to fly around a forested district at ground level to avoid the massive low cloud virtually at the top of the trees. As we cleared this Eric looked across at me and grinned, "Even the birds are walking here."

The bad weather lasted three days and then we had a flat battery when we tried to start the machine, and the plug on the French mechanic's battery trolley would not fit the socket on our

125

helicopter. Not a good beginning. The weather improved as we flew south and the Rhone Valley was beautiful. After a night in Nice we prepared for the first long sea crossing to Corsica. The Met office forecast good weather with strong north-westerly winds which would help us enormously.

We did the machine checks the next morning and I went to the control tower to file the flight plan. The young controller threw up his hands in a typically Gallic gesture and said, "Captain, it is not permitted for you to fly." Somewhat surprised, I said, "Why on earth not?" The answer came that there was a new regulation that single-engined aircraft were not permitted to fly over the sea. "With an engine failure our air-sea rescue services would be involved in a search for you," he said. "This causes inconvenience and considerable expense. Aircraft with one engine have to follow the coast round the Gulf of Genoa and on to Leghorn."

This would take an extra day and together with the time we had already lost due bad weather over France, a super-fast passage to Kuwait was well and truly stymied.

The wind was now in excess of forty miles per hour and blowing almost directly to Corsica, but not conducive to the route round the coast. It would spill strongly down over the high coastal mountains onto the sea creating turbulent flying conditions. Additionally we had not arranged refuelling facilities on the coastal route which would involve another delay. The controller told us the only person to alter his decision was the Airport Commandant. With nothing to lose I went and knocked on his door. I told him the problem but he was immoveable.

"Why would you want to fly in this wind anyway?" he said. "Are you ex Royal Air Force?" I told him my flying history and found that he had flown for the Free French in the RAF outside Alexandria before being posted to a squadron in Scotland. He looked at me for a moment and said, "Captain, we will authorise you to fly direct to Calvi in Corsica. It is a principal Customs Airport and Bastia is not. Of course, with today's wind which is predicted to increase, the crossing of the very high mountains to the east of Calvi could involve severe turbulence on your flight to Rome. A flight to Bastia would be much better for you." He moved across to a wall map and continued, "You file a flight plan to Calvi,

126

which I can permit, and when you are about thirty miles off the coast of Corsica, call us on the radio quoting adverse weather conditions and request a diversion to Bastia. How does that sound?" I said, "You must have been popular with your RAF Commandant!" "Yes," he said, "That's where I learned to bend the rules. Have a good flight."

We did exactly as we were told and my log book records: 'Plenty water, sector time two hours.' The only mishap was a bird heading straight for the cockpit near the Corsican coast. It passed over the windscreen to impact violently with the lower part of the transmission. We were conscious only of a thump and after landing at Bastia found blood and feathers but no damage.

Bastia was a primitive affair, a grass strip and a shed to serve for a basic Customs Service. It took an hour to clear Customs and effect our onward clearance to Rome. One Customs man saw the Bren gun mounts and asked what they were. Of course, Erik told him. The Customs Official nearly had a heart attack. They raced to bring a Police Inspector from the town. The Inspector spoke some English and we were able to explain the presence of the gun mounts to his satisfaction. By this time the wind had changed direction and was now a head wind to Rome. We flew over Monte Cristo where in a square by a large monastery, people waved at us. It looked the bleakest place on earth.

Very strong head winds delayed our arrival at the mouth of the Tiber. We had been airborne for two hours and thirty-five minutes when I called Rome control requesting approach and landing instructions adding that we were a helicopter. The controller came back with "Join the circuit, you are number four to land."

This was a ludicrous situation. Also in the circuit were two 707s, a DC4 and a Comet; whose circuit speed was far in excess of my maximum speed at any time. I reminded the tower we were a helicopter but the controller was adamant. We finally finished the circuit four miles out on final approach with a long haul to the runway. In the meanwhile, several aircraft were waiting my landing so they could take off.

The final leg took a long time and as we arrived we thought we would have been given clearance to hover over the tower, normal practice with helicopters anywhere else. The controller said,

"Hold your position. Taxi down the runway and clear at the intersection." So for a long time we taxied down the runway watching the white centreline slowly passing beneath our wheels, all the way to the intersection. As we cleared, an American voice over the radio was heard to say, "Why can't we have that all over again?"

The next morning we left for Brindisi, our jumping off point for Corfu. The flight was through mountainous regions where it was frequently necessary to go up to six thousand feet to clear high ground. Where a railroad or cart track coincided with our compass heading, we followed it through the valleys. There were very few signs of habitation. The land looked very inhospitable.

Brindisi, on the coast, was the opposite. Well-ordered fields displayed lots of farm equipment. The landscape resembled southern England. We landed three and half hours after leaving Rome, had a quick meal and aircraft check and left on the sea crossing to Corfu. We elected to go down the coastline to Otranto and across the straits to a small island near Corfu called Othonoi. Then we made for the northern mountainous part of Corfu and through a narrow pass to the airport. It took an hour and thirty-five minutes and we were well aware that hostile Albania was not too far away.

We were met by a large group of people who were obviously expecting us. Before the rotor had stopped turning one of them was climbing up the embedded steps on the side of the fuselage to the cockpit. He shouted something, which I could not hear over the sound of the engine. I shut down, slid the cockpit window back and politely asked him to repeat. "I am a Customs Officer and I wish to look at your helicopter." I grinned at him and replied, "Look all you like, there is no charge!" His English was not good enough for him to see the joke.

The taxi that appeared to take us into town was driven by an elderly gentleman wearing glasses and a homburg hat. He professed to be the owner of the best hotel on Corfu and would give us a tour of the island. We declined the offer but were taken to see the birthplace of Prince Philip anyway and were vastly overcharged for the tour.

The next day we enjoyed a perfect three hour flight over

numerous Greek islands including the edge of Kafallina, into the Gulf of Corinth and on to Athens, where we refuelled quickly, and were on our way to Rhodes, another three hour flight over water. Early the next morning we prepared for the two hundred and sixty mile stage to Nicosia, again over sea. Full tanks would give us enough fuel to get back to Rhodes should the weather close in. A diversion into Antalya, Turkey was not to be recommended. The heavily loaded machine would not hover and it was required to gather speed on the runway in order to achieve transitional lift. All t's and p's (temperatures and pressures) were OK but one and half hours and forty miles into the flight, although there was no difference in engine note, there was a ten pound per square inch fluctuation on the engine oil pressure gauge. "Erik," I said, "What the hell is going on?" "That doesn't look so hot," he replied.

Cyprus was still a long way off. Visibility was dropping over the Turkish coast and we could no longer see the shoreline. It was at least an hour and a half back to Rhodes. We both agreed it could be that the oil pressure gauge was at fault. Perhaps a pressure relief valve was sticking. After all there was no other sign that anything was wrong. I decided to press on.

To sit over such a stretch of water without flotation landing gear, and with the knowledge that the engine might stop at any minute due to oil pressure failure, created the feeling in the pit of the stomach that we all have in moments of terror. Erik watched the instruments like a hawk. Due to the weather I was concentrating on flying at low level. Visibility was soon down to less than one hundred yards in heavy rain. There was some sea fog close to the surface.

Having flown for two hours, we reached the plotted turning point for Cyprus and I swung the machine onto the new compass heading, all the time watching the needle on the radio compass for some sign of settling down. It had been gyrating wildly and not showing any tendency to stop. Another hour went by. We watched and said very little. If the radio compass did not settle down fairly soon and give us a lead into the Nicosia radio beacon, we could miss the island altogether. We would never know if we had passed it, and I would have to proceed on a dead reckoning course for the Lebanese coast. I had only just enough fuel to reach Beirut.

Then, to our enormous relief, the radio compass needle steadied on a course similar to the magnetic compass heading we were following. I called RAF Cyprus Control but received no reply. We were too low and barely within VHF radio range. Right on three hours and twenty minutes we called again and fancied that we could hear the very faint voice of RAF Control. Within five minutes of my ETA we were over Nicosia Airport, landing in very heavy rain.

Erik checked the engine and found that an oil pressure relief valve which was sticking had been responsible for the scare. The weather to the east was looking better all the time so we decided to press on towards Beirut. We flew across Larnaca Bay and over the water but an hour out of Beirut we started to see thunderclouds on the horizon and began to run into storms. We managed to fly around most of them and then thirty minutes out we hit a very bad one which it was impossible to avoid.

I was forced to fly through its base at sea level. Many of the hailstones were half an inch in diameter. They smashed across the windscreen and we were worried that they might damage the flimsy tail rotor. The hailstorm only lasted a minute but the very heavy rain and limited visibility continued unabated. My eyes were sore from constantly searching for land and, of course, with the large side window open to give me a better view, rain and hail got into the cockpit.

Then suddenly land appeared. I saw what seemed to be a shadow ahead which abruptly materialised into a low bank of land not four hundred yards in front of the helicopter topped by a large radio mast which we missed only by executing a hurried ninety degree operational bank. We must have come very close to its supporting stays. On making an immediate radio call Beirut International gave me a course to steer to the airport which was only five miles away but not visible due to the weather.

The agent met us at the airport and told us the Iraqui visas had not been issued. Without a permit we could not go anywhere. I tried to phone the Syrian Authorities in Damascus but got no answer. I tried again in the morning and was told the 'permit man' would not be at the airport before eleven a.m. We went out to the airport to do an inspection and refuel so that we would be ready to fly instantly the visas were issued. I was wearing my usual khaki shirt and pants. Entrance to the tarmac was blocked by a slovenly looking soldier armed with what looked like a musket. We retraced our steps to the tower and tried to get permission to cross the tarmac. Nothing doing.

Then Erik had an idea. "Paddy, put on your epaulettes and uniform cap. You know how they love gold braid." I went and got my captain's bars and hat and tried again. The tarmac guard jumped to attention and I returned the compliment with a salute.

The messenger with the Syrian permits arrived while we were having coffee. They would only let us overfly between one and four in the afternoon. There was no response from the Iraqui authorities but I determined we would go anyway.

We had to climb to eight thousand feet in order to clear the Lebanese mountains. There was considerable turbulence and the rotor blades of the heavily loaded machine were suddenly subjected to 'retreating blade' which made them momentarily stall, causing the helicopter to pitch up, roll to one side and rapidly lose altitude.

I recovered by immediate reduction in power and associated blade pitch but not before we had lost about six hundred feet. Flying back up to eight thousand we followed the pipeline across the desert.

Later, Erik tapped me on the arm and pointed down. Looking immediately below us we four Russian MIG fighters spread out abeam following the same pipeline towards the Iraq border. Then as we watched, they swung around and came back along the pipeline weaving right and left as if involved in a search. Damascus, knowing our flight plan, had almost certainly sent out the fighters to monitor our progress across their territory.

They were obviously not expecting the quarry to be flying at anything other than low level. We derived a certain sadistic glee from the spectacle. They hung around for fifteen minutes totally unaware of our presence seven thousand feet above them.

We heard Damascus calling us on the radio but we had no intention of replying and being told to land there for the Syrians to discover that Iraq had refused us visas to overfly its territory. That would have held us up indefinitely.

We dropped down to the desert floor as we passed a Syrian border post and ten minutes later we landed at an Iraq pumping station called 'T One' where we were met by an oil company representative who was also the immigration officer for the station. He asked for our passports and visas. We handed over the passports. "I see no visas, Captain." "That's because we don't have any." I said. He looked at us very carefully. "In that case, sir, you are under arrest and there is no possibility of escape." In the middle of the desert surrounded by miles of nothing, this remark seemed a trifle unnecessary.

I explained the situation regarding the visas. This seemed to partially satisfy him. "Come and have a meal and we will talk about it," he said, "Besides it is Christmas Eve and even though we are not Christians, we like to sing Christmas carols." So we tramped around the thirty or so cabins on the camp with a bottle of whisky, singing carols. It didn't seem unusual somehow and Christmas cheer and goodwill began working. The company representative made a call to Baghdad and on Christmas morning our permit to fly came through. Now we felt Kuwait was within our grasp.

We carried on down the pipeline for fifty-five miles to a junction near another pumping station, which I identified as 'K Three', and then out into the desert on a compass heading for Baghdad one hundred and twenty miles to the south-east.

A few miles on, this heading took us over the River Euphrates which I decided to follow rather than fly over barren desert. We were met at the airport by a Colonel and four of his staff and visas were never mentioned. He took us to lunch and asked if we needed any help. "The Sheikh of Kuwait is a great friend of our Ruler and you are the Sheik's Pilot," he said. That explained a lot.

We were flying on the long range fuel tanks for an hour and a half before landing in darkness at Kuwait; five hours non-stop from Baghdad. Before I could switch off the engine and with the rotors still turning, an Arab Brigadier General climbed up the side of the machine to confront me in the cabin. The large side window was open and it was clear he was extremely agitated. We were going through the pre-shut down checks but he shouted over the noise of the engine, "Captain, why you take so long to get here?"

That he could not wait until we had shut down irritated me, so I ignored him. It was Christmas Day and we had been flying for over eight hours. Erik and I were dog tired. When everything had rattled to a halt I descended from my lofty perch in the Sikorsky forcing the Brigadier to drop down out of my way. I faced him to politely ask, "What was that question, sir?"

He looked at me through spectacles to reply in an insolent manner, "Why? Why have you taken so long to get here. Why are you so late? You are two weeks coming here."

I retorted sharply, "We left England nine days ago and have done exceptionally well in view of the political problems between you and your neighbours to the north-west."

He said even more curtly, "You should have been here ten days ago." It was not the time or place to debate the question so I said, "Excuse me, sir," and eased past him to greet the Manager of the Sikorsky Unit, "Hello Cyril, what's up with our friend in the fancy uniform?"

Cyril said, "Good to see you, Paddy, come to the office."

He told me he had only been out there two months and that he was being subjected to this nonsense from all and sundry. "The machine was promised for the beginning of the month," he said. "Until they located you, the Ops Manager at Redhill did not have a pilot. When they refer to the Sheikh they really do mean the boss man. When the Sheikh says 'Jump' everybody jumps. He holds the power of life and death out here. All the Egyptian employees are terrified of him. If he throws them out, he sends them back to Egypt which is the last thing they want now that Farouk has gone."

He continued, "The Brigadier is terrified too. If the machine had not arrived in the next day or so the Sheikh would have stripped him down to Lieutenant."

We were still talking when the Brigadier pushed into the office to say, "Captain you will fly the helicopter tonight. We are putting the gun in the cabin. We will fly over the sea with one of my Lieutenants and we will try the gun."

Although I found it hard to believe and utterly ridiculous, particularly on Christmas Day, this popinjay was adamant.

It was too much and so I said, "Sorry Brigadier, we have flown

133

all day and I have no intention of going on a night flying mission over the sea until I am satisfied that the gunners are trained to the standard required. I am an ex-Officer Air Gunner and I do have some knowledge of gunnery." Cyril flinched but the Brigadier stalked out without a word.

All three machines were still on the British register but it did not stop the Sheikh arming them with Bren guns and we three pilots took turns in patrolling the Iraq / Kuwait border most mornings, ostensibly checking inbound desert camel trains for the presence of drugs.

We often practiced air-to-sea target practice on a 45 gallon oil drum which was dropped overboard for the Brigadier and his men manning the guns to aim at from the right hand open door of the passenger cabin. As to be expected in this extraordinary country, they soon tired of the novelty. The Brigadier pulled out early, no doubt to save face, as he continuously failed to hit anything. After that, we pilots, all with war service, took over and took it in turns to get rid of the large weekly delivery of Bren gun ammunition. I became very proficient at hitting the oil drum.

Kuwait city, viewed from the air, was a mixture of East and West. There were large areas of mud houses interspersed with large modern apartment blocks. There were also many fine dual carriageway roads. The Sheikh had made great efforts to improve the lot of the average Kuwaiti. He had built first class schools, a university, one of the best hospitals and the largest seawater desalination plant in the Middle East.

Money was no problem. The many thousands of trees planted throughout the city were fed distilled water. The roads teemed with cars. Many Kuwaitis had come in from the desert and a car was part of their share of the oil wealth. In many instances they got straight off a camel and into a VW Beetle. There was no law to stop them getting into a car and, without any tuition, driving it away. There were pile-ups everywhere, but few fatal accidents.

On the other hand, selling a used car was highly regulated. The auctioneer's site was in the desert and your car was parked alongside hundreds of others. Bids were made on paper and at the end of the day the highest bidder got the car he'd bid for and paid cash on the spot. If for mechanical reasons it broke down the following day, the ex-owner was promptly thrown into jail and would eventually be brought for trial. Understandably, there was a marked reluctance to try selling any car unless one was totally sure of its serviceability.

We saw a lot of the Sheikh at the airport. He appeared to trust Europeans more than his own people. He had appointed senior British officers to run the Army and the Police, but as a face-saver had placed the Arab Brigadier in overall command. He treated all around him with total contempt and it was very obvious that most were frightened in his presence. One morning he and his outriders in a retinue of Cadillacs came tearing down the road to see the two daughters of the European Manager of the Kuwait Flying Club riding bicycles. He went to the Egyptian Wing Commander on the base to say, "I have seen Captain Lash's daughters riding bicycles. I will not allow European girls whose father works for me to ride bicycles."

The message was passed on and the bicycles were put away. The next morning there were two brand new MG sports cars in the drive for the girls, a present from the Sheikh.

The Sheikh took a fancy to a Convair airliner which visited Kuwait and ordered one complete with crew. As usual he soon tired of his plaything but would not permit anybody else to use it. Even the crew was not allowed to fly unless the Sheikh was on board. One day he demanded, "Why is the aircraft not under cover?" The American Captain of the Convair replied, "Your Highness did not wish to build a special hangar for it. You said six months ago it could stand in the open."

"I have changed my mind," said the Sheikh. "It must go in a hangar. Why can it not go in that hangar," he demanded of the Egyptian Wing Commander, pointing across the airfield. The Egyptian Wing Commander replied that it was too small for the machine. The Sheikh looked at the aircraft and asked, "How many people will this machine carry?" The Egyptian answered, "About fifty-five." "How many do we usually have in our party?" asked the Sheikh. The response was "Never more than sixteen, your highness." "In that case," said the Sheikh, "if you take three feet from each wing it will fit into the hangar, and it does not need all those wings to carry sixteen people. Cut the ends off." Not

135

surprisingly the aircraft was returned to America intact.

The Sheikh disliked narcotics above everything else. A Customs Man was caught smuggling hashish. For punishment, the Sheikh forbade anyone, on pain of death, to give the man employment. He took away his passport, his house, his car and his job. In an instant the man was reduced to the status of a beggar. Cruel but effective.

A sixty-year-old Egyptian pilot worked under the Egyptian Wing Commander, both were royalists but they hated each other. One day Captain Abdul resigned. It was mandatory in such a case to go to see the Sheikh. This he did.

"Why are you resigning?" asked the Sheikh. "I am an old man, and have not been well for some time and it is not advisable for me to continue flying," Abdul said. But the Sheikh was well aware of the real reason. "Captain Abdul, I have produced the best conditions of employment, the best offices and chosen the best men to work in Kuwait. For those who are sick I have the best hospital but for those who wish to resign without very, very good reason I have the best jail, where at the moment there are three hundred of my political enemies. Take your choice Captain, work, hospital or jail!"

Captain Abdul was back at the work the same afternoon.

My chief task in Kuwait was to instruct the Sheikh's Arab pilots. I had eight men aged between twenty-two and twenty-five, all of whom had completed a commercial pilot's course in England. They had also picked up western habits and were fond of a drink. Two had married English girls and the others often escorted girls from the various Embassies.

They were all intelligent young men and while they did not particularly want to fly helicopters because their original intent had been to fly for an airline, they were good trainees but not right away. At first they refused to take lessons, even when the Sheikh informed them that after three years spent in England at the Sheikhdom's expense they owed their country something. So the Sheikh promptly made then all Second Lieutenants in the Kuwait Army and after breakfast the next morning they were issued with uniforms and ordered to attend flying training, or face a Court Martial. They had no choice but to comply.

They were all independently wealthy and most drove Cadillacs. One, Jesaam, insisted on wearing Arab dress, even when I suggested that it would not be practical to do so when flying a helicopter. He had already made his mark at the flying club by returning from a flight in a four-seater Auster minus the undercarriage. He made a good landing and when the wreck was towed away he explained that he had been practising low flying and had hit a sand dune. This obviously wasn't the whole story and a week later the truth came out.

A Bedouin tribesman said he had been watching an aerobatic display. The machine — incidentally not stressed for aerobatics — had been looping so close to the ground that in the last series of loops it pulled out so narrowly that it had wiped off the undercarriage at almost zero feet.

A prerequisite before the student was allowed to solo was a demonstration of his ability to fly the helicopter in manual rather than with powered controls. This was a safety requirement, in case of a hydraulic control failure in flight. The stick loading in manual was heavy but only dexterity rather than brute strength was required to move it. A small switch on the instrument console controlled the hydraulic power. Jesaam was so undisciplined and independent that he took a lot longer than average to go solo but I was determined I was going to get him qualified. We climbed to five thousand feet and I gave the instruction, "Level out and, when the power controls are switched off, you must fly in manual."

He nodded and I leaned over, switched off the power control brought back my hand quickly and folded my arms, to let him know that he was flying the aircraft without any assistance.

In that moment he lost the stick, which he let jump put of his hand and the helicopter slewed right over onto its side. The machine was now diving towards the ground at an ever-increasing speed and practically over on its back.

With no time to switch back the servo button, I grabbed the controls and tried to level the machine. My startled gaze took in the air speed indicator, which was now registering one hundred and forty miles per hour, and this was building. The whole aircraft was vibrating. The stick was dancing around in my hand and the desert floor was coming up very, very fast.

Eventually, and it seemed like a lifetime, the machine came back under control having been at one stage close to inverted. We pulled out of this mad dive at less than five hundred feet.

We landed and I said to Jesaam, "Now do you understand the importance of doing what you are told all the time when you are in the aircraft with me?" He said nothing for a few seconds and then, white faced, nodded. "Yes, sir," he said.

So they all made solo and received some post-solo instruction. Jesaam finished up my star pupil and three of them achieved their ambition and went on to pilot airliners.

In the third week of January, the Sheikh, with a cavalcade of thirty vehicles, had set up a camp far out in the desert some seventy miles from the capital. The vast income of the Sheikhdom entitled everybody to a share of the wealth, even the nomadic Bedouin tribesmen. We had heard that a considerable amount of gold was being carried in the convoy for distribution to them. The camp abounded with air conditioned trailers, showers, baths, and even a complete radio station.

All this had to be hauled from Kuwait including water.

Cyril and I set off with two helicopters under orders to stand by. The Egyptian Wing Commander came to us after dark and required one of us to go back to Kuwait to meet an incoming Viscount aircraft and return with two violinists. I elected to go, while Cyril manned the radio and arranged as much illumination as possible to help guide me in on the return.

The trip was no problem but trying to find the camp at night in the middle of the desert could be a different proposition. But one learned not to say "No" to the Wing Commander, the answer would always be, "You are fired today and you leave yesterday."

I flew to Kuwait and landed a few minutes before the Viscount. Only three people disembarked, two violinists and the German stewardess. The Sheikh had invited her to the camp as well. Cyril had switched on all the lights in the camp and turned on the radio in his machine so that we had intercommunication. I landed and told him, "No problems — you were lit up like a Christmas tree!"

The Sheikh called for me to sit on his right hand. When the

meal was over he turned to me and said, "You have proved yourself a master of your craft," and presented Cyril and me each with a solid 24-carat gold watch.

Later his comment was cause for ribald laughter from the more uncouth members of the Bristow Helicopter team.

In the Middle East, face saving is of paramount importance. At the end of January we were asked to put on a demonstration for the King of Morocco and his entourage who were on an official visit to Kuwait. Sitting in the co-pilot position in my machine was a young army lieutenant who had never flown before. I put on a fancy flying demonstration. Egyptian news cameras and Middle Eastern newspaper people were present. At the end of the display I made the Sikorsky bow a few times to the King and then landed.

It so happened that the side on which the lieutenant was sitting was facing the King and his party. In a Sikorsky the pilot sits on the right but, in just about every other machine, the pilot sits on the left. So, the young officer descended and, to my amusement was obviously being introduced to the King by the Sheikh as the pilot. This was great stuff, because here was a Kuwaiti who had learned to fly these helicopters so well.

In February, a De Havilland Caribou freight aircraft, which specialised in landings and take-offs in very rough terrain, arrived in Kuwait to demonstrate the plane's capabilities to the Sheikh. We flew the pilot and the Caribou crew into the desert to choose a particularly rocky area for the demonstration. The Sheikh selected a piece of ground which would have given severe problems for even a jeep to negotiate at anything other than a slow crawl and the Caribou Captain politely told the Sheikh that it would be impossible for him to land his machine there.

"This may be so," said the Sheikh. "But your agent in Beirut informed me that your aeroplane could do anything my helicopters could do." He spread his arms in a regal gesture and said, "Your machine will not land here but my helicopters can." He dropped his arms and in a quieter tone and said, "I don't want your aeroplane." Later the crew of the Caribou put on an exceptional display but it did not impress the Sheikh. Even so he gave each of the five-man crew a gold watch.

A party of Danish archaeologists which included five girl

students, had arrived to excavate some two thousand year old ruins on a very small island called Falika, about ten miles from Kuwait city. The Sheikh had spent a lot of time and money arranging accommodation and help for the expedition. During the work they found a large stone with decipherable calligraphy on it, said to be worth its weight in gold. We were sent to the island to bring back a lot of their discoveries to the city and it was always a pleasure to see the girls.

The last job I had to do before the contract ended was a photographic survey of the city of Kuwait. The photographer Ali Kamal, was in the co-pilots seat. When banking the Sikorsky so that Ali could get a better view, he suddenly grabbed a red lever on the top left side of the cockpit window. I don't know why he did it. In the event of an emergency this lever was designed to jettison the window to provide an easier exit for the co-pilot and it fell away below to spiral down towards the congested city.

It was a horrifying experience for me as Captain of the aircraft.

If this very large, heavy chunk of metal-framed Plexiglas should hit anyone, or a vehicle, resulting in a death it was going to be very bad news. We flew back to report the incident. Cyril suggested we keep quiet at this stage. We waited for two days for a report but nothing happened. Perhaps somebody had found it and sold it, one never knows.

I left Kuwait at the end of March to accept a seasonal offer as a Sikorsky pilot on the Canadian Government Polar Continental Shelf Project.

From desert to Arctic in just a week!

CHAPTER NINE

The Artic Ocean and After

THE BASE OF OPERATIONS WAS AT ISACHSEN, A SMALL weather station on Ellef Rignes Island, part of the Queen Elizabeth group of islands and almost eighty degrees north bordering on the Arctic Ocean. The project was an investigation by the Department of Mines into the possibility of developing this far northern polar region of Canada. Involved were scientists from several professions including geological, topographical, oceanographic, botanical and seismic experts.

The company I was working for was supplying two Bell 47s and the Sikorsky 55. The Sikorsky had been dismantled and transported north in a DC4 freighter. It was going to be used for carrying oceanographers and their echo sounding equipment and also employed on tellerometer survey and in the general transportation of stores. The smaller three-seater Bell 47s were to carry one-man gravity meter and magnetometer parties to areas where stations were to be established.

All the aircraft, which involved two fixed-wing ski equipped DH Otters from another company, would operate from the runway at Isachsen Weather Station. Because of the ambient temperatures of forty degrees below, the necessity of preheating the helicopter piston engines in order to get them started was imperative. The intense cold sometimes froze the lubricating oil into a solidified mass in the engine. It could take two hours or more with the special Herman Nelson hot air blower, fuelled by gasoline, before it was possible to turn over the engine. The heater was heavy and cumbersome and therefore only practical to keep at the base. The two Bell helicopters were to be flown from Montreal to Edmonton where they would be dismantled and shipped on a Bristol Freighter to Isachsen.

Russ Shand, the engineer from a previous season in Northern Quebec, was in charge of maintenance. He and I flew one Bell to Edmonton and a Danish pilot flew the other. We left Montreal on

141

April 9th and made Edmonton on the 14th. We had encountered freezing fog and snow storms along the way.

The Bristol Freighter, commonly called 'Frightener', was heated — but only inadequately. It was not pressurised and flew at a comparatively low altitude. It was intensely cold in its barn-like fuselage and we got into our sleeping bags and stayed in them until we landed to refuel at Yellowknife.

We stopped overnight at Resolute, on Cornwallis Island, and the hundred yard walk from aeroplane to heated messhall was agony. It was so bitterly cold that it was painful to draw breath, every single one felt like it was freezing your insides. Within the mess hall my frozen eyes took in a notice '*This polar hotel has all facilities; including hot and cold running chamber maids.*' At least somebody had a sense of humour.

Our next stage of the journey was three hundred miles to Isachsen where the temperature was thirty below. The base had three permanent buildings that belonged to the State Meteorological Service. We had one building as a cookhouse and mess hall and we slept in nissen huts constructed of canvas with fibreglass linings and heated with oil stoves. The floor was invariably coated with ice because we took in snow on our boots. We slept in our clothes in insulated sleeping bags. The abrupt change from baking Kuwait to freezing Isachsen came as a shock!

Peter Hort, an ex-Royal Navy Pilot, was in charge of the Autair helicopter operation. For most of the men this was their first experience of the real Arctic. We were all experienced bush pilots and most of us had operated north of the Arctic Circle, but operating aircraft under the conditions we were to find here would introduce pilots and ground crews to a completely new set of flight and maintenance problems.

It should be emphasised that due to these Arctic conditions it was generally impossible to keep to the normal safety margins stipulated for in more temperate climates. All of the many islands were covered in ice and snow with coastlines only recognisable from the air because of the massive mounds of ice thrown up by the combined action of tide and wind against the shore.

On one occasion, a hundred miles from base, we were following such a coastline trying to locate an aviation fuel cache left for us

142

by one of the Otters. The Sikorsky used two gallons of lubrication oil every hour in its large radial multi-cylinder power unit. It was necessary to carry the oil with us inside the cabin because it froze in the intense cold outside and, until thawed out could not be poured into the engine. But we could never carry enough on board for a long round trip. Hence the cache. The wind was now at gale force and snow was blowing up off the land, severely restricting visibility from the cockpit. There was not nearly enough fuel on board to fly back to base. Finding the cache was imperative.

We suddenly saw it a hundred yards ahead and hovered well above the oil drums to clear the snow before settling down to land. We then spent five hours drinking hot coffee, hoping the weather would improve and watching Artic foxes watching us as we waited for the oil to thaw before pumping it into the engine oil tank.

We had hand pumped over a hundred gallons of fuel, a miserable task compounded by the gale force wind that picked up minute particles of ice and snow and blasted it through our 'specialised' clothing.

All the crews had a rescue system. We turned out to search for crews in reasonable weather only. It was assumed that if the weather deteriorated the overdue pilot and team should be sitting it out somewhere on the ice, reasonably safe. It was common to sit out on the ice-covered sea for long periods waiting for a weather improvement and the reappearance of the sun.

Another Arctic hazard unconnected with the weather, but potentially as serious, concerned the magnetic compass. As we got nearer to the Pole the compass needle would begin to dip down towards the compass card, pulled down by increasing magnetic attraction, eventually actually jamming into the card, making the compass totally useless.

The north magnetic pole lies between latitudes seventy and seventy-five degrees in the vicinity of Prince Edward Island, which made our magnetic compass virtually unusable. We had no alternative electronic means of navigation so we relied on a 'sun compass'. This is a flat wooden board the size of a dinner plate in the centre of which is a moveable needle. The board is marked in five-degree intervals with 360 degrees representing north at the top and 180 degrees representing south at the bottom. We knew from an Almanac the position of the sun in degrees for any hour of any given day of the month. So as the relative movement of the sun was fifteen degrees for each hour of elapsed time, it was possible to fly fairly close to a required course.

At the time of year I was based at Isachsen the sun at 1200 hours GMT was due south and if this was the required course we steered the helicopter towards the sun. My passenger, often a Master Mariner, helped with the manipulation of both needle and board. If a course of 210 degrees was required two hours after noon, he moved the needle around to 210 degrees by adding 30 and again we flew towards the sun. However if another course was required, such as 280 degrees, I would glance at the board and mentally add another 70 degrees to the sun-pointing needle and use the turn gyro on the instrument panel to assist in achieving the course.

It was a rough and ready way to navigate but its accuracy could be negated by a wind on the beam adding an element of drift. Nevertheless, it was our only method of navigation close to the Pole until the excellent DECCA navigation system became fully operational later in the season.

There could be another major impediment to sun navigation. Whiteout. When the sun disappeared you landed immediately, with another hazard to watch out for. The atmospheric pressure through which the altimeter measured height changed so rapidly in these arctic regions that dependence on an altimeter reading for landing in a whiteout was unreliable and dangerous. The same hazard occurs in a desert with the glare of the sun on the sand dunes.

Whiteout is probably the most dangerous of all near surface flight phenomena and occurs where the ground or sea is completely covered with sand, snow or ice. Any visible soil, vegetation or water will shatter the illusion by providing visual contrast. Whiteout is recognisable by loss of horizon and inability to visually determine the distance of the aircraft from the ground. This condition in the arctic is usually associated with a solid overcast and often accompanied by quantities of minute ice crystals which, in the air, can reduce forward visibility to practically nil.

The towering edge of the great ice ridge in Canada
where a number of scientists were killed
about a year before I arrived to fly in connection
with the Distant Early Warning System

Ferry flying a Sikorsky helicopter from Abadan
in the Persian Gulf to the UK, and forced down by the
dreaded Mistral blowing at more that 94mph,
I was the honoured guest of the French police
until I could get airborne again

The last Days of Rhodesia
Commissioned into the Rhodesian Airforce to fight
the infiltration of Communist terrorists across its borders

We were frequently required by the echo sounding team to land between ice ridges on the polar sea. These ridges could be over 30 feet high and, in a whiteout, blending in with their surroundings, often were not seen as ridges on the comparatively flat ocean surface at all. If we were required to land between ridges we had to be very, very careful not to put down on top.

Much of the time spent on the Continental Shelf Project involved Decca Navigation. Most of the heavy equipment was already in place, the masts erected and the master and two slave stations practically ready to start. Two weeks after we arrived the stations were manned, with two men on each island station to operate the equipment. The instrumentation system was already installed in the helicopters, having been fitted in Montreal before we left. We would drop in on these two-man teams as often as possible, as we were the only fellow humans within hundreds of miles. On one trip I was offered a bottle with the label 'Parkins Perfect Plonk'. They were making their own hooch and jolly good it was too.

In flight one day we heard a frantic call from one of the Decca stations. We were not the closest aircraft, so we were not the first to reach them. A polar bear had made an unwelcome foray into the camp. One of the operators was attending to the diesel when he heard a sniffing sound and turned to see a very large polar bear peering in the nissen-shaped weatherproof canvas hut. Being relatively dark inside the hut, the bear may not have seen the man but only smelt him. The other operator was asleep in the other hut a few yards away. The bear walked around the diesel hut, took a tentative poke at the building and then went back to the water's edge three hundred yards away.

The operator raced to wake his partner and load their rifles. These were a ·303 army issue and an inadequate small bore repeating Winchester of ancient vintage. They then went looking for the bear. It was at this stage we heard the call for assistance. It took the Otter an hour to reach Borden Island by which time the excitement was over. The bear reappeared round the sleeping hut but the operators wisely held their fire, knowing that a wounded animal would be extremely dangerous. It was obvious that the bear was becoming very curious indeed about the huts for it now reared up on its hind legs and rested its forepaws on the top of the nearest one which, under the weight, threatened imminent collapse. This was too much for our heroes who opened fire in unison. The bear was probably dead before it hit the ground.

The guys had kept their heads and they were very lucky. These animals are amongst the most lethal in the world. They have no fear of man and are more dangerous than the North American grizzly. We carried rifles all the time because, as the 'leads', or broken stream waterways, became bigger there were signs of polar bear activity almost everywhere. One day in spring as the snow was beginning to disappear we landed on an island to take soil samples only to discover twenty or more polar bears less than a hundred yards away. Luckily, they took no notice of us if, indeed, they were ever aware of us. The sampling took place very close to the aircraft that day, while I stood guard with the rifle.

Much of my time on the Sikorsky was spent on a tellerometer survey on Axel Heiberg Island. My temporary base for this work was Eureka, a weather station just north of the eighty degree parallel similar to Isachsen but one of the most isolated and desolate places in the world. One supply ship a year arrived to keep the unit going and this could only get into the inlet in the height of the summer because of pack ice. Even then it was necessary for an icebreaker to force a passage for the cargo vessel.

The Axel Heiberg survey involved us in carrying a full fuel load, two tellerometer operators and the transmitter and receiver, together with a good deal of ancillary equipment plus sufficient stores to last ten to fifteen days. The work involved many mountain landings at five thousand feet or more. We were engaged in an attempt to accurately measure the distance between mountain peaks using an electronic instrument called a tellerometer, which could calculate distances from electronic signals 'fired' on the line of sight between two objects. The 'shots' were as long as thirty miles. The transmitter and its operator were set down on the first selected mountain peak and the receiver and its operator on the second and the line of sight distance between them recorded.

This was a 'leapfrog' operation with the transmitter and operator put down on the first selected mountain peak and the receiver and operator put down on the second. After the distance between the peaks had been measured and recorded, the transmitter and operator would be moved to the third peak to fire back to the receiver on the second, and so on. There was always one man on a high inhospitable mountain peak completely on his own.

Because there was always the possibility of engine failure, or adverse weather conditions, each of the two operators had to have sufficient food and survival equipment to last several days. In fact weather was the principle problem. My logbook records complete grounding for six days due to iced-up controls on the Sikorsky and freezing fog.

There were some interesting variables associated with flying an overloaded, underpowered helicopter and making landings on mountain slopes subjected to strong winds and extreme turbulence. Visibility between the peaks was a major difficulty since transmitter and receiver had to be aligned exactly, and across a thirty-mile gap it was impossible for either party to actually see the other.

Both had radio communication however, and we could use a signalling mirror over the long distances, when we could get the sun to co-operate. Or we resorted to other methods, hovering high over the receiver in the hope that the landing light would be visible to the transmitter operator.

With the ice and snow beginning to thaw, there was thick sticky mud around our base which made it impossible to walk the three hundred yards from the landing strip. There was nowhere, not even on the DEW line where the mud was so tenacious and for three weeks we landed as close to the sleeping quarters as possible to eliminate the walk.

The three helicopters were now equipped with rubberised float landing gear but only as an emergency safety precaution. Landing on water was discouraged chiefly because of the corrosive effect of brine on the airframes. Floats permitted touchdown on ice thick enough for scientists to work from, but possibly too thin to land a wheel or skid equipped machine safely. The flotation gear was also insurance against possible engine failure when flying a single-engined helicopter over ice-free ocean. The activity we were engaged in also covered various other types of survey including the collection of information on marine life such as plankton. Where the sea was solid, holes were drilled through the crust and a wire cable dropped down over three thousand feet. A portable motor then winched up this wire, which was fitted with a small grapnel, to bring up a soil sample from the seabed.

Infrequently I was required to land on an isolated iceflow. On such an occasion it was inadvisable to leave the controls or to shut off the engine because these small icebergs could, and did, split, conjuring up the picture of pilot and scientists on one flow and the machine rapidly drifting away on another.

The helicopter engines incorporated a device which injected a small quantity of gasoline into the oil lines before shutting down, thereby thinning the engine oil and preventing its coagulation or cohesion at sub-zero temperatures when a restart was attempted. It was advisable, after landing, to idle the engine for at least five minutes to reduce its temperature before injecting of the gasoline, otherwise it would rapidly evaporate and the desired effect would be lost.

My contract ended towards the end of June when I had flown in excess of two hundred hours over this difficult and dangerous terrain.

Autair sent me off to Labrador to fly a Bell 47. This was a mapping survey to determine the correct demarcation line dividing Labrador and Quebec Province. Both parties had made this border a bone of contention for years so it had been decided that a correct geographical survey would be undertaken.

On 9 July I flew in a Dak to the isolated community of Fort Chimo on the southern side of Ungava Bay, nine hundred miles north of Quebec City. It was mainly an Eskimo settlement. It had the inevitable Hudson's Bay store and trading post and numerous wooden shacks with corrugated metal roofs. It had little to recommend it except a well-maintained airport. The Americans had used it during the war and had left hundreds of 44 gallon barrels full of aviation fuel in one corner of the field.

Eskimos seldom lived in igloos. Many in Chimo were housed

148

in well appointed prefabricated buildings of metal construction provided by the Department of Northern Affairs. Igloos were only used for hunting and fishing purposes out on the frozen sea. They were not of practical use for more than two or three days because breath produced a glaze on the interior walls which affected insulation and they became too cold to live in. We had an elderly Eskimo helping with odd jobs around the helicopter. His ability to acquire mechanical knowledge was amazing. It was intriguing to watch him re-assemble complicated mechanisms which had been stripped down for cleaning.

Our Survey Crew comprised two professional surveyors and six assistants, three of whom were university students on summer work. Our crew chief went out most days in the helicopter with an assistant to conduct tellerometer surveys. These were not over such great distances as we had covered in the Arctic, but still at great heights, constantly swept by gale force winds. The survey continued until the end of September. Freezing rain and hail like golf balls were constant companions. It was a wet, windy and miserable summer.

The only things of interest in this barren, wind swept land had to be minerals. The only growing things were stunted trees and lichens on every rock. In my logbook I wrote: 'The Lord took six days to make the earth, and on the seventh he got mad and threw rocks at Newfoundland.'

On longer flights, partly due to unpredictable weather and the heavy load of metal survey markers and extra fuel, the crew chief's assistant was often left in camp and I became the helper.

The country bordering the big river west of our general operating area was very pleasant, contrasting sharply with that around the rugged, craggy and bleak survey line which we were attempting to establish and where the winds were beyond description. I had never experienced winds so strong, not even the north-westerlys coming across the New Zealand Alps. Often of hurricane force, these winds hit so hard that we frequently found old survey markers held in place by heavy rocks, but bent almost double.

The markers consisted of three aluminium legs which were placed upright in the shape of a triangle. Each leg had a swivelled

149

extension at the bottom which lay flat on the ground. Willis, the chief, and I then searched around for suitable rocks to pile on these extensions to prevent the now canvas covered triangles being blown away by the winds. The survey markers could be seen from incredible distances when viewed through a telescope. I became extremely fit carting rocks about and Willis offered me a surveyor's course so I could do it full time. I ever-so politely declined the offer.

One morning I was engaged in collecting rocks when a slight gleam from a piece of white quartzite caught my eye. I broke it and found it had a silvery streak running through it. I sent a few pieces off to a geologist friend in Toronto to see what he made of them. He said he and his colleagues were unable to say what it was. But long after I had left Labrador I discovered that the silvery streak had come from old aluminium marker legs which, because of the hurricane winds, had rubbed into the rocks leaving fragments of their metallic composition behind, deeply embedded.

When they were available we slept in deserted log cabins, but more often it was under canvas in heavy-duty sleeping bags with pine branches under them for softness. Food was plentiful but usually came out of a tin.

Occasionally there were large herds of caribou around the camp. Sometimes seventy or eighty of these attractive animals would come in close, exhibiting no fear, only intense curiosity. Apart from the caribou there was little wild life other than a lone black bear or moose. We were later camped in a more inhabited area next to an Eskimo village close to the mouth of the George River.

Up river there was a luxurious salmon and arctic char tourist fishing camp. Hollywood movie stars (including Bing Crosby) came here to fish around the rapids in the river. Below the rapids, customers arrived in their own floatplanes to spend two or three weeks in the wilderness. The Department of Northern Affairs provided three college girls every summer to give the Eskimo children basic schooling in general subjects, including English. They lived in a well-appointed log cabin and, of course, we used every lame excuse to drop in for coffee.

One of the mechanics had a habit of doing helicopter

maintenance with a cigarette perpetually in his mouth. I had warned him to dump the cigarette when servicing the Bell, but he could not be convinced that this was a potentially dangerous habit. "Watch this," he said, and dropped a lighted cigarette into a can of aviation fuel. It was promptly extinguished. "See," he said, "You're just an old worrier — no danger at all".

I left him to clean a fuel filter while I went to my tent when there was a sudden violent explosion nearby. Racing back I saw the mechanic standing upright in the space which had been our stores tent and which now had ceased to exist.

He had been cleaning the fuel filter with gasoline. His cigarette had gone out and he had struck a match to relight it. The fumes in the confines of the tent had ignited and exploded, burning the nylon tent to ash in an instant. Knowing he suffered from a slight heart problem I enquired as to his health. Both eyebrows and eyelashes were gone when he looked at me. "Durned if you weren't right, Paddy," he said. Physically he was OK, but it cured him of playing Russian roulette.

With September came the freezing rain. The rotor blades often took a covering of ice and on several occasions I was forced to land. The contract terminated in October and I flew to England for some well-earned R and R.

The company for which I had flown in Kuwait had moved its main base from Henstridge to Redhill in Surrey. I went there after Christmas and was offered a banana-spraying contract in British Honduras to start in mid-February 1961. They were flying Hiller 12C helicopters, similar to my beloved Bell and I was checked out on the Hiller. In addition, because the banana people were also flying an ancient model Hiller 12A where the cyclic came out of the cabin roof rather than the more normal floor position, a further flight endorsement was required to comply with British aviation regulations.

I filled in the waiting time to take up the contract working as a fixed-wing instructor at Biggin Hill. A Major Christopher Draper, DSC, Croix de Guerre, who was a WWI Naval fighter ace, came to Biggin for a periodic flying check to renew his licence. This was the man who was known by the newspapers as 'The Mad Major' because some years earlier he had flown a light aircraft under all the London bridges.

We flew the check ride in a Percival Proctor. After a short flight we taxied back to let me out before he continued with the necessary solo flight to gain his licence renewal. Before I got out he said anxiously, "Are you sure you don't want me to do another circuit? That last landing was a bit ropey". I replied, "Sir, you have flown for well over forty years and not killed yourself. I think it's unlikely you are about to do so today!"

The BBC invited me to appear on the TV panel game *What's My Line* before I left for Honduras. The usual team was there, Barbara Kelly, Lady Isobel Barnett, Uffa Fox and Cyril Fletcher, chaired by Eamon Andrews. Lady Barnett opened up with, "Well, you look the healthy outdoor type and a Canadian, so I'm told. Are you self employed?" To which the reply had to be "Yes," being a contract pilot and not salaried. She followed that up with, "Um, I wonder are you in any way connected with agriculture?" The outcome was a foregone conclusion.

The Republic of Honduras has enjoyed independence from Spanish rule for over one hundred years and is bordered by Guatemala and Nicaragua. It is a mountainous country and its poor economy was at that time largely dependent on the banana plantations which were generally managed and financed by an American fruit corporation.

The ancient twin-engined Curtis 46 landed on a sloping runway outside the capital, Tegucigalpa. Parked outside a nearby hangar were a number of Steerman radial-engined bi-planes. These old primary training aircraft were used for banana spraying by a rival American aviation company. One of their pilots, an Austrian had been a wartime German fighter pilot. He and his American boss (also a wartime pilot in Europe) did not get along.

The Austrian was a great believer in chance and every week bought a government lottery ticket. One morning before he left for the airfield a telegram arrived with the information that he had won eighty-five thousand American dollars. Kurt, understandably, lost interest in flying and it was two hours before he drove his ancient Chevy to the hangar.

His boss, George, was by this time livid with anger and shouted at him "If I wasn't so short of pilots I would fire you right now!" Kurt smiled happily at him and walked over to one of the Steermans. He climbed in, started the engine, and not waiting to be filled with chemical spray, opened the throttle and took off. He pulled the aircraft over on its back and put on a stunning display of very low-level aerobatics. On the ground George was jumping up and down shaking his fists and screaming with rage. Kurt climbed to six hundred feet and dived straight at George who had to drop flat on the ground to avoid the undercarriage as it passed within inches of his head.

Kurt finally landed and taxied to the hangar. George screamed, "You're fired. Get off my airfield." Very quietly, Kurt replied "You are mistaken George. I quit." He looked at his watch, "I resigned at ten o'clock this morning when I received this."

He handed the telegram to George, allowed him enough time to read it, then took it out of his hand, turned on his heel and walked jauntily to his old car. It took only a few seconds for the full implication of the message to sink in and George ran after the departing Austrian crying, "Kurt, Kurt, just a moment".

Kurt turned around slowly, and said, "Yes, George?" To which came the much quieter reply, "Say, Kurt how would you like to buy into a part of this business. I could sure do with a partner."

Typical of the industry. There are many 'Georges' and fortunately not a few 'Kurts' scattered throughout the aviation world.

I flew on the Curtis next morning heading for La Ceiba. The first stop at San Pedrosula mystified me. As we came in on final approach I could see no sign of an airfield. Suddenly the elephant grass, intermingled with uncut bush, swished by on both sides and we were down. The airstrip was little better than a cart track and was only just wide enough for my wheels. Most of the pilots were American, flying into similar strips all over the Republic. They carried anything and everything, flying visual in the most appalling weather, low over mountains or through treacherous passes.

The company chief pilot was at La Ceiba to meet me. He had flown thirty-five miles over the mountains from the base at

153

Coyoles in an ancient 12A Hiller. Another of the same type was parked on the airfield to be flown back by me the next morning. La Ceiba was squalid, fly ridden and dusty. Most of the buildings were mud brick adobe with a few modern buildings in the centre. There was a motley assortment of people including mulattos of mixed Negro, European and Calib Indian origin. There were a few Chinese store owners, some Greeks and a number of Americans and Mexicans. Here was poverty, with borderline living for many, but with a very small minority of long established Spanish families living a segregated, rich life.

Around the railway station and town centre were many limbless beggars. I asked restaurant owner, Dino, whilst enjoying a splendid crayfish dinner on the first night, why there were so many. "Well," he replied. "It's like this. There are no roads. The railway is the only form of transport for seventy miles in any direction. The natives have established their villages to use it as a means of transport. They walk along the rails or, if they can, hitch a ride on a banana train, they hang on the sides. They come back in the evening drunk and lie down by the side of the track. Sometimes their legs are over a rail and the train comes along and takes them off. They also steal a ride, jump on and sit on the roof. When the train goes round a corner, they slide off. Again, we have feuds here; many of the men carry machetes in scabbards. When they fight they don't use fists, they use swords and pistols. The result is the same."

One weekend in La Ceiba I went down to the docks to see the banana boats loading and unloading. I watched an eighty-foot wooden schooner approach on which most of its passengers appeared to be European speaking English. I asked the man next to me who they were. He told me they were descendants of Captain Morgan and his pirate crews who still lived on an offshore island. They had retained most of their English customs and habits and had not intermarried with the local Indians to the same extent as had the Spanish. They came every month or so, to shop and stock up on stores.

I flew the Hiller to Coyoles next morning. Away into the far distance there were outstanding views. The base itself consisted of a village with a few houses, two administrative buildings and a

154

club for all employees, with a sports field set in the centre. Behind the helicopter hangar was a railroad halt. A high barbed wire security fence surrounded the village with large metal entrance gates which were locked at night, and the whole area was patrolled by security guards.

One morning having completed five hundred acres of banana spraying, we pushed the machine into the hangar. We could hear the banana train arriving. Suddenly there was the distinct double crack of pistols followed by a fusillade of shots. Deciding discretion was the better part of valour we stayed inside the hangar until the shouting and shooting subsided. Then the Sheriff and deputies arrived on horseback. As the crowd parted we saw two men lying in the dust. It appeared that one man had been involved with the other's sister and then refused to marry her. This seemed sufficient to justify the subsequent killing. A few days later a wooden cross appeared on the spot. I had seen hundreds of these wooden crosses alongside the railway and I had tried to count them on one trip but gave up at two hundred and fifty.

Four days after my arrival, I met Fritz in the company club. An ex-Officer of Rommel's Afrika Corps, he was company transportation officer. Well qualified, with a German mechanical engineering degree, he was in charge of everything driven by internal combustion. He owned an old diesel powered Mercedes of pre-war vintage and had driven it since new. It had accompanied him to North Africa during the war where he had managed to retain it as a Staff Officer after it had been requisitioned by the army. He somehow got it back to Germany after El Alamein and after the war he took it with him to India and then to Honduras. It had over 400,000 kilometres on the clock and was still going strong.

Fritz also held the Iron Cross, First Class, awarded in North Africa. He had been a Captain in the Infantry when, with ten of his men he got cut off from his unit. There were several British and German wrecked aircraft lying about the desert including a slightly damaged Junkers 52 three-engined transport. One of Fritz's men was a mathematician and between them they decided they could repair the damaged undercarriage. The whole party set about doing the repairs by night; lying low through the day and avoiding British patrols. None of the group had any flying experience, but Fritz knew the rudiments of flight from his engineering course and realised that they could only carry three men so seven would have to be left behind.

They fuelled the aircraft from all the other abandoned machines and managed with some difficulty, to start all three engines, after which they practised taxiing until they could travel in a straight line. In one of the British aircraft they found two maps covering the Mediterranean and Fritz taxied the Junkers at speed, lifting it a few feet from the sand before allowing the aircraft to continue climbing. The airspeed was induced to settle at around eighty miles per hour and for the first thirty minutes this solid, large box-shaped transport aircraft with an infantry officer at the controls weaved its way in the general direction of Italy, several hundred miles to the North.

As the aircraft droned over the sea, Fritz's flying improved and the aircraft's speed climbed to a comfortable 120 miles per hour assisted by a strong tail wind. Five hours out of Benghazi they saw the Italian coastline and they were buzzed by German fighters but not shot at. Fritz made three attempts to land, twice overshooting the airfield. On the third attempt he came in very low, almost hitting a farmhouse, and only just missing the control tower.

Everybody scattered. Ambulances and fire crews raced around the field as Fritz came in for a fourth and final attempt. He hit the end of the runway and bounced, breaking an oleo leg as he came down. The Junkers skidded along on one wing towards the tower, losing part of the tail assembly, then swung round on one wing tip, coming to rest at the tower's base. He had switched off the engines after the first contact with the ground, so there was no fire. Three very shaken Afrika Corps soldiers climbed out of the wreckage to be greeted by a screaming, over-excited Italian Commandant, who could not understand how a German pilot could make such a hash of landing on his airfield.

It was seventy-two miles to La Ceiba, by train and all single track. It could take up to ten hours because the driver had to stop every five miles or so and use the trackside telephone to see if the banana train was coming from the other direction and we could wait for an hour and a half in a small siding for clearance to proceed.

The three helicopters were spraying against a fungus called sikitoka which left speckled brown rust over the skin of the fruit which was not acceptable to the housewife although the fungus did not affect the flesh of the fruit at all. So we sprayed a light oil on the plantations, about half a gallon an acre, which controlled but did not wipe out the fungus. We carried about fifty gallons of oil in hoppers. This was sufficient to treat between seventy-five and one hundred acres of bananas.

The Spraymaster used a plastic tube-like instrument called a metholic to check the wind velocity. He would not accept temperatures of more than eighty-five degrees or winds in excess of four miles an hour, so flying finished very early in the day. We started at dawn and we would often be back in the hangar by 9am.

There were five farms to spray on a rotational basis, each growing about three thousand acres of bananas. During the dry periods a constantly revolving water cannon sprayed streams of water over the plantations, only ceasing when aircraft were operating. Bananas were not allowed to ripen on the plant. They were cut in big bunches and transported green overseas, ripening en route. For this reason it was impossible to pick a banana and eat it as one rode along.

Because of the prevailing lawless conditions, there were often seven or eight violent deaths a week on the plantations, generally occurring at weekends. Three miles from Coyoles there was a bar where many killings took place after hard drinking. It was off limits to helicopter crews because the police could not guarantee us any protection but, in fact, the Europeans working for the plantation company were usually left alone.

I was not sorry to leave Honduras at the end of May 1961 to rejoin my old company in Canada and accepted an immediate posting to Pickle Lake, Ontario.

Pickle Lake was a small settlement of a few wooden houses, a

157

Hudson's Bay post, an Indian school and an office of the Department of Lands and Forests which operated an Otter floatplane on forest fire patrol. There were a number of Cessna and Piper floatplanes moored to a wooden jetty. These were employed in the sturgeon fish trade that the Indians ran on Lake St Joseph. The Pickle Lake settlement was connected to an operating gold mine at Pickle Crow by a three-mile gravel track. My company was principally interested in the location of gold bearing quartz but other metals were also targeted in the search.

One morning, en route to pick up a geologist from one of the lakes, I saw smoke coming out of a nearby forest whilst preparing to land. Flying over to investigate, it was immediately obvious that the forest floor was aflame and the fire was spreading rapidly. I made a radio call to the Lands survey office reporting the fire and its location and I was so intent on watching the conflagration below that for a couple of minutes I failed to notice the arrival of an Otter circling with me.

These specialised Otters carried all the equipment necessary to put out such a fire with water from the lake below, where it could land. But I could see that there would be a problem dragging the Otter's hoses and pumps up close through the forest to the seat of the fire. However, it was one I could solve. There was a small swampy clearing close to the fire in which I could land, so I put down on the lake, transferred the necessary gear from the Otter and then flew it and two men to the seat of the fire, returning to pick up two more men.

The next day our assistance was requested again and permission was granted by my company to help in any way possible. The aircraft engineer and I soon found ourselves on permanent fire fighting. These outbreaks, known as dry storm strikes, were usually started by lightning. When a very serious situation developed later in the month, the helicopter had to work flat out ferrying men and equipment. More numerous forest fires broke out which, fanned by high winds, spread conflagrations with frightening speed, often encircling and trapping firefighters.

There were eighteen Indian firefighters and a Forest Ranger in one incident. *The Star Weekly* Magazine dated 9th September 1961 published an article describing *The Summer of the Great*

Fires of which the following is an extract.

About 150 miles away helicopter pilot Paddy Jones, was becoming one of the few identifiable heroes of the long hot summer. A few months ago he was in Kuwait teaching the Sheikh's fledgling pilots how to fly helicopters armed with machineguns. This summer he was flying prospectors in the bush when a fire started. Prospectors were ordered to stay out of the forests during the emergency, so Paddy spent a month in the fire lines with his helicopter. The day Red Lake was threatened, thirty-nine-year old Paddy, his bald head covered by a khaki cap, broke all the rules in the pilot's book to save men trapped between two converging fires at Banagei Lake. The fires had been ten miles apart for days but the winds of July 1st brought then swinging together. Paddy spotted the danger from the air and guided eighteen men to a swampy creek where he could land. He took nine men out, three at a time. The next trip four crowded into the Perspex dome of this two-passenger seat helicopter and then the fire swept across the creek. The five remaining men led by twenty-five-year old forest ranger, Jack Armstrong, ran a race with another arm of fire to reach a clearing a quarter of a mile away. There Paddy landed, three men climbed into the cockpit, Jack Armstrong lashed himself to one of the helicopter pontoons while Paddy thrust a terrified Indian on the other. Rotors thrashing smoke in whirling eddies, he took off as trees which lined the clearing exploded with flame.

On Banagei Lake itself Dave Croal, thirty-five-year old Lands and Survey bush pilot was using his yellow Otter float- plane to water taxi men from the lake shore to the safety of a rocky island. As he began his last trip to the island the wind generated by the heat of the fire, registered on his air speed indicator as eighty miles per hour. "It was like night, the smoke was so black," he said. George Bullock, brought in from Sudbury to be fire protection boss of the Pickle Lake area, sat in the co-pilots seat of the Otter. "The pilots saved almost 100 men between them, the wind roaring like Niagara Falls," he said.

This article does give some idea of the conditions experienced during the summer of 'The Great Fires'. As a footnote, carrying a total of six people on a Bell 47 should be acknowledged as a record!

The men were landed at our main campsite near the edge of the twenty-mile long Lake Banagei. The fire was rapidly approaching this major forestry supply site, necessitating an immediate evacuation. It was courting disaster for a large single-engined Otter to attempt to take-off in the near hurricane force wind, nevertheless the pilot loaded as many men as possible on his machine. They sat on the wings, on the floats and packed themselves into the cabin. The Otter started to taxi out to a large rock (later known as 'Funk Rock') about a mile offshore. Because of the wind the pilot had difficulty in holding direction and the turbulence was building up the water into waves on the normally placid lake.

I got three men in beside me. We were unable to taxi as efficiently as the Otter and I was forced to lift-off to avoid being engulfed by the flames. There were several bad moments before I gained some semblance of control to land safely alongside the rocky island.

Fifty or more men had been evacuated from the burned out camp with many making the hazardous journey by canoe. All were now perched on Funk Rock which was about twenty yards by fifteen.

Soon it was obvious that the aircraft would have to be moved. Heavy black smoke and burning cinders were falling on our machines. We had to spray them with lake water from a fire pump to cool them from the falling ash.

There was a constant roar overhead, like a train racing by. It was the noise of a wind carrying still blazing parts of trees for four miles over the width of the lake to deposit them on the other side amid stands of old pines which quickly became a raging inferno.

The engineer and I took off for Slate Falls. We had a very rough ride for ten minutes but landed at the small Indian settlement intact. The Otter pilot had a horrifying experience when he tried to taxi clear. He was taken by the wind and lifted through a half circle before being dumped back on the lake. He took as many passengers as possible and the rest had to hug the coast in their outboard canoes, eventually arriving in Slate Falls.

When the Otter failed to arrive I went back to look for it. I found it still unable to fly because of the weather, taxiing down the turbulent lake. I called the pilot on the radio to make sure he was OK. "Paddy," he said, "this is one heck of a deal, I think I'll learn to fly helicopters." He had a point. Although slower, they fly much better than fixed-wing aircraft in extreme conditions. Eventually the Otter got airborne and made its way to Slate Falls.

The wind was by now sweeping through the Indian village and we were fearful that it would take the fire with it and burn out the hutted community. Soon the sun was obscured by heavy black smoke and once again we were covered in burning cinders and fiercely hot ash. Airliners later reported ash and smoke at eighteen thousand feet. It was so dark that chickens went to roost and vehicles had to use their headlights, but the Indian settlement survived.

Don, the engineer, was only twenty-two and confessed he had only been married three days before he came on this, his first bush assignment. He was more worried about bears and moose than fire. By September we were back under canvas on lake shores doing geological surveys. One night Don, sleeping with the helicopter spares in a tent next to mine, heard noises outside. He called to me and after a look outside I told him there was nothing there. A few minutes later he called again. I could hear nothing still then, putting my head close to the ground I heard a thumping noise. I got up quietly and picked up my rifle and lifted the flap of my tent to see a very large buck rabbit outside Don's tent violently thumping his back feet.

I delivered Don back in one piece to his patiently waiting new wife and I was back in London on leave by the end of September.

161

CHAPTER TEN

Globetrotting

WITHIN TWO WEEKS I WAS IN CALCUTTA, IN INDIA, transporting oil executives across the flat surrounding plains to map the best route for a proposed oil pipeline and, later, when it was under construction, to pinpoint any damage or leaks which involved numerous landings at pumping and booster stations.

Sections of the pipeline passed through the beautiful undulating tea gardens of Assam, where, on night stops I met and talked with tea planters. One of these I had known in Malaya as a rubber planter. "I quit that communist bandit infested country two months after you," he said.

India was a subcontinent of amazing contradictions, of incredible wealth and unbelievable poverty. One could walk the bank of a river and find peasant women scrubbing dirty clothes and pounding them on a rock, or a man in a dhoti washing himself, cleaning his teeth with a wet strip of wood, rinsing his mouth out and, squatting, relieving himself whilst, a few hundred yards down stream more women were filling pitchers with water to drink, a contributory factor to the low life expectancy of India's millions of peasants and to the fact that the fearful disease of cholera was such a killer.

Meantime, we knew that the rich and politically privileged lived lives of such luxury that any, and every, desire could be obtained and even the smallest whim satisfied.

In mid November I was flying without passengers over the hot dry rice fields heading for base at Gauhati when, for a moment there was an uneven vibration in what had been a smooth flight. This was repeated and worsened and I immediately landed on the baked ground. A cursory inspection came up with nothing. Which was even more worrying. Immediately identifiable or not, clearly all was not well.

As happened every time I landed in open country in India, about three hundred people appeared from the surrounding paddy fields to see this amazing machine. Everybody wanted to touch the helicopter and, until a police detachment arrived, curious people could unwittingly inflict serious damage. The Police Inspector phoned our Swedish engineer who three hours later drove up in a jeep. "Vots the problems?"

"I don't know," I said and told him about the heavy vibration I had encountered. His inspection of one main rotor blade, which the police had helped us to remove, appeared to indicate that it was perfectly normal. Karl, now looking more than a little concerned asked the police to help him remove the other rotor. The heavy, fibreglass-covered wooden blade was removed and Karl stripped back a small portion of the protective covering. Seconds later he looked at me and said, "You very lucky — see here." He inserted a metal feeler gauge in a crack in the wood under the fibreglass and pulled it out to reveal particles of dry rot adhering to it. The fibreglass had prevented the rotor blade from breaking away, but for how much longer? The wavy motion felt in the last few seconds of flight was the final bowing of this blade before it broke off. "A near run thing," I said to Karl. He looked at me and said, "I tink ve drink visky tonight." And we did.

The contract terminated in December and, after spending Christmas in London, I joined Autair in Montreal to fly a float equipped Sikorsky 55 for a seal culling operation near the mouth of the frozen St Lawrence river. This operation was the first of its kind in Canada to involve helicopters in hauling sealskins from a controversial culling operation.

Before departing for the east coast, the Operations Director approached me to say, "Paddy, you will need to go into Quebec Airport for refuelling, but you will have no problems there because the refuelling man has been taking care of our helicopters for many years. You can leave him to it and go and have a meal for a change." So at Quebec I took him at his word and left the refueller to do his work. Out of habit, waiting for the coffee flasks and sandwiches to be made for our onward journey, I wandered out to the machine.

To my horror, a steady trickle of aviation fuel was dribbling out from the bottom of the passenger compartment onto the ground. Glancing over at the refuelling hose I then yelled, "Stop!

163

Stop!" The 'expert' had pushed the nozzle of the hose into a circular cavity at the rear of the machine instead of the clearly embossed FUEL filling point on the helicopter's side. The cavity under the cabin accommodated a cross tube for a wheeled undercarriage and should have been sealed off by the base engineers when they refitted the machine with floats. It wasn't the multiple fuel tanks 'the expert' had been rapidly filling with high-octane gasoline it was the belly of the helicopter.

We spent almost three hours getting rid of every last trace of the aviation fuel inside the machine, particularly that around awkwardly sited electrical motors and circuits. Time and great care was needed to ensure that dangerous gasses were not trapped in these spaces to spark an explosion and fire when the electrical master switch was activated prior to starting the engine. It transpired that the 'expert' refueller had never before even seen a Sikorsky, let alone refuelled one, but in the end, he was not to blame. I, as the pilot, should have supervised the refuelling and had there been a fire I would have been held wholly responsible and rightly so.

From Quebec to Charlottetown was a five hours and twenty minutes flight with an overnight stop and then on to Magdaleines after mechanical delays. Here and there on the way we saw colonies of seals. These scampered away as we passed low overhead. The annual seal hunt in the Gulf of St Lawrence which also involved the coastal areas of Newfoundland, Quebec and Labrador had, for many years, been an essential economic factor in the lives of the people living in isolated villages and primitive settlements along the rugged coasts. Many of them were very poor and fishing, in one form or another, was the only source of income for the majority.

The seal cull was a brutal business. The herd in the Gulf of St Lawrence was huge and so was its consumption of fish. In order to survive, the local fishermen had to make a living and the men employed as seal hunters would protest that they had to live too. It was the seals which had to die.

The hunters were based on sealing ships about twenty miles out in the Gulf, ice-locked in the frozen sea. These had positioned themselves within and around the huge herd before the big freeze and were now immobilised in a vast field of thick ice and would have to await the onset of the annual thaw before they could move away with their cargo of skins. When we flew over, three of the ships were in the middle of the herd. From the air the seals appeared as thousands of crawling ants. The mature animals were clearly discernable because they were dark in colour where their offspring were white.

We set the hunters down on the ice to commence the cull and, using a pole, they piled sealskins in slings or nets naming the ship to which the skins belonged. It would have been sensible for the helicopters to uplift the skins to the ships and this we offered to do but nothing came of it.

Once the skins were in marked piles on the ice, they were steam winched to their respective ships with chains laid over the ice. Because of the pressure ridges and crevices in the frozen surface, coupled with open stretches of water, complete piles of skins could be scattered or lost. Once the ice started to break up in the thaw it was possible to launch boats from the ships to retrieve pelts from dispersed ice floes, but still many were lost. The action of the wind and tides could move floes far away, never to be found even though the helicopters regularly joined in the hunt for them. It was said that less than forty percent of skins left on the ice was ever recovered.

We had a good relationship with the ships' crews and would often join them for a meal and an evening's entertainment. However, this happy atmosphere changed rapidly after a very heavy storm caused the ice field to shift and the seal herd to break up. Pelts became scarcer. It may have been this that led to the troubles which followed.

On the Thursday following the storm the skipper of one of the sealing vessels was reported to have protested that crews operating the helicopters were lifting piles of his skins and he had issued rifles to his men with orders to fire on them. Two shots were fired at a Bell 47.

The American pilot, Charlie McKeeg, (his business card read 'McKeeg of Labrador'), landed his machine alongside an armed band and with commendable courage tackled the men, took their rifles away from them and threw them into his machine. He then flew with the rifles to the Police post at St. Peters on Prince Edward Island.

The Commanding Officer of L Division of the Royal Canadian Mounted Police said that a complaint of theft of rifles had been received, but that he declined to go further into the matter. He pointed out that International Law was involved because the alleged incidents had taken place beyond the three-mile limit.

A Newfoundland Member of Parliament reported that a sealing captain had complained that he had been attacked by pirates who took his rifles and pelts. He went on to say that seal rustlers operating from five helicopters had swooped down on the ice and taken the pelts. The Parliamentary Secretary said that the matter was under active consideration by the RCMP.

The use of the word 'piracy' aroused considerable interest and much of the nation's media was devoted to coverage of the incident. While all this was going on we were operating as usual. In one week my Sikorsky hauled 2,128 skins into Price Edward Island.

Locating heaps, which may have been left on the ice from the night before, could present problems. A floe could, and did, move more than ten miles overnight and an ownership marker could and did, blow away. When we had to search hard, looking for pelts, we could not always be certain that what we found belonged to 'our' ship. Furthermore, it was strongly suspected that some flags were switched by sealing crews from other vessels.

Accusations and counter accusations flew between helicopter crews and those of the sealing ships with much bitterness developing between them. Happily, the following season, when I was employed elsewhere, the crews of ships and helicopters concluded a workable arrangement for jointly retrieving the pelts.

Flying back to Montreal at the beginning of April, I landed near Hartland, New Brunswick, in the yard of an old farmer. His land was next to where my father had farmed during the Depression and where I had spent several years as a boy. We had flown along the wide St John River to cross the longest covered wooden bridge in the world. I had driven our two-horse buggy across this bridge many times.

In Montreal, my employer, Autair, learned that legal action

was likely to follow the wild accusation of piracy, but I was not eager to hang around, idle and unpaid, awaiting a possible call for my day in court. Instead, I accepted the offer of a job in Greenland.

'McKeeg of Labrador' had the same idea and had left on a contract to Timbuktu in the Sahara Desert. I understand there was much hilarity in court when his whereabouts were revealed.

I flew into Sondestrom Fjord in Greenland on board a Military DC6 from Maguire Airbase in Philadelphia. It was 13 April 1962. At that time Sondestrom was a large American base with about four thousand men stationed there, being responsible for the upkeep of the few existing roads and the construction of new ones. Strategic Air Command came in and out at regular intervals, their air tankers being on constant alert. In the event of a Russian attack these crews would have been responsible for the aerial refuelling of fighters and strategic bombers hitting the Soviet Union.

Our three Sikorsky 55's were equipped with Wright Cyclone engines and we were contracted to fly on a scheduled basis in support of a Distant Early Warning Line site known as DYE Site One. It was a vast dome of a building on top of a five thousand foot mountain, sixty-five air miles from Sondestrom. The unit housed around forty people and was equipped with electronic radio detection equipment and was part of the trans-Canadian warning network. The closest other site was on the Greenland icecap served by a USAF four-engined C130 turbo ski aircraft.

In general we were engaged in the transportation of miscellaneous cargoes to and from DYE Site One or in assisting crew changes on a periodic basis. The Sikorsky 55 eight-seater helicopters supplied this isolated outpost with technical spares, food, fuel, drink and of course could be switched to air ambulance configuration in the case of serious sickness or emergency.

On some occasions we were used as transport for senior military officers and VIPs. In late August, when the ice had disappeared, a Sunday 'fishing flight' took an Admiral and a Colonel down a long narrow sea inlet to where I knew the best Arctic Char could be caught. We caught two salmon and fifty-two char with normal lures on spinning gear. The char were easy to hook but very difficult to land unless you unsportingly used a line with a twenty pound breaking strain. The catch went into the freezers in the NCO's mess.

It is not difficult to imagine that there was little in the way of entertainment at Sondestrom. Scandinavian Airways had an hotel locally for ground and aircrews servicing their passenger flights to America and their stewardesses were permitted to attend dances in the Officers' Club. But as can be imagined, they were usually well escorted. Officers were not allowed reciprocal privileges. Talking to any female was a bonus, escorted or not.

There was an excellently equipped gymnasium on the base, in which many overweight personnel spent much of their twelve-month tour getting rid of unwanted pounds. I spent most of my free time here playing badminton and volleyball. I also became reasonably expert on the trampoline. One officer, arriving from Chicago weighing two hundred and sixty pounds, finished his tour at one hundred and seventy-five. His wife must have had a shock when he walked through the door.

I took a month's leave from mid July to mid August and spent it flying patrol and electronic rail inspection sorties for the Quebec North Shore and Labrador Railroad in a Bell 47. My base was at Sept Isle, known as Seven Islands. The work was periodic in nature along a three hundred mile length of line up to the iron ore town of Shefferville.

This railroad's operation was almost completely automatic. The great ore wagons were towed by three or more diesel powered locomotives and normally controlled remotely over the whole journey. Only on occasions when a passenger coach was added would there be a driver and a guard.

The country on either side of the railway was very rugged and landing places difficult to find. Often we landed across the rails adjacent to one of the electronic inspection stations, keeping an extremely keen lookout for approaching trains. We slept overnight in old railway carriages parked here and there in rail sidings.

For two weeks I was switched to Quebec Fishery Patrol. My passenger was a Fisheries Inspector who spent his time checking permits and licences to fish. Even the possession of a rod in a car, without a licence, left the owner open to prosecution and the seizure of his vehicle.

The inspector and I had some good fishing, landing twenty-four speckled trout in one day; one weighing in at five and a half pounds. At the end of the season I was invited to a party at the Fishery Patrol's Seven Island HQ. Bill, the inspector had told all and sundry about our prowess and the number of unlicenced fishermen we had apprehended. Then he turned to me and said jokingly, "Of course, you have a licence don't you?" With a wide grin I announced, "No, I don't, actually."

I returned to Sondestrom in mid August and found the ice had disappeared and small white and yellow flowers had grown among the muskeg and moss, but there were no trees to be seen anywhere. On Saturdays and Sundays a group of us from the base would get together in an attempt to break the monotony of camp and go for a twelve-mile walk out to the foot of the immense Greenland Ice Cap from where a military vehicle would pick us up and bring us back.

The ice cap was an awe-inspiring sight when viewed from the ground. As pilots, of course we saw it from the air every day, but that sight was as nothing when you stood on brown naked ground and looked up at a great vertical wall of ice about one hundred and fifty feet high. The cap stretching back in an ever increasing slope to make an ice sheet over eight thousand feet thick near the centre of the island.

In the short summer the jagged walls of this barrier were constantly melting and great chunks of ice weighing many tons were regularly breaking away to fall and splinter into thousands of fragments. A year or so before, a party of Canadian scientists had been inspecting the bottom of the ice wall, when a huge fall of ice had killed many of them.

Whilst I had been away on leave the engineers had replaced the rubberised floats of winter ice and ocean operations on our helicopters with summertime wheels. Ours were the only helicopters in that part of Greenland and were sometimes called on to mount search and rescue. In a blinding snowstorm one night we were sent out to look for an overdue yacht. With the search co-ordinator, Air Force Captain Bill Foster in the co-pilot's seat, we spent forty-five minutes out in the fjord in appalling conditions. Then we were told the yacht was moored and everyone was safe. We, however, were under full instrument conditions close to the high walls of the fjord. After a few very unpleasant minutes flying a GCA approach, we saw the runway lights and made a safe landing. "I owe you a drink," said Bill.

On another occasion an Eskimo child was lost on a hillside. This three-year-old had been walking with his parents back from a camp about ten miles inland from the fjord, They had been hunting reindeer and were returning to their fishing boat which was moored on the shore of a small bay on the fjord.

They were walking in single file when, amazingly, the child just disappeared. Of course they had retraced their steps and called his name but had found nothing. It was early morning and still dark. It was dangerous country because, although they were following a well-defined path, the ground fell away steeply on either side, in some in a sheer drop of over four hundred feet. The parents sailed their boat the short distance to the harbour to alert the authorities and we were called out again, with Captain Foster, to search.

We spent the day traversing the mountain only stopping to refuel. It was almost dark when, on a beach far below us, there looked to be something moving across a patch of sand. Bill thought it looked like a fisherman. We did not connect the figure with the child. The form looked too big for a three-year-old, although Eskimos were notoriously inaccurate when giving ages. Just to make sure, I banked the machine to one side to drop swiftly towards the person now weaving along the beach. We made a low pass for a better look and saw it was an Eskimo boy.

As we landed, Bill dropped quickly from the cockpit and the boy tried to run away, but he was exhausted. I stopped the main rotors but kept the engine ticking over. The boy's face was swollen with insect bites, both eyes were nearly closed and the whole of his face was scratched and bleeding. Bill lifted him into the cockpit and the boy started to cry. The parents met us at the harbour and went with him to the hospital.

Later, discussing the incident, we agreed that had this boy not been an Eskimo he would not have survived wandering through the night all alone and unguided. He was older than three, but not by much. We estimated he had walked at least five miles from the point where he had been missed. It could be assumed that had we not intercepted him, he might well have got close enough to the boat to be seen by his parents. Incredibly he was out of hospital and back on the boat within forty-eight hours.

At the end of the contract in October, I was sorry to leave many good friends behind as I took a welcome break before heading due south.

In January 1963 I arrived in Beirut, Lebanon. My function was to represent a helicopter company which had connections with a travel agency in London. We were sub-contracted to a local company promoting helicopter involvements in the Lebanon, in advertising, tourist trips and films.

Our first job was working on an Italian film called *The Last Plane to Baalbek*. It was an adventure movie starring George Sanders and Elsa Martinelli. Part of the action called for the helicopter to shoot up an enemy convoy in the desert close to the ruins of Baalbek. My Hiller, with a door removed to permit an Italian actor to lean out and fire a revolver, was to swoop down to ground level. They decked me out in an army uniform complete with Sam Brown belt and revolver and my passenger in a like manner. The vehicles and men in the convoy were a Lebanese Army Unit that had been hired as extras. We 'attacked' the rear of the convoy, my companion opening a rapid fire with his pistol, the soldiers returning fire, their rifles loaded — I hoped — with blanks. We were so low on these sweeps that the cardboard inserts in their blanks were spattering and impacting on the cockpit canopy.

Another scene involved a large airliner landing on a desert runway. We carried a cameraman to record, from our helicopter, the approach to landing the airliner Captain would see. As a tie-in, we were requested to meet up with an actual airliner at six thousand feet. By arrangement, the Caravelle, flying in from Beirut, circled us a few times with our camera getting the required footage.

Ami, the representative of the London company, flew back with me to Beirut. She was from a wealthy local family with good business connections, but was incapable of organising contracts and schedules with devious film directors. We had a contract with the Lebanese company for a guaranteed minimum of twenty flying hours at twenty-five pounds sterling per hour plus two hundred pounds sterling per month living expenses for my engineer and myself. This was only just adequate as Beirut was an expensive city to live in. We were soon to discover that precisely the basic twenty hours would be flown and not a minute more. The London office had accepted this contract on the verbal understanding from the Beirut people that they envisaged flying well in excess of seventy hours per month.

What London did not know was that the local Lebanese sub-contractors were hiring out our helicopter at fantastically high hourly rates to visiting Sheikhs for tours of Beirut! One morning I flew a gentleman around the city only to hear later that the local director had received a thousand pounds sterling for the one-hour flight. We were being ripped off. The injury we felt was compounded by the fact that our aircraft was the only commercially operated helicopter in Lebanon. So there was no competition.

Another project involved dropping two hundred and fifty thousand sweets, attached to a small paper parachute with the manufacturer's name printed on it. We carried out safety checks to satisfy the aviation authorities and got the go ahead. We climbed to fifteen hundred feet over the city at lunchtime with one of the local directors dropping the goodies in bunches. Not surprisingly many of the parachutes did not open. The aviation authorities banned the project after this one run because of accidents in the streets where children ran to pick up this manna from heaven.

We then became a flying neon sign over the city at night, advertising a well-known nightclub. The engineer, Stan Rowsell, was an excellent technician and an innovator second to none. Our helicopter was on a foreign registration and therefore not hidebound by any of the conditions, many of an impractical nature, which would have applied had it been registered in the

172

UK. So we legally and safely attached the long neon sign to the left side of the machine. It was operated through a transformer secured to the passenger seat and connected to the aircraft battery.

The frame containing the neon tubes stretched from six feet in front of the machine back to near the tail rotor. It held fourteen letters each sufficiently large to be read at night from the seafront at a height of a thousand feet. We rigged a complicated electrical system with some unofficial help from a friend, the UK Civil Aviation Engineering Surveyor, who was temporarily based in Beirut.

We had no problems with the flight and requested clearance to land, which was given. A minute later over to my left and on a converging course a DC8 suddenly appeared. I informed the tower and was told to keep clear. I have often wondered what the passengers thought as they looked out on their final approach to Beirut and saw this flashing advert for a nightclub apparently hanging in the sky.

There was a lot of money changing hands in this city. It was one of the few places where Christians and Moslems could jointly take peaceful vacations. We often flew wealthy men to the lavish gambling casino down on the coast and the nightspots in the city were hedonistic and cosmopolitan.

The expatriates met at the St George Club close to Beirut's principal hotel. My accommodation was the Alcazar Hotel near the sea front and shops. Stan and his wife had an apartment close by. Stan and I went to the airport together most mornings in an early diesel Land Rover, which was plagued with mechanical problems and was a real pig to start. George, the Club's barman, possessed a pre-war Armstrong Siddeley with a pr-selector gearbox. This we hired when we had no patience left to deal with the Land Rover.

We were asked to try another advertising medium — banner towing. Neither Stan nor I knew anything about banners and even less how to construct one. It had to have the name of the company on both sides, and be readable at a thousand feet. We did not even know if a helicopter was capable of towing one.

We got together to construct a banner, with forty feet of strong

173

canvas to which we attached an eight-foot long heavy steel rod. Approximately two-thirds up this metal rod we fitted one end of a ninety-foot cable and, at the bottom of the rod, a bracket to contain a number of lead counter weights. The other end of the cable was fixed by a small 'V' connection to each landing skid of the helicopter.

The steel bar had to take a perpendicular attitude in the air in order to permit the canvas to fly without distortion. After many trial flights to adjust counterweights and cable attachment points, we incorporated a jettison release in the event of serious problems. We had some interesting moments doing these trials.

Initially, flapping in the slipstream caused the canvas to tear at the ends. We solved this by attaching a length of common fish netting, so that the slipstream could pass through. For three weeks we flew over Beirut advertising a well-known cola, an automobile, candy and the like.

Two days after the contract finished I received a cable from the London office. There was an urgent spraying job in Cyprus where two thousand acres of wheat had to be treated to combat insect infestation. The Cypriot Government would pay two thousand pounds and they would supply the chemical. We anticipated little difficulty with the job; both Stan and I had considerable experience. The question was how to get to Cyprus in the shortest possible time. Going by boat was not feasible. We would have to fly over.

Nicosia is about one hundred and seventy miles from Beirut including a sea crossing of one hundred and forty miles. The maximum airborne time on a Hiller with full tanks was one hour fifty minutes, a wholly inadequate time for the journey. Even if an informal cruising speed of sixty miles per hour could be maintained, assuming no adverse winds, airborne endurance in excess of three hours would be necessary.

Something else had to be taken into consideration, compounding the problem. Because the operation in Cyprus had to commence within twenty-four hours, two large chemical tanks would have to fly with the aircraft together with the attached spray booms. Tanks and booms would add a combined weight and drag factor and reduce the machine's speed by at least eight miles a hour. So, in fact, a total of four hours airborne endurance would be needed.

Stan and I worked on the problem and thought we had an answer. If we could get the chemical spray tanks cleaned out we could use them for extra fuel and Stan would come over by airline to save weight. A local firm helped us by steam cleaning the twenty-five gallon cylindrical spray tanks. We then connected them through a T-junction, from which a length of hose led to a hand operated wobble pump we'd fitted on the left side of the cockpit within my reach. From the pump we planned to run yet another hose down to the normal fuel tank inlet located low in the belly of the Hiller.

The only piece of hose we could find of the right type turned out to have too small a diameter to fit snugly into the inlet aperture on the fuel tank, but we had to make the best of a bad job in the short time available. I knew that if too much fuel was pumped into the main tank from the spray tanks it would overflow at this point and be lost.

We carried out a flight check, half filling the spray tanks with fuel and tried pumping in flight. It was soon obvious that fuel was going through the pump from the spray tanks to the main without any effort on my part. As the main tank was well below the level of the bottom of the spray tanks, fuel was in fact siphoning down. We carried out a rough overhaul on the pump, replacing two gaskets and we both agreed that the pump would not then permit fuel to go through it except when it was actually pumped. This was to prove a grave error of judgement.

Next morning, with twenty gallons of fuel in each spray tank, I filed a flight plan for Nicosia. When asked for a return date I vaguely replied, "Should be back in a couple of days." This satisfied the controller and he wished me a good flight.

The extra forty gallons was enough to permit over four hours of flight, allowing for head winds, providing a safe margin on what should be only a three-hour flight. Stan had secured a dinghy to the right hand passenger seat — this Hiller was piloted centrally — and I wore a Mae West jacket. The extra weight of the dinghy proved to be something of a final straw and after several abortive attempts to get airborne, we offloaded it. Even then I scraped along the grass on the side of the runway before struggling into the air. I was at a very low level over the sea until I had used up enough fuel to gain some height.

It was a glorious day with excellent visibility and I could see the lenticular cloud often located over Cyprus. As a safety precaution I had decided not to operate the hand pump until the helicopter was about forty-five minutes out of Beirut and then, according to my calculations, the fuel gauge in the cockpit should be reading slightly over the halfway mark. If, after using the pump, the needle on this gauge had not commenced to move up towards FULL, this would indicate a fault in the pumping system and return to Beirut could be achieved in safety because there would still remain over one hours gasoline in the main tank. The plan was sound and, I thought, reasonably foolproof, until I realised that the contents needle had not moved across to the FULL position by even a fraction.

It was then reasonable to assume that the spray tanks were siphoning into the main tank without my assistance and there was no means of knowing how much of this highly volatile gasoline was overflowing the loosely fitted hose and across the tail assembly. I switched the electrics off momentarily and the fuel gauge needle plunged to EMPTY immediately. Switching on again it went back across the FULL mark and so it seemed almost certain that my fuel was siphoning into the main tank.

There were valid reasons for not flying back to Beirut, one being the near certainty that our Lebanese ex-employers, who were thought to be unaware of my intended departure, would know by now that the machine had in fact gone and also where it was going. They had attempted to prolong their contract with the promise that this would be rewarded by a substantial increase in the rental rate. But even before receiving instructions from London I had been keen to move on. Another reason not to immediately return to Beirut was that I thought it highly probable the aviation authorities might ask some awkward questions about my flight plan, which required evidence of intent to return to Beirut before clearance for take-off would be given.

Therefore, I decided to continue. The weather was fine and the sea was calm. I had no immediate problems. The next one might,

Crossing the Line
New York Marathon 1985

I have always enjoyed
marathons and have
run in London, Berlin and
Hamburg. Berlin after the
Wall came down
was probably the best

Self with Bell 47 helicopter
Lancaster, PA, USA
June 2004

Check pilot on a Gazelle

Eighty-plus 'Copter Pilot — still smiling

or might not, arise as one hour and fifty minutes of normal endurance approached. At one hour forty minutes into the flight I decided to start pumping, moving the wooden handle gently to and fro. For about half a dozen strokes there was some resistance then, it was suddenly gone. It was now obvious that the spray tanks were empty and, hopefully, that all that fuel had siphoned into the main tank. The electrical fuel gauge for the main tank had dropped to slightly below FULL and it had to be hoped that this was accurate as the remaining distance would require flying time of something better than one hour.

But worse was to come.

The hands on my watch slowly ticked towards one hour fifty and at about one minute short of it, the engine coughed, spluttered, partially died and then picked up again. I was at three thousand feet. My finger found the transmission button and I called "Mayday, mayday, mayday," and transmitted my position. There was no response. The engine was firing and misfiring all the time and I was losing both power and height. There was still no response to my calls. The backfiring was now accompanied by increasing vibration and it seemed certain that the engine was about to stop altogether. However it continued to fire and misfire and it was about this time I realised that shortage of fuel was not the problem. An empty tank does not permit an engine to turn over, no matter how slowly, so there had to be another reason for this partial engine failure. But what was it? And would I ever have time to find out?

The machine was now descending rapidly with the engine still running and I was frantically trying to work out the best method to ditch and survive as the sea came closer at an alarming rate. I grabbed the Verey pistol and two cartridges, jamming them between my Mae West and coat. Then, at less than five hundred feet, the engine suddenly roared into full-throated life and responding to the throttle regained full power. The sweat was running off my face and my shirt was soaked. My relief was intense.

I persuaded the machine to climb. The engine began missing again intermittently but the next twenty minutes passed fairly well. Forty-five minutes later the coastline of Cyprus came into view. I was still transmitting position reports but with no response. Famagusta Bay passed underneath me and I was tempted to land and try and sort the problem, but the thought of explaining to the authorities why I had landed at a place other than a customs airport was too much. I landed at RAF Nicosia, and parked by the control tower. I shut off the engine and climbed wearily out of the machine, took off my Mae West and, feeling ready to drop, walked across to the tower.

"Why didn't you call earlier?" asked the Flight Lieutenant.

"Didn't you hear me call?" I said. "No", he said, "Nothing at all. Your radio must be on the blink."

I decided to maintain a discreet silence about the drama over the sea and to get a technician to repair the radio.

Stan arrived by airliner. He took the carburettor to pieces and found minute particles of rubber obstructing the fuel flow. These had obviously come from the rubberised connecting hoses. Continuous siphoning must have taken place throughout the flight, based on the fact that there was less than twenty minutes of fuel left in the main tank. How many gallons went into the Mediterranean was anyone's guess.

The RAF radioman examined the transceiver installation and pronounced it completely unserviceable, which didn't come as a great surprise. The most remarkable thing about the whole episode was the timing of the engine malfunction coinciding, to the minute, with the normal airborne endurance at one hour fifty minutes on a full tank.

The wheat to be sprayed was one complete block of two thousand acres near Paphos. Stan and I flew the Hiller across, passing over high country en route but keeping well clear of Mount Olympus. On the map, the height of Olympus was shown as six thousand four hundred feet and it was awesome. The strong winds blowing down over the high ground made for a turbulent uncomfortable flight. As we landed at Paphos, Stan remarked he wasn't keen to do the return trip on the same route. I remarked that after my sea crossing it was a piece of cake.

The area to be treated was completely flat and the strong wind created little turbulence. To get the highly toxic Parathion into the crop and, as far as possible avoid potentially dangerous drift, demanded a degree of skill. The long spray booms almost scraped the surface of the crop at a higher than normal speed of seventy miles per hour. As normal spray runs were cross-wind, and the agricultural experts discovered that not only was there excellent penetration, but the wind was driving the chemical spray through the crop at a lower level than usual to cover considerably more than the usual sixty foot swathe, the experts authorised one hundred and twenty foot sweeps. The results were good and we were finished in two days.

We were now asked to spray orange groves near Limasol. These were fairly extensive and from the air looked like a patchwork quilt but this was a more dangerous job. Each field was of little more than four or five acres enclosed by tall yew trees that acted as wind breaks. Going in and out of each miniature clearing had its moments. The confined squares trapped the toxic chemicals and although we wore masks we were subjected to both spray and fumes on clothing and skin. This sort of spraying is much better done on the ground with mechanised spray equipment and well-protected personnel.

I had a business trip to England and left Stan and the helicopter in Cyprus. On my return I had another ferry flight lined up, this time from Cyprus to Turkey. During my absence in England Stan had taken great care to modify our unique long-range tank system. He had found and installed a much improved pump with a non-return valve to eliminate any siphonic action and had overhauled the aircraft completely. He went on to install aircraft fuel hoses that I brought with me from London. The Royal Air Force had been very helpful with the radio which was now fully operational.

It was a beautiful day in Nicosia and when I called the tower for take-off clearance, the controller cleared me and added, "I hope the tank works this time." Another voice then chimed in with "Have a good flight." I had thought my adventure was not common knowledge. Obviously I was wrong.

The heading was north to cross the three thousand foot mountain range of Kyrenia and then out to sea for the fifty mile crossing to the Turkish mainland. To my great relief there were no sticky moments and the Turkish coast came into view with a range of mountains in the background. An hour later a medieval castle in very good repair on the edge of a rocky beach slid by. According to legend a local overlord had built the castle to house his daughter. This was to stop her being carried off by a rival ruler and she remained there all her life and never married.

The coastal route into Adana was extremely turbulent, caused by winds coming from the northwest over the mountains down to the sea. We suffered a severe drop from seven hundred to two hundred feet from the force of the downdraft. I followed a coastal railroad to the cotton plains and identified Mersin, and so on to Tarsus, to land in thick fog.

The local police were most helpful. Although they had no English they eventually understood that the helicopter was en route to Adana to spray cotton for the Government. One old man could speak a little English learned after being taken prisoner in the Great War near Galipoli. "Kapitan," he said. "Welcome to Turkey. Go to Adana and take care of our cotton." We had no difficulty at all in obeying. The total flying time from Nicosia was three hours twenty-five minutes.

I took an airline flight back to Nicosia via Beirut the next day to ferry our standby Hiller to Adana. This machine had been flown into Nicosia by DC3 where Stan had reassembled it. Another set of our 'specialised tanks' worked like a dream, much to Stan's relief. He was getting good at this.

Adana was on a hot, swampy, low lying plain, infested with mosquitoes and other noxious insects. A large US Air Base was close by, but we saw few Americans. This was not a surprise, for Adana was the most depressing place I have ever encountered in my whole flying career. The helicopter crews, consisting of three other pilots, four engineers and two wives, were all accommodated in one house on the edge of town. There was no room there for me, so my accommodation was in a hotel on one side of the town square. The room was barely eight by ten feet, only just large enough for a bed. With no air conditioning, the sticky humid heat in this cubbyhole and the smell and noise from the market in the square, added up to something beyond description.

I lay on the cot with rivers of perspiration running off a half naked body and no sooner had the light been extinguished than the mosquitoes dived in for the kill. Their droning would have kept me awake even if the foetid heat failed to do so. Opening the patched window didn't help because there was seldom any wind and it only encouraged more mosquitoes to enter the room. In short I was a picture of downright misery. The second night I borrowed a spray gun from the company and saw some improvement.

It appeared that the local farmer's cotton had been attacked by a bug and they were insistent that we spray immediately or they would lose their entire crop. They were apparently oblivious of the fact that their own government was withholding permission for us to operate. Then everything suddenly changed. We later heard a rumour that a little money dropped into the right hands had succeeded where more orthodox methods of persuasion had failed.

Shortly after my arrival from Nicosia another pilot arrived from London. He was a friend of the co-ordinator at Adana, both of them having flown from the same naval carrier in the Second World War. The new arrival had little recent flying experience and none on spraying operations. His last occupation had been a liquor salesman. I suggested that he be given dual spraying instruction before venturing out into the labyrinth of telephone and electricity cables which criss-crossed many of the small enclosed cotton fields. This advice was ignored by the co-director on the grounds that non-revenue flying was not in the interests of the company. Where had I heard that before? Disillusioned, I pulled out and returned to London where I arrived to the news that the new pilot had crashed and completely wrecked my newly delivered Hiller. Fortunately he was not injured.

During this stopover in London a seasonal job came through with Helicopter Services, a subsidiary of the David Brown Company, flying old Bell 47D1 model helicopters which could run for six hundred hours before complete overhaul. I joined the company in July as the Chief Pilot. In fact, to begin with, I was the only one. There had been an industrial dispute and the Chief

Pilot had quit and taken the other pilots with him to a company at Biggin Hill. They had left a lot of uncompleted work, much of it spraying against blight on Scottish potato crops with copper sulphate solution. So by August 2nd I was in Perth. 'Chalky' White, the engineer, drove up with our support vehicle. The chemicals and tankers were supplied by the Chemical Spray Company of Perth.

Between the 3rd and 25th of August we sprayed potato and bean crops around Forfar, Falkland, Kinross, Errol, Montrose and Cupar. One afternoon, spraying in Kircaldy, the machine hit, and sliced through, a high tension wire. Fortunately the impact was taken by the vertical securing tube on the skid undercarriage and not by the rotors. Several runs had been made under the high tension wire but on this last pass it disappeared into the boundary hedge close to an oak tree. It took me only a split second to realise that the sag in the wire was too low to fly under and that it was too late to go over it, so I would probably strike either the tree or the wire. I chose the wire — the tree had been there a long time.

The impact with the helicopter could only have an adverse effect on both pilot and machine. In one movement I jettisoned the chemical and tried to climb in a futile attempt to clear the wire. It caught the landing gear with the effect of retarding forward flight. I applied maximum power and the sudden increased thrust when combined with the weight of the machine and its inertial forward motion, broke the power cable with a vivid flash and a strong sulphurous smell in the cockpit.

As a result the vertical support of the landing gear on the Bell was deeply scored. This was the only damage. The local electricity chief came to the hotel later with a broad smile. "You were very lucky," he said, "Let me buy you a drink." I tentatively enquired what it was going to cost us for cutting the cable. "Well", he said, "Ordinarily it would cost you twenty pounds but we've just had some new splicing material from America and up to now we've not been able to try it out. We now know it works a treat."

We finished the potato spraying in Scone. In three weeks we had sprayed four thousand acres and we moved on to Carlyle and south-west to Wales.

As well as crop spraying in Wales we had a gravel and cement

182

job near Harlech. This was to help with the construction of a dam close to an atomic research power station on a mountain side. On the first day we made over one hundred short flights to the construction site carrying underslung loads. The following day we moved forty-one tons in a like manner. Mundane though these jobs were, there were incidents which interrupted the tedium.

The loading point for the helicopter was the closest spot the trucks could get to the site on the mountain. There were no buildings around except a very isolated church. Sunday morning we had paused for coffee and sandwiches when a figure in a black cassock made his way slowly up the hill towards us and in a strong welsh accent he bade us "Good morning."

"Good morning to you, sir," I replied and with the suggestion of a smile he said, " We in the village have much admired your work on the mountain involving not a little skill and possibly some degree of personal danger."

I said, "Thank you, you're very kind," and waited for him to continue.

"You know that machine of yours is a trifle loud and I have a sermon to deliver," he said indicating the little church. "No problem," I said. "We'll stop flying for the duration of the service." He beamed, "I understand you are Canadian, may I know you're name?" "Jones," I told him. "Ah!" he said. "I knew it. Your family came from Wales!" I made no mention of Ireland.

Later in another remote welsh village, we gave a ride to an old lady of ninety, who only spoke Welsh. She lived within thirty miles of the sea but had never seen it. She saw it sitting beside me as we circled at two thousand feet on a clear sunny morning over her cottage.

We were used by the Forestry Commission to lift fencing equipment. Loads were made up of around five hundred posts, wired together and flown into position. High winds and associated turbulence made for difficult flying conditions into the high ground where new boundary fences were to be erected. Much of the terrain did not permit ground transportation and men and horses were the only other means of moving the gear.

The last job we had in Wales was spraying in the Hafod Forest prior to flying back to Luton in September. Before leaving for

South Africa I checked out a new pilot named Odell and my logbook records that I put him through ten engine-off auto-rotations to a full stop — poor man!

CHAPTER ELEVEN

No Time to Draw Breath

SEPTEMBER 1963 AND I WAS BACK IN SOUTH AFRICA, spraying grapes in Cape Province.

We had two Bell 47's and three pilots. The company was based in Worcester, seventy miles north east of Cape Town. We were spraying in the beautiful Hex River Valley, a long, narrow defile. Hills, almost small mountains, lined it in on both sides with its width little more than three miles. The vineyards had been hit by a serious infestation of blight.

Company Director, Tim Clutterbuck, met me off the Viscount at Cape Town. Tim could have been a double for the film star Fred MacMurray and had been the first pilot to land a Mosquito on an aircraft carrier without the use of an arrester wire. He'd had an emergency over the sea and landed with only his wheel brakes to stop him shooting off the other end of the deck into the briney.

His first words were, "Boy, do we need you! This job's a complete bastard."

Much of the trouble stemmed from the very small fields in which the vines grew. Some of these were less than an acre in size and they were covered with wires of all kinds. These included cables on tall poles to power the irrigation pumps located in the centre of each field and which stuck out above the wire frames on which the vines grew. Also through the valley went the main Cape Town to Johannesburg highway with its telegraph poles and the railroad with its tall steel supports for its catenary wires. These factors together with high winds funnelling down the valley made for very unpleasant and dangerous spraying operations. One pilot had already gone through a power cable and wrecked a set of rotors.

Next morning, taking a load of chemical spray out over the patchwork fields, I found all too quickly that Tim's description of the hazards had erred on the conservative side. On the second

185

spray run one of my skids hit and cut a cable. The helicopter wasn't damaged but the incident did nothing at all for my self-esteem.

In any spraying operation it is vital to know the exact acreage to be treated and the precise nature of the spray medium. This is in order that the correct output calibration can be made by the sprayer and an accurate application rate per acre (or in south Africa per 'morgan' of 2.11 acres) can be assured. Unbroken continuity of supply of the medium is also vital.

On this particular job I soon discovered that these three vital factors which contribute to a successful spraying operation could not be guaranteed. Which meant that we frequently ran out of spray when supposedly loaded for a particular area.

The local chemical spraying company — though part of an international organisation — was grossly inefficient and the acreage figures supplied by the farmers often inaccurate. The ground support was also very poor and it was not uncommon to wait two hours for the arrival of the ground crew and water truck in order to start. By which time a change in the critical wind factor could prevent us from flying.

In this haphazard manner we managed to labour through two thousand acres before transferring to the town of Ceres twenty miles away. Here we were spraying with Parathion for a type of caterpillar known as 'army worm' which chewed its way through wheat crops. Again, because of turbulence, we had often to quit by ten in the morning.

A journalist from the *Cape Argus* newspaper came to interview me. I had been on Cape Town radio and given a talk on some of my experiences.

The *Argus* headline read: *Paddy, the spray pilot, has had an exciting life.* The news item went on to say:

> *Mr JAT 'Paddy' Jones, a 41 year old Irish born helicopter pilot, at present crop spraying by helicopter in the Worcester district, has crammed more adventure and action into his 41 years than most people manage to achieve in double that time. His unit, based at Worcester, is at present spraying young vines. The road to Worcester for Paddy has been a long one winding out*

186

over far away places. He has been a wartime rear gunner, a miner, a merchant seaman, a bush pilot in Australia and a rubber planter in Malaya."

Towards the end of October, Tim said, "One of the Bells has to be flown up to Salisbury. Do you feel like a ferry flight?" I replied, "Anything to get away from Hex Valley!"

From Worcester to Salisbury was about fourteen hundred miles. It was a relatively simple navigational exercise as both highway and railroad were routed into Johannesburg almost a thousand miles to the north. Much of this distance involved crossing the Great Karoo. This desert expanse of brown, flat, intensely hot, sparsely bushed country was relieved occasionally by isolated homesteads where a wind driven pump maintained the lawn, the only patch of green for another forty miles.

We refuelled at Beaufort West on the edge of the Great Karoo. We also filled six jerricans to carry us over this great expanse.

A quote from the *Rand Daily Mail* dated 4th November, 1963:

After flying for more than ten hours from Worcester yesterday Captain JAT Paddy Jones, Irish born helicopter pilot, crossed the Vall River at dusk yesterday afternoon and found that without navigation lights he could not legally land at his destination, Baragwanath. So he put his machine down in the gathering darkness beside the dining room of a hotel, ten miles from Vereeniging, stepped out and asked the startled waiters for dinner. Paddy took off from Worcester at 6.10am yesterday and dropped down for fuel at Beaufort West. Hanover, Bloemfontein and Kroonstad. At Hanover he settled beside a wayside garage pump, the attendant took some time to recover from his surprise before he could serve the strangest looking vehicle he had ever seen.

Next morning after filling up at Baragwanath Airfield (altitude six thousand feet), due to a combination of fuel load and altitude density, the helicopter would not hover. It had to scrape along the morning damp grass before gaining enough transitional speed to get airborne. The flight into Rhodesia was uneventful but the

187

failing light made both a landing and a night stop necessary in Beatrice, a small village about fifty miles short of Salisbury. The helicopter was landed in the school playground, the only place both flat and secure, in the beam of the landing lights.

The English headmaster and his wife fed me before driving me to the local hotel. Both were worried about the declining political situation and I got the feeling of great discontent in the rural communities.

I left the machine at Mount Hampden, an airfield outside Salisbury, and took the airline back to Worcester. I sprayed tobacco plants and the rest of the potato plants. This machine was then required in Johannesburg for publicity shots for a film studio. An actress, Madeleine Usher, was driven in the newly arrived Chrysler Turbine car to a hotel in Sandown and then flown by me to the studios at Lone Hill for a film test.

The Automobile Association had been investigating the possibility of traffic direction by means of helicopter. I picked up the Secretary General of the AA, Mr Trew, from his home at Bryanston to conduct an aerial survey of the roads. They also wanted to use helicopters as ambulances during peak holiday periods. Once again what I was doing was written up in the *Rand Daily Mail*.

From mid January for three weeks I worked in the Eastern Transvaal spraying corn, citrus, maize and potatoes with the chemical Rogor. I finished at Sanderton where at an agricultural show I put on a demonstration of spraying technique. More and more incidents of beatings and robberies were being reported in the newspapers and there was a general air of unrest. I was relieved when the contract was over and I could depart.

On March 10th I was en route from Abadan, in the Gulf, to England in a Sikorsky 55 on another ferry flight. I had done this trip in the opposite direction some time before with a few worrying moments. This time we had no problems at the outset but the engine-driven fuel pump failed as we were approaching Baghdad and I had to rapidly switch to the electric standby pump, normally only used when starting the engine. The failure caused a three-day wait for eventual lift-off whilst a replacement fuel pump was flown out from England.

The engineer and I then flew on to France despite the bad weather and the leg between Baghdad and Rome took seven hours of flying on instruments. On the 16th we left Nice but soon hit by headwinds generated by the Mistral and was forced to land in a field next to the Route Nationale at Gardanne. The police were very helpful, put a guard on the Sikorsky and gave us accommodation in the police headquarters overnight. They also helped with the formalities that such an unscheduled landing invariably requires. Their Chief entertained the Bristow engineer and myself in a local estaminet and remarked, "You are very lucky, Captain, our military helicopters cannot fly in these conditions."

My logbook records ground speed as being less than fifteen miles an hour accompanied by very severe turbulence just before we landed. The rest of the trip to Redhill was uneventful and the four thousand mile flight was completed in eight days. It would have been five days without the wait for the replacement pump at Baghdad.

I left the helicopter at Redhill for a complete overhaul and went to Leavesden for a turbine engine course connected with the replacement of the piston engine in the Sikorskys with a turbine version known as the 'Gnome'. After passing the mandatory ARB written and oral exams, Bristows sent me out to Das Island in the Persian Gulf.

Das Island is an isolated island patch of sand, a hundred miles east of Doha. It measures about one and a quarter miles long by about three-quarters of a mile wide, and bears virtually no vegetation. At one end was a small harbour and an infrequently used airstrip ran along part of the length. Light twin De Havilland Dove aircraft brought in a golf team to play the oil company golfers on the white sand eighteen-hole golf course, using red balls. A broom was kept by every 'green' to sweep away the footmarks after putting, but the bunkers were for real. Women were not permitted on the island other than visiting golfers or female aircraft pilots.

One morning a Dove landed, piloted by a long time lady

friend who greeted me with, "Dr Livingstone, I presume?" "No Elizabeth," I replied, "And you certainly look nothing like Mr Stanley."

Accommodation and messing was excellent; a bottle of whisky cost one dollar American. The regular Bristow crews (which did not include me) were required to stay on Das Island for one year and, because the food was so good, keeping the weight down was a problem. Lack of physical exercise and sitting long hours in the cockpit also conspired. I started to cut down on my food intake and commenced the daily ritual of a perimeter run each morning before flying, passing very close to the immensely hot Gas Flare located at the top end of the island. The combination of Spartan diet and exercise achieved a drop of twenty pounds in under two months. Since those days, running has become a regular habit and turned me into a marathon runner. I have seven London Marathons under my belt now, along with various others, but my best time was four hours twenty-one minutes in the Berlin '87 at the age of sixty-five.

On the work side we had three machines and three pilots, rostered so that two helicopters flew each day with the third on standby in case of emergency. The greater part of the flying was over long sea distances to the rigs. We carried out replacement crews and brought back the time-expired ones. We also carried underslung loads of up to 1500 pounds from rig to rig. There was the occasional long haul of equipment from the Island base out to the sea location, though the really heavy stuff was shipped out on an oil company vessel.

Some of the loads we carried were extremely valuable pieces of electronic equipment and computer components. One morning the Chief Pilot inadvertently released such a load into the sea at a point too deep to permit salvage. It was not a popular move with the drilling superintendent.

The Westland Sikorsky 55 turbine helicopters were something of a novelty in that a piston engined machine had been converted to turbine power. The new type engine installation occupied the same position in the nose as it's piston predecessor but was much more powerful and a lot lighter. To maintain the original centre of gravity more weight had to be added to the forward section and this was accomplished by transferring heavy electronic equipment, normally housed at the back of the machine to a forward location nearer the engine.

There were other major differences between piston and turbine, one being that the pilot's control over power was through a computer box. There was no manual throttle control for normal operational conditions. A manual throttle *was* fitted, however, but only for use in emergencies. Operationally everything was processed through the computer in response to up or down movement of the collective pitch lever operated by the left hand.

The 'box' efficiently controlled power co-ordination but it was prone to malfunction occasionally. When that happened, from whatever cause, and even if we reverted to manual throttle immediately, it was more than likely that an emergency landing at sea would follow.

This was because engine revs would have dropped promptly below the level where they were self-sustaining. The engine would stop and an in-flight restart would take too long to keep the machine airborne in view of the low altitudes at which it was customary to fly.

Our helicopters were equipped with efficient float landing gear, but the waters of the Persian Gulf were often anything but smooth and, perhaps more importantly, were full of sharks.

So most of my low level inter-rig work with heavy underslung loads was conducted on manual throttle. With practice one could become proficient even though the smallest movement of the twist grip throttle could produce a very rapid increase or decrease of five thousand revs, with the possibility of stalling the compressor, almost certainly to be followed by the destruction of this very expensive power unit. Nevertheless, I persisted and developed a sixth sense with the 'box' as well.

With the machine in constant proximity to the sea any salt spray ingested by the turbine was removed by running fresh water through the engine. Moreover, since the engine accumulated large quantities of carbon this had to be cleared by an internal kerosene wash. Both operations, usually a daily ritual, required great care and co-operation between pilot and engineer.

The aircraft hangar and workshop were within two hundred

yards of the shoreline and partially because of this, corrosion was an ongoing problem. We had a surfaced landing pad in front of the hangar which was kept watered to limit the effect of blowing up sand from the aircraft's rotors which otherwise created a miniature whirlwind prior to touch down. The three rigs were equipped with radio beacons that helped us approach from any direction to home in on the rig. Visibility out at sea was often reduced to less than a quarter of a mile by a mixture of sea mist and blown sand.

Having successfully located and landed on a rig to drop off passengers, it was frequently impossible to locate the next drop close by because of sea mist and these work platforms though numbered were not fitted with radio homing devices. On occasion we were even forced to return on a radio bearing to the rig and wait for improvement in visibility.

Das Island was often also subjected to high winds which raised a type of sandstorm which could make it difficult to locate the island itself when inbound. Once, flying in from a rig eighty miles out to sea, we ran into a blinding sand storm, making it impossible to proceed visually and I had to continue flying on instruments. The radio directional aid on the Island required 'line of sight' for efficient homing but we were too far out and too low to pick it up.

As is often the case in a sandstorm, vertical visibility at low altitudes, though limited, is much better than forward visibility. In this instance, at five hundred feet the sea always remained visible, a consoling factor in the event of an emergency landing. I decided to remain at this low altitude and steer on the magnetic compass until the Island's beacon came within range. Understandably, the first sighting of the Island's large jib crane on the harbour breakwater came as a great relief.

I finished on Das Island on 11th July and by the 17th I was flying a Sikorsky on a photographic survey over Montreal. By the end of the month I was flying on a commercial film assignment in Scotland. Busy, busy, busy. Sometimes it seemed there was almost no time to draw breath.

A film company required a pilot to fly a three-place Hiller on a movie location at Ballachuilish near Glencoe. A Rolls Royce took me to Heathrow to catch a flight to Edinburgh. There, another car took me to Perth Airport where I collected the helicopter and met John Upham, the engineer. We flew the short distance to Ballahuilish and landed on the lawn of the hotel which, because there had been a mix up with the bookings, was full. They were extremely helpful however and found us accommodation on the shore of Loch Leven. Here the Loch was little more than a hundred yards across and a barge type car-ferry operated at frequent intervals to save a twenty-mile journey around the Loch.

The film unit was producing a documentary for an international oil company. One of the scenes was to show a fast, expensive sports car moving along a straight stretch of road at very high speed and, on coming to a sharp corner failing to take it and plunging into the Loch.

The director required me to skim low and as fast as possible over a selected road to simulate the car. The forward mounted movie camera was to capture the relative movement of the road with the loch on the far corner growing closer by the second. Being new to this movie making business I asked John why they didn't just drive a car along the road and film it. "Truth is," he said, "the car manufacturers were most reluctant to donate more than one car for the 'write-off' and then they had a hell of a job finding a volunteer to drive it into the Loch. That's why we're here." He had a point.

Finding a straight stretch of open road without hazardous trees or telegraph poles for us to fly over fast at low level was not easy. Furthermore, the director required a stretch of road where the telegraph wires were close enough to be in camera. Also to comply with the script the Loch had to be seen lapping the point where the road took the disastrous right hand bend and, in addition, impressively high Scottish mountains were required as background when the car disappeared into the water.

At this time of year Glencoe was a great tourist attraction and the roads were full of traffic. We needed a road clear of traffic for the numerous repeat low level runs that would almost certainly be required before the director was satisfied.

Jim, the camera operator, had considerable airborne camera

experience. He suggested we mount his equipment outboard on the right external cargo rack rather than attempt to shoot through the windscreen. We rigged the rack to take the camera with Jim, well secured, facing inward behind his equipment. All helicopters are subject to varying degrees of vibration that adversely affects the camera in movie work. I enclosed the camera in a type of elastic bungee frame which certainly assisted in reducing the problem. Later, the threat posed by vibration was eliminated with gyroscopic camera mounts.

We tried for several days to find the perfect location for the sequence but without success. The weather was foul with rain, mist and wind. We tried a different area. We took the station wagon and drove round the Loch. Eventually we found a stretch of road, half a mile long with a turn at the end on a smaller Loch some miles away. The only snag was two trees, one of which had branches almost brushing the side of the road two hundred yards back from the bend. Then somebody suggested we could chop the trees down.

I grabbed an axe and quickly dropped the first one. Work on the second had commenced when we heard the tap, tap of a walking stick and the murmur of voices. An elderly man in tweeds accompanied by a lady in similar garb, appeared round the corner followed by a little black dog. It crossed all our minds that perhaps the Laird and his lady would not take kindly to see their trees being downed before their eyes. Nothing daunted the second tree was finished off and we jumped back in the car and drove past the surprised couple. I looked back to see the man staring in a perplexed fashion at our now fast moving car. Jim said, "I wonder what they are thinking right now — two trees demolished and a bunch of chaps racing away like criminals. They probably figure we're all escapees from a mental institution."

Later a more suitable location was found with a mountain background. The flight went well with the local police keeping the road traffic free. On reaching the acute angled bend we carried straight on to skim the Loch, fly under both a power cable and a railroad bridge then easing back on the control column to climb with the camera recording the name of the oil company against a background of Scottish mountains. When it appeared in Cinerama, one got the distinct impression of sitting in the car, reaching the corner and hearing the screeching of tyres as the vehicle attempted to take the bend. Then swiftly, the blue, placid waters of the Loch rushing up to engulf the car as it crashed headlong down the bank. This illusion was only dispelled as the cable and bridge flashed overhead and erased as the oil company name appeared. Only then would the viewer realise that what he had witnessed had been shot from a helicopter.

In August, before I left for New Zealand, I borrowed an Auster and flew my sister up to Halfpenny Green in Shropshire to meet up with friends. In the late afternoon I landed back at Redhill to be met by the police. They had been waiting for us for quite a while. One of the great train robbery gang had escaped and they thought we had something to do with it. It transpired that we had been seen flying at low level following the M1 motorway close to the jail from which the prisoner had escaped. Somebody with a fine imagination had thought we could have landed in a field and picked him up.

They soon realised that my sister was hardly the person they were looking for and we heard nothing more.

CHAPTER TWELVE

The Antipodes Again

I ARRIVED IN WELLINGTON, NORTH ISLAND, NEW Zealand in November 1964 to fly Bell helicopters on agricultural spraying operations on both islands.

I had been given time in Wellington by the company HQ to get my licence validated for operation in New Zealand. They had booked me into a local hotel on the waterfront and I took a taxi there on arrival. It was a ramshackle wooden building with broken steps up the front door. I turned to the taxi driver and said, "You have to have something better than this in Wellington." He grinned. "Oh yes, we do indeed, but they cost a helluva lot more than this dump." I was shown to a room by a large lady with a Scots accent. On the way past she pointed out the only toilet and bathroom in the whole place. "You'll have to be up early," she said, "to get a wash." She was right, it was like a stampede.

Next day I moved to the Waterloo Hotel. I still worked on the old maxim 'if you insist on the best it is surprising how often you get it.'

In the following days 'Windy Wellington' lived up to its reputation as one of the windiest cities in the world. Gusts through the streets are strong enough to require supports at hand level along the majority of the pavements. In places the wind was too strong to cross over the road with safety.

With all the Civil Aviation formalities completed I left for Nelson, South Island to collect the Bell 47 and take it back across the Cook Straits, a crossing of twenty-five miles. A gale force wind buffeted the machine and I landed at Parapuram Airport with considerable relief. I continued on up through the North Island to Te Awamutu my destination. It was on the highway leading to Hamilton. We had been contracted to spray the gorse and blackberry which were smothering the grassland and seriously reducing the number of animals that it could graze.

Gorse was not indigenous to New Zealand but had been

imported by the early settlers near Canterbury to create natural hedges but it had soon got out of hand taking over cleared farmland and smothering grasses and clovers. It often attained a height of fifteen feet and was too thick to negotiate on foot. The common blackberry was almost as serious a problem and often took over vast tracts of land, and was so dense and matted that large unshorn sheep could be trapped by it and die slowly of starvation unless found and released by the farmer. Many thousands of sheep died in this way every year.

For eradication of both gorse and blackberry spraying by helicopter proved to be extremely effective. The machine was capable of getting into gullies and along the sides of the steepest hills, almost anywhere that a man on foot could not penetrate.

Before the arrival of the helicopter, sprayers had tried to use Tiger Moths but could not get the spray deep down into the plants. Then Miss Eleanor Rudnick of Bakersfield, California had arrived. With one Bell helicopter and an American pilot she experimented with sprays. The results were better than anything tried before. Accordingly she acquired a second aircraft and, as Rudnick Helicopters, went into the spraying business in a serious way. Prior to my arrival, she had returned to the States having done a deal with a local company boss, John Reid. He had shot down a German Jet 262 fighter in WWII and had been a test pilot in England during the early days of rotary-wing development.

Where it was practical to operate ground equipment such as on open flat pastures it was usual to apply up to three hundred gallons of water mixed with a weak solution of chemicals to every acre. To apply this quantity of spray per acre from a helicopter was economically prohibitive. In practice fifty gallons of water with the proportionally stronger addition of hormone chemical 245T was applied. Two runs had to be flown over the same swath in opposite directions to effect better penetration of thick matted growth.

Field marking was impossible in dense areas and so, with practice, 'eyeballing' was made to suffice. Of course, after arriving back on the field after refilling the spray tanks it could be hard to see exactly where one had broken off on the test run. Dropping paper markers proved to be impractical. They worked well in potato or wheat fields but not on gorse. What did help was to notea a large bush sticking up above the rest, a gate, a crooked tree, anything just a bit different.

The hormone we used had a systemic effect, the more active the sap in the body of the plant the greater the possibility of a reasonably good a result.

One morning my engineer, Noel Waugh and I entered a coffee shop in the local town and spent a pleasant half hour. Three days later we returned to be greeted by the owner. "You're something to do with agriculture, aren't you?" We nodded. She went on, "Look at these plants, they are all wilting. They're in a terrible way, what do you think is causing it?" I looked hard at Noel who avoided my glance. We offered basic advice like too much or too little water. On the way out Noel remarked, "Good gracious, Paddy, we've done it this time!" I grinned. "OK, no coveralls in there next time."

Incredibly the minute quantity of hormone fumes coming off these protective garments as we came in straight from the field had been sufficient to affect the plants on the previous visit — making them wilt. Happily they recovered. Where any broad leaf plants were affected by inadvertent hormone treatment but not killed, they would recover and sometimes grow to monstrous size. This was particularly noticeable with clovers.

Early one December morning we flew to Panetapu to spray a block of gorse. Part of this was on the side of a steep slope with three very heavy high-tension cables strung across between steel pylons which, to get at the gorse it was necessary to fly beneath them. They were high and well clear so it was safe to do so. The third load had been sprayed out and the helicopter was now in a steeply banked, almost vertical turn under the cables, well above the gorse. This manoeuvre, intended to facilitate a quick return to the tanker in the valley lower down, terminated abruptly when the engine stopped half way through it.

A small swift-flowing creek about twelve feet wide ran down through the middle of the gorse, past our parked tanker. Both sides of this shallow creek offered nothing like a safe landing spot, being steeply sloped, rutted and partially covered in well-developed gorse. I had no choice but to make a forced landing in the creek itself. This was full of rocks, waterfalls and in some places obscured by gorse and small trees jutting out over the water. Just visible in the split seconds left was the one spot in this inhospitable creek which appeared to be almost clear of obstacles. In complete silence, other than the swish, swish of the autorotating blades, the machine rapidly descended until retarded by application of increased main rotor pitch ahead of landing, followed by a grinding crunching sound as the aircraft lurched to the left. It settled at an angle of about thirty degrees. Miraculously the right landing skid had impacted on a submerged rock to hold the helicopter in a steeply banked attitude — the rotors still rotating but gradually slowing down.

Providence was very kind to me that morning. If the left bank of this shallow stream had been at the same level as the right, it would have smashed the main rotors, but as it happened it was considerable lower. Also the pronounced lopsided attitude of the machine had prevented the rotors from striking the much higher right bank, which at high rotor speed would have wrecked the helicopter and, almost certainly, also have resulted in the wreckage cartwheeling down the hillside with serious injury to myself.

Noel came rushing to the scene, his bulky frame covering the ground with remarkable speed. He skidded to a halt to make sure I was OK before going to take a look at the helicopter. His amazed expression was a picture as he took in the jagged rocks, the water lapping the underside of the machine and the branch of a stunted small tree within inches of the tail rotor.

"It's bloody impossible!" he exclaimed.

He then leaned over the fuel tank to look inside, and turned to me to say, "Paddy, you've committed the cardinal sin. You're out of gas."

That was not strictly accurate. The machine was intentionally low on fuel to keep down the weight, so we could carry heavy loads of chemical, topping up as required throughout the working day. Unfortunately this Bell model, an old type, was not fitted with the newer version of two saddle tanks, one on either side of the machine, but had one large tank fitted flat above and across the engine, with a single centrally located exit pipe to the carburettor.

This fitting was an exact replica of the Bell fuel tank seen on the Bell helicopters in MASH.

Because the fuel quantity was low my steeply banked almost vertical turn under the cables had caused it to move in a mass across the tank, momentarily starving the exit pipe and almost immediately stopping the engine. It was due to the angle of the ditched helicopter, that when Noel removed the cap the tank seemed to be empty.

It was impossible to get mechanical lifting equipment into this place so we enlisted the assistance of local Maori farmers. With spades, crowbars and pickaxes they cut away both banks and axed out the rock to level the helicopter and I flew it out that evening.

At first sight aerial spraying by helicopter or fixed-wing seemed an expensive way to dispose of a noxious weed on both islands. Income tax in New Zealand was astronomically high, but agricultural spraying, top dressing of pastures with artificial fertilisers and fencing of hill country all earned substantial tax relief under the title of 'land improvement'. So rather than pay surplus profits to the government in income tax, farmers hired the helicopter and the fixed-wing top-dressing plane to spread super phosphate over their sheep and cattle pasture.

It was a time when a city man with no agricultural knowledge could purchase a farm, stock it with sheep and generally leave it unattended other than possibly dipping against maggot fly and was able to double his money quickly on the proceeds of the wool clip and the sale of mutton.

All agricultural pilots in New Zealand were required to pass the government 'chemical rating' and one had to know not only the helicopter aspect of spraying but also the fixed-wing side of the business. A good knowledge of chemicals, herbicides, fungicides, and insecticides, together with rates of application was also essential before a pilot was permitted to commence operations. I worked over the textbooks for four weeks before being awarded certification for passing the chemical rating examination in Wellington.

Naturally we had complaints of damage to gardens and horticultural establishments. One lady sent in a claim to the company for seventy pounds for damage to her flowers. It was the policy of the company to settle small claims out of court, even when we knew that it was unlikely it was our spraying that had caused the alleged damage. The following year the same helicopter was back in her district and the same claim was sent off to the company. However, unknown to her, the pilot was not spraying herbicides but insecticide on wheat to kill maggot fly. This was completely harmless to flowers or any other plant. The good lady received a sharp note from the company solicitor. Nice try.

Wind was our greatest operational enemy. Any air movement in excess of five miles per hour was too much to ensure efficient spray penetration. If the area to be sprayed was some distance away we would attempt to phone the farmer before leaving the hotel at four in the morning, to get an idea of the weather and particularly the wind. We may have left the helicopter and tanker on his farm the day before, maybe twenty miles away from the hotel, in the hope of putting out a few loads of spray in the early morning before the inevitable wind stopped us. Many a time we would phone and get a positive weather reading only to find that, by the time we had driven out, the treetops were being bent over by the force of a westerly.

By and large this type of spraying was a thankless, frustrating task involving very long hours with little to show for it; but I was to return to New Zealand for the next four spraying seasons.

Late in March 1965 a job was offered to me in Kununurra, near Wyndham in North Western Australia. This area was the site of an experiment by the Australian government in growing cotton and involved a number of American cotton growers who had taken over tracts of land recently irrigated by the construction of a dam. But a bug had now got into the crop and we were required to spray DDT and Endrin.

When I arrived at camp I was surprised to discover that the three helicopter crews were not using masks nor were there any buckets of clean water provided in the field. Nobody washed those parts of the skin not covered by overalls and consequently two or three days later some of the ground crew complained of severe headaches. I took what precautions were practical, insisting that

201

continuously changed clean water was made available and religiously washed exposed parts of my body after each second load. Additionally I made every effort to stay well clear of the previous swath, the hot, chemical laden air often drifting across the return run. Because of the heat we usually flew without the aircraft doors in the Bell helicopter.

Then the cotton companies switched to a chemical called Bidrin because DDT and Endrin were not considered effective enough to eliminate the bug and it was found that this highly toxic chemical did the job. My flying logbook for April 4th records: 'Worried re. Bidrin spray. Two men in hospital and several including pilots with low blood counts have stopped work.' April 5th records: 'Quit company due to poisoning.' That morning I had an extremely severe headache followed by vomiting.

However, at this point an emergency of another kind occurred and I was requested to fly to the small and barren Mary Island, on the north coast, three hours flying time away. A young inexperienced American pilot had run out of fuel and crashed there, wrecking his Bell. He and his engineer had escaped unhurt to be later taken off by boat and I was requested to fly with an engineer to inspect the wreck and attempt to salvage it. I was flying a Bell 47 equipped with a more powerful engine making it a model 47G4.

We flew into Wyndham for a night stop and carried on the next day to the Kalumburru Roman Catholic Mission, arriving at seven in the morning after a one and half hour flight over some of the most desolate areas of West Australia. It was an isolated destination in every sense where one would not wish even one's worst enemy to be involved in an engine failure.

We were met at the grass airstrip by Father Abbot, an elderly man who drove us to the Mission for breakfast. The Mission was located on the right bank of the King Edward River, a wide swampy waterway emptying into Deep Bay. The Mission people used the river to irrigate their large farm and also as an access by boat to Aborigine settlements at various places along the coast. The farm was an extraordinary self-contained unit. An inlet from the nearby river drove a homemade water wheel which operated a stone grist mill. Through a clever system of sluices and water

202

wheels much of the farm was irrigated by damming the relatively fresh water from the King Edward River. The settlement had an unreal air. It was literally in the middle of nowhere, without an access road.

After breakfast Jim my engineer, and I took off for Mary Island. We intended to conduct an inspection of the wreckage and hopefully make a decision on the best method of salvage. We flew low level along the swampy shoreline of Napier Broome Bay. Twenty minutes later we were streaking over the shark infested straits which separated Mary Island from the mainland to find the helicopter sitting in a partially collapsed state on a sun-baked clay pan on the northern side of the barren island. How it came to be in this sorry state serves to illustrate the fact that failure to use common sense is as much to blame for aircraft accidents as mechanical failure.

The machine had been contracted out to a company whose function was to check the accuracy of survey points. Due to the density of the bush it was much easier to do this from the air. The original pilot, who was experienced in this demanding kind of work had been relieved and replaced with a new pilot who had a total of only seventy flying hours on helicopters, but who did happen to be the son of the company's Chief Director. He had never worked on a bush operation and, being American, had never worked in such inhospitable conditions. Moreover, the engineer sent with this young inexperienced pilot was equally new to this type of operation. He had no helicopter maintenance experience at all, having come from working as a mechanic on large airliners. He was honest enough to admit to me his inexperience later, not so the pilot, who was almost proud of the escapade. I wonder if he is still alive.

The mechanic told me that on the day of the accident they had visited a number of 'trig points', dropped off some mail and set course for Mary Island. As they reached it the engineer pointed out that the fuel gauge was reading empty and they landed and checked the fuel by dipping the tank. The stick came out dry.

They were not carrying any extra fuel, no water or survival gear and were now sitting on the equivalent of a desert island with no hope of getting to the relatively close mainland. The pilot realised that they were in urgent need of fresh water and decided to take off and fly around this very small island in search of some.

The temperature was now over ninety degrees and getting hotter. The engineer protested that to take off with a near empty tank was not exactly a smart thing to do. The pilot replied, "Don't worry, there is still some fuel. Not finding it with the dip stick means nothing, due to the angle of the tank." So he took off and at eighty feet the engine stopped. The Bell fell rapidly, crashed and the main rotor hit the tail boom, cut it in half and carried on thrashing the rest of the helicopter. Fortunately pilot and engineer managed to escape uninjured and by sheer good luck the crew of a small fishing boat witnessed the accident and took them off the island.

What we didn't know at the time was that the crashed helicopter had been on a mission to pick up two men and fly them out of the bush.

We inspected the wreckage and decided that by removing the engine from its retaining frame, thereby splitting the total weight, it should be possible to lift both sections and lower them onto the deck of a salvage vessel. Word came that a Mr Pritchard, an officer from the Department of Civil Aviation was landing at the Mission airstrip later in the day and we flew him to Mary Island so that he could carry out a survey of the crash for his department. Later that afternoon the three of us returned to the Mission to be told by the survey company representative, who had flown in from Wyndham, that he was worried about the two men who were to have been picked up from the bush and he wanted us to search for them. Mr Pritchard volunteered his services with map reading, as he knew the area well and we located and landed at the 'trig point' but there was no sign of the men there.

We searched their camp for a note or any clue of their intentions but found nothing. We started an intensive search of the area but as darkness fell we refuelled from our jerricans and headed back to the Mission. During the night two completely exhausted, torn and bruised men walked in. The monks bathed and fed them and they slept for twenty-four hours.

Several days later we returned to Mary Island equipped with a lifting hook and rope strops. The company had hired a fifty-five foot sailing schooner, masted and normally under sail but also fitted with an auxiliary diesel engine. The plan had been to lift the helicopter onto the boat, but the schooner's masts got in the way, so we worked out another plan which involved removing what was left of the main rotor blades, and the bolts holding the engine in the tubular frame fuselage. I would then hover low over the wreck to allow Jim to attach the engine through the shackle in the aircraft's lifting hook. All went according to plan and I applied power very gradually, slowly hoisting the engine and attached gear assembly clear of the airframe. I eased it down onto the beach and from there it was manhandled into a longboat and ferried out to the schooner.

How to ship the wrecked airframe posed the next problem. We finally decided to have the longboat tie up alongside and we would sail it out. The floats had been damaged in the crash. Normally constructed in a series of sealed airtight compartments, they were very difficult to repair when they were holed. However, Jim managed to make them serviceable after a struggle, and we then pumped all four full of air. Then hovering low over the framework, I lifted it out over the sand dunes to lower it gently onto the water.

The longboat was attached to one of the pontoons and accompanied by Jim, was sailed gently out to the schooner, where the airframe was lifted aboard by a hand-operated winch. Twenty-five men lived on this fifty-year-old schooner which leaked like a sieve. The bilge pumps were working all the time. The rigging was very frayed and worn. Very slowly it made its way to the mainland.

Late in April and my base was Halls Creek about three hundred and twenty miles inland from Wyndham. It was hot, dry, dusty, and fly infested, but possessed a hotel with good service and very good food. We were engaged to do geological survey work looking for copper over brown parched country with short hops and many landings to take soil samples. My logbook for April 20th records one hundred and eighty take-offs and landings in a total of six hours and twenty minutes flying time.

May found me at Louisa Downs, a large cattle ranch owned by a Mr Stein, and it was muster time. Drovers were employed to round up semi-wild animals, many of which were in dense bush and very difficult to get at by men on horseback. I suggested that the helicopter might solve this problem. With Stein as a passenger, we stampeded the cattle out of the bush by ground hovering behind them accompanied by the incessantly loud, highly disturbing roar of the engine. This operation was judged highly successful and thought to be a first for Western Australia. However, I can claim no credit for the idea, having seen it done in Africa on many occasions.

This type of mustering in fact became commonplace until the animals became used to it and ignored the helicopters. Then Science came to man's rescue with a specially adapted electric probe fitted below the nose of the machine. This usually had the desired effect when making contact with the backside of even the most stubborn of animals.

One of the other pilots said to me, "How come you don't wear a flying helmet instead of that scruffy baseball cap?" "You ever fly into the early morning sun on a spray run?" I asked. "Of course I have," he replied. "But I just pull the visor down on my helmet." "Oh yes," I smiled, "but what if the blinding rising sun is appearing not quite straight ahead but from the side, what then?"

He hesitated for a moment and I continued, "Your visor doesn't permit independent rotation like this," and I swivelled my peaked cap slowly from one side to the other. "Note that my head has not moved and had this been a spray run the peak attached to this cap would have reduced much of the angled glare from the sun, without diverting my attention from the crop a few feet below my rapidly travelling helicopter and, more importantly, allowing me a clear view ahead to see any flock of birds rising off the crop and leaving me time in hand to take evasive action."

He said, "But what happens if you have an accident and roll over. You have no protection."

"OK," I said, "Go and put on your helmet and sit in the pilots position." This he did. "Right" I said, "Just look straight ahead as if you were flying and without moving your head, tell me when I become visible on your left. I'll walk past you from the rear and about three yards away from the helicopter."

This point was slightly ahead of the abeam position.

He then removed his helmet and I repeated the exercise. This

206

time he saw me a lot earlier. "The most important thing," I told him, "is to ensure that you do your very best to avoid accidents. That comes first. In the spray business we can do without artificially created blind spots. The eyes and not the helmet are by far the best insurance against injury in crop spraying. The helmet, worn in hot humid climates also causes profuse sweating. Give me my old baseball cap every time."

After completing this contract I went back to England and in June was spraying in Essex. All was going well until I cut through a power cable with a rotor blade outside Thaxted. No damage to me but the blade had to be replaced the next day. I had cut off the village's electricity supply and the fish and chip shop had to close for three days. I was not universally popular.

Subsequently, due to the efficiency of the ground crew and air team we broke the record for Essex by spraying 665 acres in one day on 27th July 1965.

I arrived in Bombay in August 1965 and booked into the Taj Mahal Hotel. I was to spray cotton in a Bell 47, but before work could get underway Pakistan and India went to war.

Several other pilots at the Taj were contracted out to the same company. There was a tall Frenchman nicknamed 'De Gaulle' because of his height, a German WWII fighter pilot, two Englishmen (one of whom, Bill Farnell, I had known for years), a Singalese and me. The authorities would not let us fly so we spent mornings in the lounge of this lovely hotel drinking coffee and watching the Navy in its anchorage. 'De Gaulle' remarked, in front of several Indian Naval Officers, "Your ships, they come in but they never go out." It was true, nothing moved, even though Pakistan was reputed to be shelling installations further down the coast.

The Singalese pilot, twenty-four hours after war had been declared, had been flying a Bell on the Kashmir border when he heard the sound of fast moving jets and looked up to see three Pakistan fighters in close formation pursuing two others. He landed in his base village, taking off at dawn to spray a crop a mile down the road. Again he heard the noise of fast approaching engines. Two machines swept low over the village, there were a number of dull thuds and the building in which he had slept, and beside which he had parked his helicopter, went up in smoke. Needing no third warning he flew back to Bombay keeping a wary lookout.

Very early one morning the loud warbling whine of the city's air raid siren woke me, followed by urgent tapping on the door by a hotel servant. "Air raid, Sir, the Police say you have to go to the cellar." I trudged down several steep flights of stairs without any power for the electric light to find the cellar packed to capacity with people. Those wishing to leave Bombay were temporarily unable to do so as the international airport was closed. No bombs at all fell on the *Taj* during this brief war, but some fell in surrounding streets.

A short distance away from the *Taj* was a first class leisure centre called Beach Candy, frequented by pilots and aircrews during the emergency. It had an excellent pool beside which I was lounging some days later gazing at the sky when I suddenly became aware that new puffy white clouds were appearing as if by magic above us. Then dull explosions reached our ears from about twenty-five thousand feet. There was the deafening sound of discharging anti-aircraft guns not too far away. I pulled the girl I was with (a stranded airline stewardess) under cover and shouted across the pool "Get under cover, there'll be chunks of metal falling here at any moment." But they missed us.

An extract from my logbook for 20th September is self-explanatory: 'Local — Bombay. Delayed security clearance India/Pakistan state of war since 28 August, blackouts, air raid warnings, China just extended ultimatum.' As the world suddenly knew, the Chinese appeared to be on the verge of attacking India through the 'back door.' The situation looked extremely grave. In these circumstances, bearing in mind my experience in Malaya, my intention was to volunteer as a helicopter pilot on behalf of the Indian Army should the Chinese invade.

As it happened the conflict terminated on 23rd September 1965 and Chinese forces pulled back from further confrontation with India around the same time.

I was now engaged on blanket spray coverage over vast areas.

This was to rid the crops of a serious bug infestation. Between 24th September and 10th October I sprayed something in excess of twenty thousand acres. Sadly and for the first time in my experience, fish life in some of the rivers bordering the cotton also suffered, many floating dead on the surface. This was because at the height and speed required to cover the countryside, it was impossible, in this hot climate, to anticipate the drift factor of spray with any accuracy and so, many of the streams and rivers were contaminated.

However, in mitigation, many of the people occupying the area were very poor and they were dependant for survival on the cotton crop. You may ask what direct effect the spraying had on the human population. There is no clear answer, but at their request we regularly sprayed Sudanese mud villages with a similar chemical in the evenings, to rid them of mosquitoes and hordes of black flies. So far as I am aware, there was no adverse effect on the inhabitants of these villages in which we pilots and engineers were housed. There are many spray pilots in the USA and Canada well into their seventies and still working the crop seasons. With skill and proper care almost any chemical can be applied in safety.

Then it was back to England and crop spraying in Essex again, I had a complete clutch failure carrying a full load of chemical on a cross-country ferry to a distant farm. I made an unannounced emergency landing in a field between Fyfield and Dunmow. In full autorotation and wreathed in smoke from the burning clutch, I dumped the load as the machine hurtled in for an arrival more than a landing. The spray booms were damaged and one blade of the tail rotor slightly dented. Otherwise the helicopter was OK.

In the local pub that night I was approached by a couple, Mr and Mrs Baines. "Are you the gentleman spraying the crops?" I admitted that I was.

He soon made it abundantly clear that crop spraying, which had to involve the death of bees and other beneficial insects, was most harmful to the environment and if only from the view of a gardener, he heartily disapproved. I told him that I came from generations of farmers and that we were not spraying to kill insects but applying fungicides to control blight on potatoes. We became firm friends and for two seasons their house became my home in England.

By September I was flying for Autair again in Athens. We were spraying the olive groves on Kefallinia, an island thirty miles from the mainland. The Bell 47 had been flown by Clem Bateman, a retired Commander R.N., and my job was to relieve him so he could go on home leave and I would finish off the contract.

Clem greeted me with "Am I glad to see you! The people are great but the ground support is hopeless as is their concept of punctuality. By the way, I hope you have a strong stomach because the food and accommodation is the bottom of the pack." Clem was not guilty of exaggeration for the short period I spent on this island was to be the most frustrating of any agricultural operation before or since.

The ground support was utterly inefficient. The water supply from a primitive tanker was almost always dirty and blocked the emission jets on the booms continuously. This meant frequent interruption of the operation, it being necessary to land back near the engineer and, together, remove, disassemble and clear the numerous jets. Moreover the personal risk of contamination by the highly toxic pesticide was dangerously increased, it being practically impossible to avoid chemical contact when cleaning and clearing these units.

My Logbook entry for September 12th reads: '73 loads. Blocked jets all day. Flying time 6 hours 35 minutes. September 15th: Strife of every description — inadequate water — wait three hours for transport.'

So it went until we eventually struggles through to completion by the 22nd. The relief I felt flying the helicopter onto the deck of a ferry at Sami for the fifty-five mile crossing to Patrai on the mainland was indescribable. From Patrai we took the machine over the impressive Corinth Canal to Athens where we landed on the deck of the ferry for the long sea crossing to Traklient on Crete.

There, before the ship berthed, I flew the helicopter off the deck to land at Iraklion Airport, to await the arrival of a jeep which the engineer was to drive across the island to rendezvous with the helicopter at a place called Ano Viannos. He was later to tell me that the road through the mountains was appallingly bad and almost impassable in places.

Within sight of the sea, Ano Viannos was a large village in the mountain foothills about two thousand feet up. The olive groves were mainly planted on the hillsides which made spraying difficult and the unpredictably strong winds blowing in from the sea caused turbulence which added real danger. Also what we didn't know about at the start was the vendetta between villages which made them pigheadedly, both refuse us water from their communal wells, even though the bug we were spraying for was destroying the olive crop on which they both depended. On two occasions we had to threaten one of the villages that we would not spray their olives unless they agreed to let us take some of their ample supply of water to their no-go neighbour. And this was only successful because they knew that no spray meant no crop.

The organisation of the operation was as bad as Kefallinia although, to be fair, this was the first time they had worked with a helicopter. Previously they had depended on a donkey cart hauling a few gallons of spray and a hand-operated sprayer. The effect of the switch to a noisy beast that could cover an area in ten minutes that had previously taken the donkey cart and hand-sprayer twelve hours must have been mind-boggling. In one day we sprayed a hundred and four loads for a total flying time of eight hours and twenty minutes.

At the end of the contract we were to fly the reverse journey back to Keffallinia and then travel by airline home to England.

It was not unusual to receive write-ups in local newspapers as helicopters were still something of a novelty. In November I was back in New Zealand for the spraying season and a Nelson, South Island paper published the following under the caption: 'High praise for pilot.'

The Forest Service gave Captain JAT 'Paddy' Jones high praise for his mountain rescue this morning of injured deer culler, Mr

Barry Longhill, in very turbulent conditions. "We are well pleased with the Search and Rescue operation," said Forest Ranger, Mr JD Corboy, today. At over 5,000 feet this was the highest rescue in the northern part of the South Island, said Mr John Reid, managing director of Helicopters (NZ) Ltd, Nelson. Paddy Jones is a highly skilled pilot with 10,000 hours on helicopters, but the Army men on the spot said the conditions in the Glenroy were worse than those experienced recently at Mount Cook when an Army exercise was called off. Captain Jones, a 45-year-old single man and freelance pilot, flies the summer season in New Zealand each year and returns to the Eastern Mediterranean for the northern summer. "There are not many places he can't go with a helicopter," said Mr Reid. The rescue took place in a gale force blizzard at 5.500 feet

Another press cutting of the same day: 'Set Record'

The Irish Canadian helicopter pilot Mr Paddy Jones who featured in the deer culler rescue in the Murchison district today set a New Zealand record in agricultural spraying by helicopter on Monday. Working in the Cheddar Valley, he covered 189 acres of broom infested country in eleven hours. Altogether 9,450 gallons of chemical were used and gross revenue for the day amounted to over £2,500. The previous record was 160 acres in a day at Kaiteriteri, Nelson.

Autair asked me to fly a machine to Benghazi in Libya for a special event. It was to be a challenging operation: From *Helicopter World* December 1966:

Just too late for inclusion in our last issue comes the news of an unusual long-range ferry flight made by the well-known free-lance helicopter pilot Captain JAT 'Paddy' Jones. The flight in a BEA Whirlwind under charter to Autair Ltd was a solo journey from Gatwick Airport to Benghazi, North Africa. Starting at midday on Sunday 19, the flight terminated thirty-one flying hours later on Wednesday October 19th, just over three days later. The route was Gatwick — Paris — Auxerre — Nice — Ajaccio (Corsica) — Cagliari (Sardinia) — Tunis — Djerba — Tripoli — Marble Arch — Benghazi.

Perhaps the most outstanding aspect of this flight was that only a minimum of navigational equipment was carried, for example no radio compass) on a flight that covered sea, mountain and desert. Captain Jones carried out all servicing during the flight, since no engineer was carried. The tanks and an extra fuel supply were carried in jerry cans in the cabin. During the latter stages Captain Jones landed in the desert to replenish the fuel tanks from the cans by hand. There were a number of everyday problems from the servicing point of view, including a generator defect and an apparent loss of engine oil pressure, all of which were dealt with by the pilot. One more irksome snag was a leaking blade damper reservoir which had to be refilled at every landing.

Captain Jones told Helicopter World that generally speaking the trip was a pleasant one. The worst period, he said, was the first stage from Gatwick to Paris due to bad weather in the English Channel sector. Battling against a headwind, the Gatwick — Paris leg took over three and a half hours to complete. The helicopter will be operated in Libya by a BEA pilot and engineer on behalf of Kingdom of Libya Airways for what Captain Jones described as a 'sentimental journey'. The King of Libya who does not fly, wishes to visit the land of his grandfather and will travel by camel. The helicopter will fly as support and supply aircraft for the camel train, maintaining communications between the King and his Ministers of State.

While making no claims, Captain Jones believes that this ferry flight may well be a record for flights of this kind.

The one hundred and seventy mile sea crossing from Cagliari to Tunis was certainly not without problems. The generator which supplied the electrical current for the radio and other auxiliary units failed, which meant that should the engine driven fuel pump cease to function, as occurred on an earlier ferry flight, there was no back-up electrical pump to supply gasoline to the power unit.

213

The machine was on wheels, with the consoling factor of floats very much missed when the generator warning signal came on. At around the same time the persistent fluctuation of the needle on the gauge recording engine oil pressure became more marked. At Tunis I checked the oil system as far as possible. The fuel consumption and temperature were normal and there were no obvious leaks. This slight oil pressure fluctuation could, I knew, be due pressure relief valve malfunction. Once airborne again everything behaved itself.

On the leg to Djerba, I landed in the desert to refuel from the jerricans. I kept the engine running while I did the task and just as I finished a cavalcade of nosy camels came trotting out of the blue to see what I was up to. I got airborne in a real operational manner as the first of them thundered in.

Djerba is an island airport but the local Customs and Immigration kept me waiting for clearance into Libya for over two hours. Fortunately there was external electric power available for start-up and so the engine was shut down during this frustrating wait. Eventually a vehicle arrived with the officials and numerous forms to be completed. This done I lifted off and eventually arrived at a French oil camp near Sirte having followed Mussolini's tarmac road from Tripoli. I explained the problem with the generator and without any hesitation they removed it and within an hour had effected a repair and recharged the battery. I stopped overnight at the US Navy camp (Loran) near the airstrip known as 'Marble Arch' and the next day arrived at Benghazi. The entry in my logbook reads: 'Fluctuating oil pressure right through whole trip. Also generator trouble plus u/s damper. 31:50 hours for flight. Self very busy as Pilot/Navigator/Engineer!'

The South Island of New Zealand had for many years been plagued by great herds of deer. The early settlers brought in these animals and like most things introduced into New Zealand they prospered and having no natural enemies multiplied at a fantastic rate. The problem became so acute that the Government stepped in and employed hundreds of professional hunters on a full time basis, who spent most of their time out in the bush hunting the

214

deer and leaving the carcasses where they fell, merely removing the tails to collect the bounty. They made large sums of money out of this occupation and one man of my acquaintance bought a large farm on the proceeds. It was slaughter on the scale of buffalo hunting in North America, but unlike the fate of the buffalo the hunters failed to reduce the vast herds of deer by any noticeable numbers.

The deer cullers were rugged men, taking a three-day hike into the mountains, remaining out for two or three months and finally returning to civilisation having enjoyed only their own company since they left. They hauled their deer tails in sacks, backpacking them out for several miles where the terrain was too rough even for a horse. Consequently a Canadian pilot, Milton Sills, saw in the helicopter a means of transporting deer carcases out of otherwise inaccessible areas to the outside world. Various experiments were tried in different areas and all were successful. A number of individuals and companies then became actively interested in the helicopter as a means of both hunting and killing the animals and, in particular, getting the meat out.

In March 1966, a young man approached me in a hotel bar and said, "I'm Tim Wallis. I understand that you are finishing up very shortly in New Zealand and I wonder if you would be interested in flying a helicopter for me on deer hunting?"

He had a brand new helicopter from the States and a helicopter Private Pilot's Licence. Very soon after his acquisition he had crashed into a gorge, but nothing daunted, had hired another helicopter and was looking for a pilot. He later wrote an excellent book on deer hunting. He made me a good offer and I accepted. We picked up the Bell 47G4, more powerful than earlier models, and flew it to Luggate, a few miles from Lake Wanaka. The view from Tim's house had some of the most beautiful scenery in the world, with a long deep lake and towering mountains to one side, many of the peaks of which were covered in snow into the early summer.

One morning as I took off from the house, a casual glance over to my left revealed a long cavalcade of big cars moving down the main road. It suddenly occurred to me that they must be escorting The Queen Mother who was on an official visit to Canada and was currently staying at the Wanaka Hotel. I knew only too well the air regulations governing any kind of flight near a royal personage and without hesitation the helicopter was rapidly turned around to make a hasty landing at base, where I took one of the cars and drove off down the road to park next to very tall policeman lining the route. We had exchanged greetings when he happened to look into the rear passenger seat of the car to see three Belgian FN semi-automatic rifles and a vast quantity of ammunition.

I quickly explained what was going on and with that the Royal car came round the corner. The Officer said, "Well, that's that. What's the chance of a lift into Wanaka?" I replied, "Sure, hop in." I remember he had to remove his helmet to sit down because of his height. We swung into the road and had gone a little over a mile when a glance in my mirror revealed another convoy of cars with what appeared to be a police car in front coming up behind us. My companion yelped, "My God, it's the Governor General. Turn round and get me back!"

I made a very hasty U-turn two hundred yards ahead of the cavalcade. "Faster, faster!" shouted my new friend as we zoomed round a long bend in the road. "We're leaving them flat." I told him. "They're not in sight anymore, and anyhow what about the speed limit?" He said something remarkably rude about New Zealand law, barked "Stop!" and jumped out smartly and replaced his helmet to come to the salute as the Governor General came round a bend.

One early morning in May, luck was very much my ally. I had landed the helicopter with two deer hunters on a ledge on the side of this particular mountain. I had earlier dropped off two other men in the valley far below where they were to deal with the deer carcasses as they were shot on the 'tops'. The carcasses would then be flown down by my helicopter and removed to the factory by light aircraft from the local airstrip. My two passengers departed to go higher up the mountain and I secured four carcasses left from the previous days hunting, with a rope strung through their legs and paid out around the back of the landing skid and then forward under the machine to the cargo lifting hook. My mistake, which was to cost us the helicopter, was in failing to get the two hunters to supervise the positioning of the rope as the helicopter manoeuvred to slip off the ledge with a heavy load of deer meat.

The engine was started and enough power applied to slip a few feet away from the bank and the slightly overhanging ridge of rock under which it had been necessary to make a landing. As the power increased for lift-off, in an instant the helicopter spun violently and there was a momentary vision of breaking rotor blades, and a disintegrating Perspex bubble all accompanied by the most infernal noise immediately followed by a dull crump and explosion.

There was a blast of hot air and severe pain in my left hip as the lap belt broke and the force of the explosion blew me out of the machine to land, miraculously still intact, on my feet several yards away. My heavy wool jersey was on fire as were my baseball cap and trousers. I tore them off and rolled over and over several times in a large puddle to put out any other flames. I backed off from the blazing machine still not understanding what had happened. Suddenly, above the crackle of the flames, there was a whistling noise past my ear followed by a series of sharp reports. My past experience as a rear gunner recognised the sound of exploding ammunition. The whistling noise was made by the empty cartridge cases flying past. I threw myself behind a large rock until the fusillade died away and the heat made my funk hole untenable. In less than five minutes my helicopter was burned out. The only recognisable surviving part was the tubular tail boom.

There was a smell of singed hair but apart from a throbbing pain in my hip I seemed to have sustained no serious damage. What was left of the helicopter was now inverted and it was not difficult to come up with the reason. On lifting off, the rope attached to the cargo hook had slipped across the protruding tail end of the skid and, when power was applied, the weight of the deer carcasses was taken by the skid instead of the cargo hook and flipped the helicopter on its back. The fuel tanks had then burst spreading high-octane fuel over the engine causing instant fire. I had to have been upside down when the strap broke on my hip and I was extraordinarily lucky to be alive.

The logbook entry (in red ink) reads: 'Aircraft crashed on take-off. Exploded and burned. Escaped with singeing but jersey and cap on fire. Rifle, camera and other items lost. Helicopter burned out. No passengers involved. Cause believed snagged sling rope attached to four deer and caught skid heel causing complete loss lateral control shortly after attempted take-off. Walked out thirty-five miles. Exhausted. There but for the Grace of God. Altitude approx. 5,000 feet on Mount Cunningham."

The two hunters rushed up, concerned for my safety. "Are you OK?" to which I can remember answering, "Yes, I'm OK, but my feelings are sure as hell hurt to blazes." Had the helicopter been equipped with the later mandatory, more positive, restraining shoulder harness instead of the single lap strap version, I would have been firmly held and burned to death in seconds.

Getting down to the wide cattle basin far below was a painful ordeal as my left hip stiffened up and four hours later, after a very steep, difficult descent, the three of us arrived in the valley to join the other two. Due to the weather, no fixed-wing aircraft had landed all day and the two hunters waiting at the airstrip were not aware of the accident. We five were now faced with walking out with about twenty-eight miles to go.

Our emergency food had been lost with the helicopter but we ate a quantity of raw liver from the deer carcasses at the airstrip. We crossed the swift flowing, glacially fed Dart River at least four times. The sides of the valley were almost precipitous in places and we had to follow the animal tracks. Darkness set in and two of the hunters went on ahead to get assistance as I was having increasing difficulty in walking.

Later, in the dark, the drizzle, which had been with us most of the day turned into torrential rain. Eventually Evan called a halt because I was stumbling along using a stick, trying to keep on my feet but in excruciating pain. Somehow, in the appalling weather, the boys got a fire lit and I stretched out alongside the flames. We carried on the next morning only to find that further progress meant crossing the river yet again, and at a very deep point. Evan cut a long thin pole and I was placed in the middle. We struggled, three abreast, through the turbulent, fast flowing, freezing water, hanging to each other and to the pole to avoid being swept off our feet.

We were still moving down river late into the afternoon. I was in considerable pain when we saw two horses. With relief we realised the two who had gone ahead had got through and help was on its way.

A mounted horseman leading another horse followed the first two. They mounted me and after going down river three miles I was transferred to the hood of a tractor, and sitting astride, bumped and jolted over what must have been the roughest farm track in New Zealand.

It was a week before I could walk without a stick, but nothing was broken and I made a complete recovery. At the end of May, Tim and I were at Wanganui, North Island to take delivery of a Hiller 12E helicopter, which we flew back to Luggate. Two days later we were back to lifting out deer carcasses. But then Tim and I had a disagreement and I terminated my involvement with Luggate Game Packers in June.

I did several different jobs including crop spraying; lifting a twelve foot duralumin tower onto a cliff top for the new Gable End Lighthouse near Gisborne; stringing eighteen miles of power cable across support poles; and transferring fencing materials into hilly terrain.

Later I was flying for another deer recovery company out of Christchurch. We were operating a Hiller in the Southern Alps in January 1967 and were banked over at a very acute angle high up in the mountains when the sharpshooter with me inadvertently put a bullet through the main rotor blade. four feet from the tip. Fortunately it missed the main spar and we got down without further excitement.

My last season, and last flight in New Zealand, was to return a Bell from Waipukarau on the North Island into Nelson, and I well remember experiencing the usual turbulent winds over the Cook Strait.

219

CHAPTER THIRTEEN

Filming and Fighters

BACK IN THE UK IN 1967 I WAS FLYING AN ALOUETTE II on publicity photography for a film company. On behalf of ITN we went out to greet and film Francis Chichester off the Lizard inbound to Plymouth. *Helicopter World* had this to say:

> *ITN chartered an Alouette II from RBA Helicopters Ltd. This machine was used to fly out a movie cameraman to the yacht and the films shot were brought back to the mainland for processing. Flying the helicopter was Captain JAT 'Paddy' Jones, the well-known freelance pilot who was fulfilling an engagement with RBA. Using the Alouette's standard camera mounting, the ITN charter was a conventional filming operation.'*

This however turned out to be a disappointing experience.

We had successfully intercepted the yacht *Gypsy Moth* well out to sea. Francis Chichester was at the helm as we approached but quickly went below as I manoeuvred the helicopter into a suitable position for filming. We took pictures of the vessel under sail and presumably on self-steering. We waited for him to reappear but to no avail. I commented on what appeared to be a premeditated discourtesy, and the cameraman tersely remarked, "Maybe for commercial reasons." We took airborne shots of the ceremony when he was knighted on the Thames and on this occasion got excellent footage.

The crop-spraying season of 1967 saw a greatly reduced requirement for the Hiller in Essex and Kent. It had been unusually dry and potato blight only thrives in wet weather. Experts were also bringing in environmental restrictions.

At every opportunity I drove over to Reading to fly the Alouette including a demonstration to the Police Force, landing and taking off on a very small lake close to the Police College at Bramshill.

Subsequently I flew the helicopter in connection with an advertising campaign for a car tyre. The manufacturers claimed that their tyre had a specific advantage over their competitor's tyres in that it was less prone to aquaplaning. To illustrate this they had acquired a surfboard and a leggy blonde to demonstrate aquaplaning by gliding in on the long Atlantic rollers near Newquay. We in the helicopter were to capture this scene with a specially fitted movie camera on a gyro mounting but it was immediately obvious that the lady couldn't surf. After numerous attempts on her part to give the cameraman an 'establishing shot', all of which failed, the director called us back to await instructions and these were delivered the following morning when the helicopter engineer came up with an intriguing question. "If she couldn't do it yesterday," he said, "why would they think she can do it today?" "Not a clue," I replied, but we soon found out.

We watched the girl carrying the surfboard climb into the boat, which then headed out to our rendezvous area. I hovered well clear and waited for her to make another attempt. To my utter amazement she completed a perfect run into the shoreline to be followed by several more runs. The lithe blonde even did a few tricks as she rode the surf.

The 'blonde', we discovered was actually a man of slim build, an expert surfer and lifesaver on holiday from Bondi Beach. He was dressed in a bikini and blonde wig with full makeup and told to get on with it. I heard later that the real blonde claimed that as a member of Equity she was entitled to payment for all the action, including 'repeat money'.

During the summer the Alouette was used in a variety of ventures including crossing the Irish Sea to promote a brand of Irish butter. The action took place over a field in Wicklow where our camera-equipped helicopter recorded the peaceful scene of a herd of Jersey cattle munching grass, with the sea making a lovely backdrop.

In June there was photographic involvement at High Wycombe airfield for the TV series *Thunderbirds*. A wartime ATA pilot, Joan Hughes, flew a tiger Moth from a concealed position in the cockpit with extraordinary skill. The open cockpit appeared to be occupied with dummy figures of Thunderbird pilots. In the

Alouette we tracked this veteran aircraft to capture, on camera, the required sequence.

A few days later I was to have an abrasive encounter with a member of Equity at Pinewood Studios. We were engaged to fly into the 'mocked up' African village in a TV adventure series called *Man in a Suitcase*. The action called for a landing in the village where, in the script, the natives were all on strike and not disposed to assist in the off loading of passengers and freight. For this reason the hero and his lady were dependant on the pilot (me) to help them out of the helicopter.

Because of a degree of tension associated with the strikers this was to be accomplished, followed by an immediate take-off. By locking the controls it was both safe and practical to stand close by the now open door to assist the girl and take the hero's small suitcase as he vacated the aircraft. The script called for the line "Thank you, pilot," and I was to reply, "You're welcome," as I handed him the case. The Equity representative objected to me uttering these two words and, moreover, insisted that after the machine had landed, one of the actors was to replace me in the pilot's seat. I attempted to explain the situation but was told he would not permit me to say any words.

I responded quietly with "You or any of your staff are not permitted behind the controls of this helicopter with the engine activated and its rotors turning, if only due to a dangerous factor known as ground resonance, and anyhow, its out of the question, if only for insurance reasons. You had better decide whether or not to continue." He was not happy but bowed to the inevitable.

As is the norm in movie making, we made no less than fifteen take-offs and landings at the village to hear "Thank you, pilot," and "You're welcome," For the umpteenth time. Nevertheless it was a fun experience and I had an excellent lunch in the studio canteen sitting next to James Robertson Justice.

In August we were engaged by four lovely ladies to fly them from Battersea heliport to the Isle of Wight. They were members of the Bee Gees Fan Club. The pop group's work permits had apparently expired and the application for extension had not been approved. The girls had a petition to present to the appropriate Minister. One of the girls gave me a rough sketch map depicting a hamlet and the position of a house where the 'target' and his wife were spending the weekend. I set them down in a nearby field before taking off to refuel at the local airport. I heard later that they had made for the front door of the holiday home only to find that their target had fled out of the back door. They reported, "We left the petition on the dining room table."

The spray season was now upon us and whilst we were not employed in it very actively, flying the Hiller was not without an element of unlooked for adventure. Mid morning of June 19th near Bishop Stortford, carrying a full spray load to a field of beans, the tail rotor gearbox seized. I hurriedly dumped the load and hard landed onto a nearby grass field, the only damage being a slightly bent spray boom. A tail rotor failure of this nature is usually bad news and to escape so lightly should be put down to luck rather than any element of skill. On June 22nd, the left side engine exhaust stack broke off while flying the same aircraft and half way along a spray run. It scared the hell out of me.

On the 11th July, flying the same machine, an engine exhaust valve failed in flight and the engine spluttered to a stop. Fortunately it was a positioning flight and a successful full autorotation was made but very close to a really smelly sewage farm. Three days later, with a replacement engine — to quote from my logbook — 'Engine packed up at 400 feet, landed in beet field u/s.' Another full autorotation, somewhere near Dunmow. Later in the afternoon the helicopter was loaded on a large truck and taken to Cambridge for another engine to be installed. It was test flown there and said to be serviceable. It was flown down and handed back to me late on the evening of the 18th. We positioned over the operating site close to Lydd Airport early next morning and by 11.00 hours we had sprayed two hundred and eighty-five acres of potatoes.

The next load was intended for a potato field barely one hundred yards from our tanker and, because its headland was in a direct line with my take-off path, the intention was to spray this first, thereby lightening the aircraft. For this reason the helicopter was carrying an overload of spray, enough to finish the field without being obliged to return for more. In the meanwhile the tanker would move onto the next loading site.

223

Due to the somewhat heavier than normal load, full throttle was needed to ease off the ground into a low hover before gradually moving forward at increasing speed to encounter transitional lift. This occurred somewhere between twelve and twenty miles per hour and permitted a power reduction without loss of height or speed. When starting spray runs such a reduction was a necessity in order to maintain both a low altitude and a relatively low airspeed.

As the helicopter glided under a power line on the edge of the field, I switched on the spray and, in one movement, attempted to retard the twist grip throttle in order to reduce power. Nothing happened. The throttle was stuck and no effort on my part could move it. It was an unbelievable situation with the helicopter climbing slowly away from the crop and its engine bellowing at full power.

Because the throttle was stuck wide open, the reduction in the main rotor pitch required to descend could not be applied by the pitch lever held in my left hand without involving massive over revving of the engine. This could result in severe damage to it, if not its destruction, and also severe damage to associated parts in the transmission.

The helicopter was heading out to sea fast and still steadily climbing when I mentally worked out a plan. By now it had become obvious that the first thing to do was to get rid of the chemical load to lighten the aircraft, and to ensure that any descent would be safer and easy. In the circumstances it appeared best to spray out the chemical rather than use the emergency dump gear, when the sudden weight loss of six hundred pounds at a high forward speed might result in uncontrollable instability.

My plan was to spray it out over the sea, which I did, fly back over the airfield, switch off the engine and make an autorotative landing. Meanwhile back on the ground the engineer and tanker crew were watching my ascent with astonishment.

I had called the tower to alert them of my predicament and intended course of action. I switched off over the field and dropped very fast for the first few hundred feet before the rotor blades' new profile permitted me to make a good engine-off landing next to the fire truck and ambulance.

I phoned the Cambridge base to inform them of the drama and the operations manager got his priorities spot on, asking first if his machine was undamaged. I told him and added, "You might like to know I'm OK too." He continued as if he hadn't heard me and asked, "Why didn't you land in a field next to the airport, now we'll get a bill for landing fees." I was too astonished to think of a suitable reply.

Mo, the engineer, and I had a good look at the throttle linkages but we could not locate the fault and the throttle was now apparently working freely. Two days later we located the problem. The carburettor had been incorrectly assembled at the maintenance base before being fitted to the new engine and was liable to stick in both fully open and fully closed positions. I was not amused. The operating company may have legally complied with maintenance regulations but the dismal failures of that season left a lot of questions unanswered. By the end of the summer we had covered eight thousand one hundred and thirty one acres with four hundred loads at approximately three gallons an acre. Good work — but I was glad to say goodbye.

I went on to cover the Isle of Wight power boat race and the photographer got a scoop. One boat was travelling at about seventy knots. We had flown alongside to obtain close-ups when without warning the boat burst into flames and stopped dead in the water. We swung round swiftly and being float equipped prepared to take off the crew, but a non-racing vessel slid alongside and got the three men off even before we were positioned to do so.

In August I did some film work on Dunstable Downs for the film *Chitty Chitty Bang Bang*. We had to shoot movies and stills of a partial mock up of a manned power operated small gaudy balloon.

One of the last jobs that season was to fly Mr Barley, an American lawyer, to the house of J Paul Getty near Guildford. I was to fly him in, and then pick up a photographer and make several sweeps across the house and gardens for him to film. Mr Getty did not make an appearance and when I sent in a message offering him a flight to look at his house from the air, he declined but said his secretaries would like to go.

In two separate flights I took up five very beautiful young ladies and later had tea with them on the lawn. A pity not all jobs ended like that.

In late September there was another film called *The Strange Affair* starring Jeremy Kemp, part of which was to be shot at Battersea Heliport. My machine, a Sikorsky 55, was supposed to be carrying fourteen passengers when I landed. This Sikorsky was an eight-passenger helicopter which could not legally carry fourteen people and due to an anomaly in the licensing of this particular machine it was not in fact permitted to carry passengers at all!

The business was well faked, however, with the empty aircraft making an approach and landing at the heliport, my radio exchanges with the tower controller Dave Ward, being recorded for the film and with the helicopter in camera until shortly before the shutdown of the engine on the landing pad. We then crammed the required number of passengers into the cabin and in airline uniform, a 'stewardess' and I stood by the door to open it and, as the cameras turned, graciously help our 'passengers' out.

The final shot was of the stewardess coming over to me to say, "Captain, what time should I report here in the morning?" To which my reply was "Nine o'clock will be fine — we are going across to Gatwick empty, but will be picking up five passengers and some light cargo for Calais." She echoed "Nine o'clock. See you in the morning." And with a cheery wave tripped daintily away. As with filming at Pinewood, numerous retakes were required but, on this occasion, there was no Equity man to complain.

The director came across to me and asked if it was my Mercedes parked nearby. I had just taken delivery of a brand new white Mercedes 250SL. I told him it was and he asked if I would agree for it to be included in a take to show a general view of the heliport. The car, bought and collected by me in Stuttgart, was an Americanised version. Eventually it went to my lawyer brother in Toronto who has it still.

The Sikorsky was then engaged for another film called

Hammerhead starring Peter Vaughan, Judy Geeson and Vince Edwards. Much of this film was being made in a small town twenty miles west of Lisbon. I was contracted to ferry the helicopter to Portugal, work on set as required and ferry it home again. It was to be a solo flight but for the presence of a film company official. Because of the 'no passengers' clause he had to be on the manifest as crew, and so, that day, Dick Whittington flew in the co-pilots seat. He proved his worth by map reading and assisting with customs and immigration formalities.

The flight from Gatwick took nineteen hours, much longer than planned, entirely due to adverse weather in Spain. The route was Cherbourg and Biarritz, to Bilbao, where we refuelled. After Bilbao I climbed to six thousand feet in a futile attempt to cross the very high Cantabrian Mountains, a western extension of the Pyrenees, and from there drop down into Portugal. A gale-force headwind accompanied by severe turbulence forced me to abort that venture for the day. Two days later we tried again to cross the mountains to Salamanca but it was no better. We diverted to Santander and followed the coast down to Oviedo and then on to Santiago. High ground, gale-force winds, and severe turbulence forced us back to the coast where dense fog made us fly for over an hour ten miles out to sea on a westerly compass heading, hopefully, parallel to the coastline. We eventually made landfall at Corunna and went on to Santiago to refuel. From there we flew to Vigo and on to Porto and Lisbon. My co-pilot muttered something to the effect that next time he would take the airline.

In the movie, the mission of tough guy Peter Vaughan was to dispose of the bad guys on the mainland. This was to be achieved from an offshore luxury yacht. My function was to put Peter ashore and later bring him back. The aft deck of the yacht was too small to fly the helicopter from, besides which the masts and radar aerial array on the boat would have got in the way. The director then came up with the unique idea of lifting Peter off in a sedan chair. At the start of the sequence Peter had to be seen seated in the chair on the deck. Then there would be a shot of the hovering helicopter with its winch cable attached to the chair the whole to create the impression of imminent lift-off. The cameras would then stop and Peter would get out and a dummy would be put in

227

his place which we would winch up and be filmed heading for the shore.

The return to the ship would be the same thing in reverse. The Triton yacht was moored about a mile offshore and subject to tide, wind and waves which caused it to swing round its anchor. When hovering twenty feet above the deck the considerable downwash from the main rotors had sufficient force to move the vessel around. This hover was more efficient when the aircraft was facing into the wind but the proximity of the ship's mast, little more than eight feet from the tips of the rotors left no room for an error of judgement.

To help we devised a system of simple hand signals which when made from the foredeck were visible from my cockpit. There were three signals; both hands and arms up to request lift-off; the reverse of this to land; and both arms in surrender attitude with palms showing to indicate 'hold your position'. From my cockpit direct visibility downwards was not possible so I watched the man on the foredeck to tell me everything. I knew that the American deck boss and his English assistant were not on the best of terms but I thought this was no concern of mine. I was about to be proved almost fatally wrong in this assumption.

On the technical side of flying the sedan chair, we'd had some problems. The wire cable twisted as the chair rotated in forward flight and ultimately severed, with the loss of the chair in the sea. A rotating swivel fitted to the cable showed some improvement. The relatively light weight of the chair, it being a mock up, caused it to rotate when moving forward at any speed. After losing a second chair in a practice run, Ricky, the engineer, asked how many more chairs were left. "I've no idea," I said. "Perhaps we had better check." There was only one. So no more dummy runs. Next one was for real.

It had become obvious that the sedan chair operation was to involve an unavoidable element of danger. Working closely with people who knew nothing about aviation — a minority of whom were emotionally unpredictable and withut with the discipline so essential for survival in our line of business, we tried to impress upon everyone the potential hazards. In particular I emphasised the vital importance of correct hand signalling from the foredeck.

Ricky was standing by on the winch and would keep a watching brief on the cable and in emergency could cut it.

Hovering, the roar of a straining radial engine overwhelmed all sound from below so hand signals were all we had. The initial stages of the lift-off went without a hitch. It had been decided by the director to film the incoming flight first. We put the chair on the deck, the cameras cut and the dummy was removed and replaced by Peter and the door closed. Again in camera he was seen to leave the chair and with both the helicopter and chair in view was then seen to walk across the deck.

The next flight was intended to simulate the shore-bound departure of our hero. After holding me in the hover for what was undoubtedly longer than necessary the English assistant on the foredeck finally threw up both arms and, with a feeling of relief, I gently eased up to lift-off.

To my surprise I needed considerably more power than I had anticipated, indicating that something more than the flimsy mock-up sedan was now hanging beneath. Losing patience with his American boss the assistant had thrown up his hands in exasperation, so we took off with sedan chair and Peter Vaughan inside it. This extra weight was the reason I had to apply the extra power, which in turn created an increased reactionary downward air blast from the rotors, and moved the ship's stern rapidly to one side.

I was forced to slide out of the hover in an attempt to gain transitional lift in order to prevent the now rotating chair from hitting the water. At this stage any attempt to put Peter back on the deck was impossible. I decided to fly a short, low slow circuit and in a steady controlled approach get him back on board.

The engineer, now acutely aware of the problem and knowing that the chair was a mock-up and not stressed to carry anything at all, let alone Peter's weight began to winch up the chair very slowly to wedge it near the underside of the helicopter, but he couldn't actually get Peter into the helicopter because the door on the sedan was in the wrong place for transfer. Nevertheless his timely action stopped the chair's rotation and very slowly and with infinite care we manoeuvred back to the ship. We commenced a very low approach and I could now hear an over-excited director shouting in my ear, "Bring him back — bring him back. He's my star!"

We were both now fighting to ensure a safe arrival, the engineer standing by to lower the chair as we hovered to place it on the postage stamp deck. We got in OK and, unknown to us, a German camera crew had filmed the approach and landing of the chair with Peter's perplexed anxious face peering out of the its side window.

I had a loud discussion with the deck crew.

The Sikorsky performed excellently throughout the filming until a week before I was due to ferry it home. The machine was on a solo local flight when it sustained a total hydraulic systems failure. The flight controls were only power assisted in the right-left movement of the cyclic control stick; the fore-aft movement being non-assisted and wholly manual. Nevertheless, for a few seconds the helicopter was almost uncontrollable, but as speed was rapidly reduced a semblance of control was regained. There was only sea and rocks below and, as they say, 'nowhere to go'. After a hazardous three minutes, a landing was achieved on the flat roof of a long disused fort. Logbook entry: 'Complete hydraulics failure in flight. Landed Fort. 10 seconds to spare.'

We found that the oil seals in the four-way hydraulic oil box had failed. These were replaced and the machine was operational next day. Ricky and I left for Porto on 15th October 1967. David Miller, the director and his team bidding us farewell having stamped my personal logbook with 'Irving Allen Ltd. Hammerhead a/c.'

From Porto our attempt at a direct transit to Bilbao via Salamanca was aborted due to weather and, taking a northerly heading, we arrived and stopped overnight at Coruna, before flying on next day through northern Spain into France. The flight across the Channel and onto Luton was perfect. Total flying time a fraction under seventeen hours.

I was back in Canada in May 1968 engaged on a unique operation flying a Piasaki Vertol 42A. This machine was a long twin rotored aircraft with capacity for sixteen passengers. It was powered by a

Wright Cyclone radial engine of approximately one thousand horsepower. The six main rotor blades were of mainly wooden construction, similar in composition to those fitted on early model Bell and Hiller helicopters. They were installed on both ends of the machine in sets of three and as they were contra-rotating they cancelled out torque effect, eliminating the need for a tail rotor.

It had a tricycle undercarriage and the pilot flew it from the right-hand seat. Many of these machines were Korean War surplus and their twelve years of storage had left much to be desired; particularly where the wooden rotors were concerned.

White River was a railroad town with a mandatory curfew and young people of less than seventeen years of age were not permitted to be on the streets after a certain hour. The locality included a railroad maintenance depot and there was a scattered shantytown nearby. The engineer, Red McKinnon, and I were based at White River for a period and our biggest problem was the persistent fog which rolled off the lake and grounded us for hours at a time.

Before I could take off in the Vertol I had to have a full company conversion course under the supervision of 'Shorty' Ferguson. He had ten thousand hours on type and was the most experienced helicopter pilot of 42As in the world. All this experience didn't prevent him hitting power cables in a thunderstorm and he was killed instantly. He was ferrying a Brantley 305 four place helicopter back to base on completion of a contract at the time, and was believed to be following a railroad when disaster struck.

A small grass airstrip near Wawa was used for the initial flying training followed by ten hours on actual fieldwork, which involved stringing nylon rope over the cross arms of tall electricity pylons. Cables carrying hydro-electric power were to be strung over a fifty mile line of these steel towers, several thousand of which marched across the rugged country which separated the Wawa and the White River districts of Western Ontario — two small areas connected by the Trans-Canada Highway on the north-eastern side of Lake Superior.

But first, before the cables themselves could be lifted into place, nylon rope had to be strung across the towers attached to

231

which the cables would follow, inched into place by a ground crew. In our training, apart from learning this gentle art, we also practised using a grapnel, a small anchor hook with claws which, attached to a long line, could be used to hook up any string which had missed a tower and become entangled in bush below. As may be imagined, the manoeuvres required to retrieve a wayward line and re-string it required the very close co-operation of both crewmembers. In fact, from start to finish it was very far from easy.

The thin but strong nylon rope came on wooden reels, somewhat like enlarged cotton reels, each of which carried a length of nine hundred feet of rope and weighed approximately two-and-half thousand pounds.

The carriage and operation of this large, heavy reel slung under the aircraft was, to say the least, rather tricky. Although it was supposed to smoothly rotate and release nylon rope as the aircraft moved forward at a sedate five miles per hour just above pylon height, the rope would — and without warning — frequently jam, calling for an immediate expert reaction from both the pilot and from the engineer lying prone by the open door.

Unlike the pilot, he could actually see the rotating reel swinging directly below him and could often anticipate an imminent jam if he saw smoke wisping up from an overheated bearing in the wooden reel. Red McKinnon, my engineer on this operation, was later to die when flying to put out a forest fire. His underslung bucket snagged on a treetop and brought down the helicopter, killing both Red and his pilot. In this job you can't be too careful.

Red and I were on the intercom throughout the whole of the very slow journey between and over the towers, laying a line across one side of the cross-arms, emptying a reel and replacing it with a full one and so proceeding mile after mile. Frequently the reel would jam and the taut nylon rope drag the aircraft to a full stop. When that happened, the reel had to be hovered into a space between the towers and held there, no easy manoeuvre, whilst the ground crew sorted things out.

As backup, a friend of mine, Dale Simpson, flying a Bell 47 carrying two ground crew, would always be close by to land and deal with the problem if no other help was at hand. Dale later crashed the Bell, but escaped unhurt.

So, section by section, at least a mile at a time, as we completed stringing one side of the cross-arms the ground crew would winch that strand of the cabling up into place and we would return to string the next designated point on the arms, now with the added hazard of a heavy steel cable linking the towers beneath us. Then a third cable had to be strung and winched and finally a fourth, the conglomeration of perilous cables high above or close to the ground calling for the closest co-operation between Red and me.

During this period, my teeth were proving troublesome. I asked about the dentist in the motel at White River. The manageress said the local man was on holiday but there was another at Marathon. She hesitated and then added, "If you go to him, always go in the morning." I made an appointment and found him an excellent dentist who was his own dental mechanic. He made me a very good gold bridge. But by two in the afternoon I doubt he would have been able to see his own office let alone a patient's teeth.

As the work progressed, the transportation of ground crews by any means other than by air proved to be appallingly slow, so they were usually flown in from 'University Camp'. This was a large site about twenty miles from Wawa filled with air conditioned and well equipped trailers and the only place where one could escape the mosquitoes. The food was as good as in any first class hotel. 'Fergie' the cook was French Canadian and, at the end of each summer contract with Ontario Hydro, he and his family departed by car for the long drive to Acapulco. They stayed there for the whole of the Canadian winter returning in the spring to start cooking again.

Nearing the end of the job, two Hydro crews had been flown to where work had ended the previous day and Dale had landed there with both Hydro bosses from Toronto after my second crew delivery flight. It was windy and getting more turbulent by the minute, preventing any further work, so late in the morning we gave up and returned one crew back to camp. With fourteen passengers on board and flying close to the line over a rough dirt

233

track at five hundred feet, I felt a thump of some strength, followed by severe vibrations. Within seconds the machine was shaking violently. My immediate reaction was to enter autorotation profile but I kept the engine running, my intention being to attempt a landing on the track. My instincts told me that the violent vibration might not be the result of an engine problem. The shaking became severe enough to cause the collapse of the instrument console located on the floor next to my position and I instantly applied full power and managed to get down on the track but the machine was now shaking so much that it seemed about to break up.

We evacuated the machine and I shut the engine down to follow all the rest out. We stood in a cluster well clear of the still rapidly free wheeling rotors until they shuddered to a stop. Looking at the rear set of rotors the trailing edge of one blade had torn away and had holed the other two. There were also abrasions from flying debris.

Later, another engineer was to infer that I had hit something on the ground when flying at low level back to camp. The Line Foreman who had been on board wrote a letter stating we were at least five hundred feet up as he could see the lake more than ten miles away. As he wrote: 'No way can anybody see the lake from the treetops.'

The attitude of the management to the occurrence is best demonstrated by the words of a senior Board member who said, "These blades are perfectly safe. I had one shed its trailing edge right here outside the hangar when testing the helicopter in a low hover and it stayed in the air." But I heard later that this was the third rotor trailing edge to disintegrate in the previous three weeks.

So much for Korean War surplus.

In August I was offered the job of ferrying a Sikorsky 55 to Munich for BEA. This was intended as the initial stage of a far longer trip to West Africa. But, in the event that projected second stage did not take place. I did a routine proficiency check with Captain Cameron, chief of the helicopter division and was ready to go

234

when the weather allowed it. The flight assistant was a friend, Dr Phelan, a medical practitioner in London.

There was quite a lot of paperwork to clear so it was late evening of August 13th 1968 when we left Gatwick for Lympne on the Kent coast to refuel and night stop. Next morning we cleared customs and took off for the Channel crossing to Dunkerque. We were wearing Mae West jackets because with no pontoons, floats or life raft, they were our only hope of survival in the event of a channel ditch. There were no problems and from Dunkerque we set direct course for Cologne. The route took us into Belgium and very close to Brussels, a section of the journey which was accomplished in two hours thirty-five minutes, but we had, unwittingly, infringed on protected air space. We were at eight thousand feet to take advantage of a very favourable tailwind and they had me on radar. There had been considerable 'chatter' from one of their controllers, most of it unintelligible but it was made very obvious that we were not regarded with favour and strongly suggested that we leave immediately if not sooner.

In mitigation, it should be said, that our radio was not a great unit. Moreover, other than this VHF set we had no other navigational equipment, not even a radio compass. We had to rely entirely on map reading and, as part of our route across Belgium was above broken cloud, ground features were impossible to identify. Whilst in these conditions, we had only the magnetic compass to rely on and attempt to compensate for wind drift, the controllers in Brussels were sitting in front of a mass of electronic equipment and living in another world.

The remainder of the flight was a good map reading exercise for Michael. We were met at Cologne by the BEA representative on his bicycle. He immediately made arrangements for refuelling commenting, "We were not expecting a flight this morning. If you and your co-pilot would like to go and eat, I give you vouchers." It was easier to accept this gracious offer than to explain why our machine was in airline livery, although not being operated by them.

From Cologne we followed the River Rhine southeast watching the barges on the way. We passed Bonn, Koblenz and Heidelburg. We left the Rhine to follow the Neckar to land at Stuttgart — a flight of three days. At Stuttgart we acquired a pot of paint and erased the BEA insignia on the tail.

It was a straightforward flight down to Munich, following the autobahn. We were again at low level in the hope of avoiding a repeat of the Belgian experience. Somewhere between Augsburg and Munich we were suddenly confronted by a jet fighter, which passed underneath us. With some dismay, I realised that it was in the final stages of take-off and that we were crossing the end of a military runway in use. My instinctive reaction, probably abetted by the background of an experienced spray pilot, was to hug the ground, to fly at a few feet across flat farmlands and only gain height to clear any wires which were too low to go under.

Later that evening Michael said, "From your seat you may not have seen it, but there was a second fighter coming down that long runway and not quite airborne as we shot across the end." One wonders what their radar operators were doing. Perhaps an early indication of the military potential of low level heavily armed helicopters for in-and-out undetected attacks against such targets.

We parked the aircraft in a special compound for aircraft destined for a warring faction in a Central African state connected in some way with a General Ojuku. There were other aircraft of various types in this enclosure, but their final fate was never revealed. Our machine eventually arrived back in England. Michael and I waited for further instructions for a few days but as no word came we flew back to London by airline.

In early April 1969, Autair asked me to test fly this same Sikorsky for a renewal of a Certificate of Airworthiness and to check out the newly installed radio for certification. These flights and the paperwork were satisfactory and Maurice Rose and I left on the forty-five minute flight to Redhill to arrange storage for the machine.

It was a bright spring day with excellent visibility and we elected to fly a circuitous route in order to avoid the London Control Zone and other restricted airspace. We crossed the Thames at Greenwich and were approaching the small town of Oxted at eighteen hundred feet where we intended to turn west for the eight mile run into our destination, when Maurice inadvertently operated the jettison lever for the very large Perspex sliding window on his side. This took off with a loud whooshing noise followed by a blast of cold April air into the cockpit. I swung into a steep descending turn to see the window gyrating from side to side with the sun's rays reflecting off the Perspex like a flashing light. The wind effect slowed its descent into a haphazard glide rather than a headlong dive.

We watched the direction of the fall with apprehension as we were over the very busy A25. It was obvious it was going to fall very close to the road with potentially dire consequences — its metal frame and attachments adding up to much more than the weight of a Perspex sheet. To our immense relief we saw it land in a leafless tree not more than half a dozen paces from the roadside. None of the cars on the road stopped so we had reason to hope that nobody seen the incident.

In a less populous area I would have landed in an adjoining field and retrieved the window, but there were cattle in the next field and I didn't want to upset them. We made a careful note where the tree was located and headed off for Redhill. Maurice had his wife waiting there for us in the car and we drove back to the tree but the window had gone. We decided to go to the Police Station at Oxted in case somebody had handed it in.

So we drove there and found a large Constable at the desk. Not wishing to advertise the fact that I had dropped something from an aircraft, we played it cool. "We have lost a large Perspex window while travelling on the A25 and wonder if you have any knowledge of it?" Maurice chipped in with, "It's a large sheet of Perspex in a metal frame." Ponderously, the officer climbed to his feet and vanished into an adjoining room to return with one intact Sikorsky co-pilot's window. Looking at me he enquired, "Is this yours, Sir?" "Yes," I said, "Indeed it is." He handed Maurice a small cardboard tag bearing the words 'Returned Property' and said, "Please sign this to indicate that you have got the article back. By the way what is it?" Before Maurice could open his mouth I garbled, "Its to do with a storage project down the road at Redhill." Not entirely untrue.

The Constable told us it had been picked up by a little old lady in a battered Morris Traveller who had seen the window on the roadside and brought it in. She had not left her name and

237

address. We gave the Police Benevolent Fund five pounds.

I did some top dressing of phosphate fertiliser for the Scottish Forestry Commission on young pine plantations around Loch Fyne and then moved on to the Isle of Arran to cover forty acres of hilly forestry. The work completed, Bill Coyne and I headed back across the six-mile stretch of water separating the Island from the mainland. We were almost at Skipness Point when the engine coughed, almost stopped and then picked up to run very roughly for the last two miles over deep, cold water. I spotted a red marker buoy and I had this in mind if we had to ditch. I turned to Bill and said, "Can you swim?" A very white faced Bill shook his head and said, "Not very well."

The helicopter, its engine backfiring, staggered into a long disused graveyard near the ruins of an ancient castle. Over the next hour Bill and I removed the spark plugs, many of which were oiled up and obviously not firing. Bill, as he replaced the last of the twelve plugs turned to me saying, " We have a sick engine. I've replaced some of the worst affected plugs with the few spares we have and I hope they get us back." "I hope so too," I said, " A forty mile hike over the Scottish Moors is for the birds."

We made it back to Lochair were the engine was removed and sent to the maintenance base. They confirmed that it was, in effect, worn out. The helicopter had been purchased from a Middle Eastern operator and the hourly figures entered in the engine and airframe logbooks were nothing like the truth. This was not an uncommon ploy, widely practiced to enhance the book price of the machine. The introduction of integral engine recorders partially, but not entirely, eliminated this scam.

Aero engines have a legal life expectancy calibrated in operating hours. Government regulations require that an engine be removed for a complete overhaul, or withdrawn and replaced, when the specified hours are reached. Mandatory overhaul hours are based on a number of factors originating with the manufacturer's recommendations. These may be backed by operational experience under varying conditions reported by users, and may, in some cases be an extension of the recommended hours. The responsibility for the maintenance of the engine and keeping correct records must rest with the operators and the relevant government authority. To ignore or misrepresent these rules leads to accidents and, in some cases, death.

In this instance, Bill and I were extremely lucky to get away with only a bad scare. Survival in the icy waters around the Scottish coast might well be only minutes.

In July 1970 I was based in Donegal. The contract was to fly press visitors, journalists and photographers — to a Citroen car Press Party where they got to drive new Citroens on the Irish roads. Autair supplied the Sikorsky 55 again and I flew in from Manchester (spending the overnight stop very pleasantly in the Officer's Mess at RAF Ballykelly) to land at Rosapenna in the Republic.

There were about twenty Citroens, many of which, driven by my passenger 'motoring experts', were wrecked on the narrow winding roads of Erin having impacted on stone walls, often in a successful attempt to avoid horses and donkey carts. It was said only four of the cars were intact after five weeks of Irish roads and 'expert' drivers. We flew, on a daily basis, a dozen overseas press people into Rosapenna from Ballykelly. They arrived from many European countries in a Falcon jet which would then embark the previous day's visitors for the return flight to their country of origin while we took the new arrivals to Rosapenna Strand.

Either way this thirty-minute journey was a mundane operation with little to commend it. The flying activity being limited to little more than an hour a day. In fact the five weeks sojourn would have been very boring if it hadn't been for the riding horses kept by the hotel. I proved to the Stables Manager that I could ride well and on several occasions was asked to accompany the hotel guests on rides along the beach.

One of the expert drivers was German and over a drink I learned he had been in the Luftwaffe and had recently retired with the rank of Colonel from the German Air Force. He had an artificial leg from a wartime incident and I mentioned Douglas Bader. He said, "Yes, I know Bader. I met him after he was shot down over our field on the French coast. You may remember seeing a photo of Bader sitting in the cockpit of a Messerschmit

239

109 with a German Officer standing by him and apparently holding a pistol at hip level."

I replied that indeed I did remember the photo because there was no way Bader could take off in the 109 as the wheel was chocked.

The Colonel laughed and said, "Well, I was the officer and the 'pistol' was this," and he touched his right hip where a pronounced bulge was visible. It was the fitting section of his tin leg.

He said that they had entertained Bader in the Mess after he had parachuted down minus his legs. A spare set was dropped the next day by allied aircraft. As he remembered, Bader had his legs on when he sat in the 109. The Colonel was my co-pilot for the trip to Ballykelly the next morning.

James Casey was the youngest Commandant in the Irish Air Corps and a long time friend. He was on leave and on the Sunday morning he attended Mass before we took off. His machine, an Alouette, had no radio, which was in for repair. There was no problem as we flew in loose formation with me talking to Air Traffic for both helicopters. The Colonel asked me how efficient the radar at a military base was and I replied, "Well, we are at fifteen hundred feet and you will have heard the operator reporting our height, distance from the field and two contacts. It's Sunday morning with no other reported activity and I know the controller on duty; so we will test it out."

We dropped rapidly away from the Alouette and down to sea level having given Jim Casey a hand signal for him to maintain his height. We were now approaching the base at low level and skimming only feet above the waters of Lough Foyle. I called for a position report. The radar operator coming back with, "Three miles, one thousand feet, two contacts." We had crossed the railway line which ran parallel to the shore at a height of ten feet and were heading for the control tower when I called to say I had them in my gun sights!

It was obvious they had picked up the Alouette and had assumed that the relative positions of both aircraft had not changed and reporting two contacts was an assumption. The Colonel was vastly amused.

Because James had to return to military duties, Irish

Helicopters asked me to conduct several flights for them to collect motoring journalists. To my amazement one of them was Loghlin McGlyn who I had last seen at Curragh military camp in 1941. That was a memorable night in the hotel bar.

I left for Redhill at the end of August but had to return to Belfast because of developing fog at sea. This kept us on the ground for three days. We took the shortest sea crossing to Stranraer in misty conditions which persisted down through the Pennines and the flight south. The Thames was crossed at Gravesend and we arrived at Redhill twenty minutes later in visibility of less than half a mile.

I was back in Ireland in September to fly Lt. Colonel James Holloway, Commissioner of Irish Lights, together with Captain Kelly Rogers onto the newly constructed helicopter landing pad fitted to the Irish Lights Vessel *Granuaille* in Dun Laoghaire harbour. This was the first ship of its kind to be equipped with such a facility in the Republic. I picked up Captain Rogers, a legendary pilot and a founder member of Aer Lingus, from the garden of his pretty cottage by the sea. The plot of land was only just large enough to land the Alouette. We made several test take-offs and landings from the *Granuaille* after which Kelly Rogers looked at me with a satisfied smile and said, "This has crew transfer by longboat and Atlantic rollers beaten to hell!" I had to agree but had mental reservations about landing in turbulent winds, often at gale force, on a very small landing pad.

A Mr Mulcahey, an American pharmaceutical millionaire, was to play host to President Richard Nixon during an official visit to the Republic. The President's wife had a Quaker ancestor thought to be buried in a hamlet called Timahau. It was only a dozen or so houses on the edge of a vast peat deposit called The Bog of Allen. The President had expressed a wish to visit the grave, but it was discovered that burials of that period had no markers. A senior policeman came from Dublin to make the arrangements and found a resident aged one hundred and two in the local hostelry. He asked him if he knew where the grave might be and the old man indicated a field with cattle grazing I it. We went down to have a look but found no evidence of burials.

I suggested a short trip in the helicopter, as sometimes such abnormalities can be seen from the air. The policeman suggested we take the old man with us. I harboured a sneaking suspicion that the ancient Irishman had about as much idea as we had as to where the grave might be and simply fancied a trip in a helicopter.

We landed no wiser after twenty minutes, but the police accepted the field where the old man had indicated and started to make all the arrangements needed for the visit. The field was cleaned up and the cows evicted. A large stand was erected to hold the world's press and a slight protrusion at one end of the field was seen as a possible burial ground. "How can you be sure this is it?" I said to the policeman. He looked at me with an engaging smile and said, "Sure now and does it really matter?" He had a point.

The President landed by helicopter and made his way to the nominated burial site. There he was met by two large men who were said to be Quakers holding placards saying Nixon was not welcome. Four of the largest policemen I have ever seen moved in quietly, gently lifted the two men completely off the ground by their elbows, reversed direction and without any fuss deposited them in the road with the admonishment "Don't come back."

I spent a week acting as pilot for a Mr Stint of the NBC company following the Nixon progress. There were a few demonstrations of dissent but generally Mr Nixon was well received and popular in the Republic. In Limerick there were so many people I had to hover out over the canal to avoid accidental damage to the machine by the multitude. Later, I flew three bags of undeveloped film to the airport, for onward transmission to the USA.

Before I left, the Irish Department of Transport and Power nominated me as 'check pilot' for the issue of type ratings on helicopters.

CHAPTER FOURTEEN

Last Days of Rhodesia

AUTAIR APPOINTED ME OPERATIONS MANAGER FOR Woods Helicopters Pty in Perth, Australia. This was a partial subsidiary of Autair and the local General Manager was Jimmy Woods. He was an Australian legend. He had set a number of flying records between the wars and operated a small charter company.

He had never learned to fly a helicopter and knew even less about how they worked. Autair had supplied him with two Bells together with the flying and engineering personnel to operate them. Woods had no fixed-wing aircraft at all and when I arrived in January 1971 the company was being maintained by constant injections of money from London. My function was to reverse this trend but from the start Jimmy resented my presence as anything other than a pilot. An increasingly abrasive relationship with him gave me massive problems trying to get the show off the ground. For example, I worked very hard to get a sixty hours contract from a mining company in the city. Jimmy promptly vetoed it. When I challenged this decision he replied, "Not enough hours."

This was an incredible attitude. We had one serviceable Bell 47 but no work. We had no money to pay the office overheads, the secretary or my accommodation in a Salvation Army Hostel. The Bell 47 was in a poor state of mechanical repair because of irregular maintenance and no engineering presence for some time before my arrival. The second Bell was grounded awaiting a twelve hundred hour inspection and an engineer to carry it out. With Head Office approval I overruled Jimmy and went ahead with the contract.

Without an engineer, but with Ian Shawyer, a young man who drove the support vehicle and refuelled and cleaned the helicopters, I headed out to Kalgoorlie. The job was a reconnaissance trip and we flew thirty-five hours in six days. The remainder of the sixty hours were flown at a later date. Kalgoorlie had little to commend it. The flies, extreme heat and aridity had to be experienced to be believed. Every landing outside the town blew up a cloud of red laterite dust which invaded every bodily pore and every crevice in the machine.

Captain Woods retired in March and the company was restructured as Wescopters Pty Ltd. I regret we did not part amicably.

An old friend, engineer Danny Patel, arrived from Singapore. We were more than pleased to see him. Jimmy's secretary, Mrs Revell, told me, "It's a relief to see an engineer at long last. Flying without any mechanical assistance must be a little hard on the nerves." She had been working for Jimmy over a number of years and went on to say how little maintenance was required for the twin aeroplanes compared with operating helicopters. Danny gave the Bell 47 the once over and said, "It's a bit of a rogue; but I've flown worse."

He soon had both Bells in better shape. The twelve hundred hour inspection was accomplished and, by April, we were in Dampier doing soil sampling. Most of this barren, hot and utterly dry district was in the Hammersley Range where heights seldom exceeded twelve hundred feet above sea level. We were based at the Westfield Camp one hundred and seventy miles from Marble Bar, said to be the hottest place in Australia.

I often helped in taking the samples so we could extend the range of the machine by dispensing with the second geologist and substituting his weight with extra jerricans of fuel. The camp was comfortable but the flies were impossible. The aviation fuel fumes probably killed hundreds as it seemed to have a fatal attraction for them as we hand pumped from forty-five gallon drums. Soon Union Carbide employed us for a geological survey at Port Headland which, combined with the Westland contract, bolstered the company's finances.

For this, the helicopter was required to carry two passengers plus a heavy load of wooden stakes for the claims pegging contract at Port Headland. We had to stake the ground at predetermined points to legally validate the claims. In addition extra fuel was carried in jerricans on cargo panniers for the more distant missions. The temperature rarely dropped below one hundred degrees fahrenheit. The flying called for multiple take-offs and landings. My logbook records one hundred and eighty four on one day.

These conditions meant that the helicopter was operating at near 'maximum possible power' which may have contributed to the following incident. We had noticed a slight bounce in the machine four or five minutes away from Jandakot airport. It needed investigating but I decided to continue on in to Jandakot where I could change machines. Danny soon found the cause of the trouble: a crack across the main rotor blade's metal strap. The bounce so clearly felt was the result of the strap's grip on the blade beginning to loosen — which could have had fatal results. My logbook reads: 'Very, very lucky. Not very nice. Another of the nine?'

Leaving Danny to sort out a replacement rotor blade and a new engineer — for he had plans to return to Singapore to set up his own business — Ian Shawyer and I left for Port Headland. We had arranged to refuel and refill two jerricans at Moora, more than enough to get us to Geralton, the next stop. We were in cruising flight about one thousand feet above the main highway when, attempting a slight adjustment to the throttle, I found no movement was possible either way. For the second time in my career the throttle was jammed.

I decided to continue on course as far as possible on the fuel in the tanks and, when they were indicating empty, shut off the ignition to make an autorotative landing in a suitable place close to the highway, where help might be available if required. I called Geralton but getting no reply realised that it was probable that our line of sight VHF set was too far away for contact. We had been airborne a few minutes more than two hours when I selected a field near the road, next to another containing a small herd of Jersey cattle. I alerted Ian to switch off the engine when I gave the word so I could keep both hands on the controls. We circled the selected field, Ian shut off the engine and we started an engine-off descent. The initial noise of the helicopter passing overhead may have caused some panic in the cattle who broke through the fence as we landed. On inspection it was found that the throttle linkage system had vibrated loose from a retaining bracket near the oil pump and this had cause the throttle to jam. We bodged this up and refuelled from the jerricans surrounded by very inquisitive cows. We landed at Geralton without any more mishaps.

Dropping into Marble Bar one day we landed on a small knoll close to the pub. It was midday and the temperature was one hundred and fifteen degrees Fahrenheit. We booked rooms for the night and moved into the bar. We were standing with our backs to an open window sipping our beers when I was suddenly aware that something wet and furry was pressing against the back of my neck. Turning round I found myself face to face with a camel. This was the pub pet who was exceedingly fond of as much beer as he could cadge from customers.

I left Australia for a business trip to England and the London Operations Manager asked me to act as a relief pilot on a spraying operation in Lincolnshire. His pilot was to attend an investiture at Buckingham Palace in connection with his previous military service. I agreed, but on arrival found that another pilot was to fly the Bell 47 and that I had been assigned a very old Bell D1 that had been brought in from Belgium and that had manual rather than servo-assisted controls. From my experience in Borneo with similar equipment, I realised that to go straight into low level spraying, which required adept handling of controls in abrupt turning manoeuvres was a recipe for disaster with this machine unless I first acclimatised myself on a more mundane operation.

Accordingly I told the Operations Manager that while the original agreement was fine, the new scheme was unacceptable, which provoked a response of, "Now our bloody pilots won't fly our machines." Having pointed out that I wasn't his bloody pilot and that I was still around because I knew how to say no to such schemes, he had no choice. If he wanted the job done, he had to revert to the original arrangement.

My logbook entry for the day reads: 'Spray 146 and a half acres potatoes and beet, Holbeach, Lincolnshire. Swiznik killed today testing Bell D1 which I was asked to fly and refused. Reason for accident not determined.'

I returned to Australia in September continuing operations much as before. Every day, as the summer advanced, the weather

246

was getting hotter. It was so hot that it was inadvisable to stop the engine for refuelling because the gasoline in the carburettor vaporised so that a rapid restart was impossible. We would often refuel with the engine running and as this was usually with jerricans, the procedure required great care on the Bell 47 with its overhead fuel tanks since on this model an idling engine was accompanied by a rotating main rotor. The only advantage was that this kept the flies away. Eventually the temperature became so high that the operation was abandoned until the end of the summer.

Because of the conditions we had several partial engine failures due to valve malfunctions. Fortunately Bernie Rose and his company, Helix, helped us by loaning a helicopter to finish the contract.

In July 1972 an interesting situation developed in Cyprus. A few months earlier the Presidential Hiller 1100 jet turbine powered, four-place helicopter was shot down by an opposition political faction near the Government Palace at Nicosia. The President, Archbishop Makarios, was on board but escaped uninjured from a badly damaged machine. The incident occurred just after take-off from the President's helipad and the partially wrecked Hiller was pushed into a hangar in the Palace grounds.

The Chairman of Autair now said to me "I may have a deal to acquire and sell on their piston-engined Bell. Why not go out and take a look at the machine and. if possible, fly it."

I asked how the Presidential Bell fitted into the picture. "The Palace," he replied, "is selling it together with the shot up Hiller. It was not involved in the ambush and is said to be perfectly serviceable."

The Hiller was beyond economic repair but the executive Bell was in fine shape and with a prospective purchaser from Beirut on board, I carried out a series of flights around Nicosia and struck a deal. It was deemed preferable, for several reasons, to fly the machine to Beirut, rather than dismantle it for delivery by sea. Maurice Rose, Autair's representative grinned like a Cheshirre cat and said, "This should be easy for you; haven't you done this trip before? Don't worry though I'll be flying a Cherokee aircraft to act as escort for the water crossing." "That's OK," I said. "When you ditch I'll be able to direct the rescue boat."

The President's helicopter had a similar performance to other Bell 47s but was markedly different in appearance. The long conventional tubular tail frame was encased in a stressed metal skin. The bubble enclosed cabin had been replaced with a longer, wider elongated box structure which, in addition to the central position for the pilot, provided side by side bench seating for three passengers in the rear.

The delivery flight was scheduled for early September and in the meanwhile a plan had to be worked out for in-flight refuelling as the machine's twin overhead tanks could only contain fuel for a two-hour flight. Very much in my mind was the last time I had done the inbound flight from Beirut, when the time taken had been over well three hours.

During the waiting period, potatoes, beans and other crops received my attention in the Fens and meantime a scheme was evolved for the ferrying flight to Beirut. For safety, fuel for four hours endurance was necessary. The weather and aggressive Israeli air activity around Beirut could force a premature return when close to the destination. The fuel was to be transferred from jerricans in the cabin to one of the two self-levelling tanks fitted to the helicopter. A small bilge pump was obtained from the Esso Boat Marina at Newhaven together with tank and tubing from the same source. These were made of a plastic material and neither of us knew what effect high-octane gasoline would have on it. We soaked both tank and tubing in high-octane fuel for a week just to be sure — with no apparent adverse effect.

It was found to be neither safe nor practical to pump fuel from the jerricans up to either tank through the normal point of entry. But a plug associated with fuel calibration, which was sited on top of the left hand tank, could be screwed out and replaced with plastic tube, clamped with a band to ensure that it remained in place. There was the danger of static electricity being generated and consequent risk of fire when using the bilge pump to transfer the fuel, and in an attempt to eliminate this an anti-static paint was applied to cover the pump and tubing. Twenty-eight gallons of extra gasoline were carried in jerricans, a can each side of my pilot position with the rest, for centre of gravity reasons, further back. These were attached by light ropes to be hauled forward as required during the flight.

When this occurred the manipulation of a jerrican and the insertion of the suction pipe from the pump required the use of both hands, thus leaving the flight controls to their own devices momentarily. Equilibrium was maintained by locking the less critical pitch control lever on my left with a friction nut and maintaining straight and level flight with knee pressure on the cyclic stick. The heat was intense on the day of the flight, the cabin temperature reaching 120 degrees Fahrenheit. This, and the fumes from the gasoline in the cockpit caused a perpetual headache and on two occasions, vomiting. The sliding window panels did nothing to reduce the problem. I was grateful for the comforting presence of Maurice Rose in the escorting Cherokee.

At an early stage both the magnetic compass and radio went unserviceable, but I managed to steer a sun bearing. Two or three times I lost sight of the Cherokee in the heat haze. The Israeli air force had attacked Beirut Airport half an hour before I landed. Although not seen by me, Maurice saw them leaving. The flight time of two hours and thirty-five minutes was good, but it was certainly not the most comfortable of flights.

In June I went back to Canada and was having lunch in Calgary airport one day when a man I didn't know approached me and asked if I was Paddy Jones. He introduced himself as 'Howdy' McPhail. Everybody in aviation in Western Canada had heard of HD 'Howdy' McPhail. A bomber pilot in the war, he had been shot down over the Swedish coast on his first operation. He and his crew had baled out and were interned for a few weeks by the Swedish authorities and then quietly returned to England with a load of much needed ball bearings. At the end of an operational tour he was awarded the DFC and leaving the RCAF he started a fixed-wing crop spraying business in Saskatchewan.

"I need a pilot urgently," he said. He was about to hire a three passenger Alouette Two helicopter, turbine powered. Howdy explained that the contract was for forest fire control on behalf of the Department of Northern Saskatchewan.

Mel O'Reilly came along to be engineer — in fact, it was he who had recommended me to Howdy — and we flew for two and half hours to Battleford, Howdy's base. The next day we flew on north another two hundred and thirty miles to Buffalo Narrows following the only gravel road. The swampy terrain and densely forested areas were not conducive to emergency landings.

Buffalo Narrows was an overgrown village on the southern side of Churchill Lake. The lake itself was twelve miles wide and thirty miles long with a very narrow neck of water separating it from the larger Peter Pond Lake. It was along these narrows that the settlement was built, hence the name. There was no road past this point, but there was a track called the Semchuk Trail which continued on north. There were said to be ten thousand Indians in the area, many of whom were unemployed and living off Federal or Provincial benefits. Some were 'Treaty Indians' with villages on lands ceded to them by Queen Victoria in the last century.

Buffalo Narrows itself had one hotel that included a beer parlour. In addition there were two general stores. There was also a busy floatplane base from which Beaver and Norsemen light aircraft operated from the lake. Some of the local people worked on forest fire prevention in the season, but alcohol consumption was often a problem. Logbook entry for 24th June 1973 states: 'Two lightening fires — one twelve miles east — aircraft Perspex window damaged by Indian getting out — they very dangerous around helicopter — unpredictable when sober; many of today's dead drunk.'

The offloading of portable fire pumps and hundreds of feet of coiled hose, axes and other implements called for skill and some element of training, even when operating from a well prepared pad. Our operating conditions included flying in dense wood smoke, evading burning ash embers and offloading over uneven, swampy surfaces so bad that the helicopter had to be held in a rock steady low hover while the fire crews jumped out.

One evening, a visiting English doctor and I were enjoying a drink in the beer parlour when, without warning, a very drunk young Indian produced a rifle. Shouting obscenities he started shooting up the establishment. Those who could left by the door, others took flying leaps through the window and within seconds

250

the bar was empty. The Indian boy reloaded his weapon and ran outside. He stood beside an ornamental old time Prairie Wagon, as the doctor and I crouched by the rear wheel on the other side. The doctor, who had consumed more than a few drinks, then decided to act the hero and shouted to the boy to put down his weapon and give himself up. The reply was a fusillade of shots. Result — the doctor and I set off crawling along a very wet ditch on our way to the helicopter.

What I didn't know then was that the doctor was ex British Army SAS.

We got airborne in the dark to fly across the lake to the Mounted Police post. They were all absent on a boat trip to Dillon. We set off for Dillon and flown about ten miles when we saw the lights of the police vessels. They arrested the Indian boy after he had expended all his ammunition.

We finished the contract at the end of August with no major conflagrations to extinguish and, on the whole, it was an enjoyable summer.

December 1973 found me flying geological surveys again but with a marked difference for now I was in the hot mountainous regions of Saudi Arabia. Special Flight, an American ancillary of Saudi Airlines, operated a DH Beaver and two Bell 47s based in Jeddah. Most of the work was in the vast deserts behind the mountainous barrier running near Mecca, paralleling the Red Sea, and was on behalf of the Ministry of Petroleum and Mineral Resources but also involved the Americans and the French. I spent Christmas Day with the French contingent in a most comfortable tented camp. The Gallic inmates had the best of both food *and* drink in this liquor-banned state.

One of the sites we surveyed was an ancient gold and silver mine which dated back two thousand years or more. The foundations of some of the original living quarters for slaves were still recognisable. Several crushers for breaking rock were still there. Pieces of gold-bearing quartz had been crushed into powder by an up and down thumping motion of a heavy circular stone attached to a baulk of wood. Records show that the ancients extracted the gold by primitive but effective methods. A quantity of crushed quartz was processed by modern methods but seldom even a trace of gold resulted. The ancients had got it all.

We took a trip from the site of the mine to a village called Kut, from where Don Hadley, one of the passengers, wished to fly on to An Numas, another village near the edge of the escarpment. He'd heard that the village store had a large numbers of old guns and pistols and he was a collector. The fifty-mile flight was slow due to the strong head wind and took almost an hour and we spent another hour in the village finding that most of the 'old' pistols were of very recent manufacture. We were about a thousand feet up on the return flight when there was a distant thump enough to shake the helicopter. The flight became noticeably smooth and we were making much better time on the return.

Fifteen minutes or so after take-off Don said, "Surely that can't be the camp can it? Not so soon?" I started to say, "No way" when I recognised our tents and huts. I reduced power to commence a steep descent, as we were now in real danger of overshooting the camp, when suddenly the earlier thump was repeated, immediately followed by a rapid deceleration of speed. Weird!

Later we checked the exact distance for the return leg and the elapsed time and our resultant return ground speed worked out at one hundred and seventy two miles per hour; this in a helicopter with a normal cruising speed of around seventy.

It became obvious after some research that both thumps had been produced by a jet stream coming in from a high altitude over the Red Sea. This flowed continuously across the escarpment at around eight thousand feet, and at an air speed in our lower level of around one hundred miles an hour. It would sweep across and above the band of lower and much slower environmental air and at about one thousand feet. With both quite separate air masses possessing widely differing speeds we had passed through from one to the other and the thumps must have been due to a momentary change of aerodynamic forces on the main rotor as we crossed the invisible barrier.

One camp was at a height of seven thousand two hundred feet, two miles from the northern border of Yemen. I had made several landings with the geologists and this was to be the last landing of the day. The passengers disappeared into the bush and I sat on a large stone with a knife, whittling a stick which I intended to use for walking. I was so intent on this project I did not notice four men enter the clearing until I heard voices.

Startled, I looked up to see not ten yards away four heavily armed youths with rifles, side arms and knives in their belts. We had been warned by the Saudi Police to take great care when working the border areas as gangs of bandits operated on both sides of it.

This group did not look threatening, merely curious. I got slowly to my feet and, smiling, I addressed them with the little Arabic I possessed saying "Salaam Alakem." To my intense relief they replied in like fashion. They walked past me and inspected the helicopter with some intensity. They ignored me and touched the machine and chatted among themselves and, after ten minutes or so, they moved off into the bush.

I got airborne in an urgent search for the geologists before the Arabs found them. Inside five minutes I saw them clustered round a rock outcrop. I landed, locked the controls with the engine running and yelled at them, *'Get on board, now!'* They protested they hadn't finished and I informed them in no uncertain terms that they had. When we got back to camp we told the local police who told us we had been extremely lucky.

That same stick I had been whittling went with me all over the world. At Calgary airport many years later it caused a minor furore. A security official insisted that the stick could not be taken onto the aircraft as it could be used as an offensive weapon. After a long argument with petty bureaucratic officials it eventually travelled with the crew in the cockpit. I still have it, and frequently use it, today.

I completed four short contracts in Saudi over a three-year period, the final one ending with a kidney infection. I suspect the drinking water in Jeddah was to blame and it was very painful and frightening at the time. The first indications occurred out in the desert, fifty miles from camp when urination was accompanied by copious quantities of blood. The hospital at Riyadh sent me to England for specialized kidney treatment and as I went to catch the plane the Aviation Manager barked at me, "This is one hell of a number, you're leaving me right in the lurch. What am I going to do for a pilot?" Thank you for your concern! But it's not an unusual reaction from Operation Managers around the world. X-rays at Wolverhampton revealed traces of a past infection but the kidneys appeared to be in good shape.

Back in London with a clean bill of health Autair approached me to go to Kuwait to fly two Sikorskys that I had originally flown out from England to Beirut fourteen years before. The people who owned the Sikorskys also had two DH Dove aircraft which the Government had used for pilot instrument training in the Sheikdom. Both the Sikorskys and the Doves were still on the British Register and so required a British licensed pilot to fly them. I didn't have a Dove on my licenses but the British authorities issued me with a 'ferry permit' for both aircraft, endorsing my licence to this effect.

Unfortunately both the helicopters were not in an airworthy state. They had been badly stored over the years and the engineers had failed to protect the engines to against internal corrosion. The very heavy main rotor blades had been left in place on the aircraft and had drooped under their own weight causing many interconnections to loosen. With years of extreme temperatures the resins used in the manufacture of the blades had also deteriorated.

A local British engineer and I still managed to get both machines serviceable enough to be flown and, as there was little more than four hundred hours of total flying on each helicopter, in theory they had a lot of time left before their mandatory overhaul. I made a series of test flights in both aircraft and the results were not encouraging. The blades would need replacing and none were available. We abandoned any idea of a long hazardous flight over both desert and mountain ranges to Beirut and sent them by road instead.

Gerard Barrau, French engineer, had purchased the Doves for the Beirut company. He would fly with me as aircraft engineer in the co-pilot's seat. Both aircraft were in the same hangar and although not flown for some time, appeared to be well maintained and in much better shape than the helicopters. A Kuwait Air Force Instructor, Captain John Armstrong, gave me a conversion course including asymmetric flight, the ability to fly and maintain height on one engine. He said he did little real flying these days as he was an instructor on the flight simulator and had I ever flown one? I had to confess I had something less than one hundred hours in a wartime Link Trainer. He grinned, "Come with me and have a go with modern technology." I did and immediately 'crashed!'

Gerrard and I, flying G-AOUG, left Kuwait on 31st January 1974. We flew across southern Kuwait into Saudi Arabia to pick up the pipeline at Al Quaisumah pumping station. Three hours and forty minutes later we landed at Bedanah to refuel and Gerrard pointed to the northwest where a dark menacing cloud formation was becoming visible. We got airborne within the hour and very soon the weather deteriorated. I had planned to fly the next leg to Turayf, close to the Jordanian border, to refuel and then fly on into Syria. Half way to Turayf we began to be hit by snow flurries and I dropped height to be able to still see the pipeline road. Suddenly the threshold of a runway appeared diagonally ahead. With a quick reaction, I reduced speed, lowered the landing gear, applied almost full flap and veered right as power was adjusted, to land half way down the airstrip. By braking violently I managed to stop just before the runway's end. We had found Turayf.

We inched out in what was by now a heavy snowstorm to park alongside a Beaver aircraft, immediately recognisable as the one from my old base at Jeddah, and got transport to the accommodation reserved for guests and senior visiting officials. Here we were greeted by the Jeddah crew and their passengers. "Where have you come from?" asked the pilot who had cheered me on my way to hospital in England. He continued, "We landed about an hour ago with visibility down to three hundred yards and very low on fuel." I looked him in the eye and said, "They gave me a new set of kidneys in hospital which vastly improved my eyesight. I just eyeballed the road — easy." Howls of laughter all round, in which he joined.

In the hurry to vacate the Dove we had off-loaded all items of value and taken them to our rooms. Fortunately the customs did not inspect our bags because, without thinking, I had brought three bottles of whisky with me. There was no thought of taking the whisky back to the aircraft as the customs might decide to initiate a search before take-off. The next morning there was over a foot of snow and we were going nowhere. That night seven pilots polished off all three bottles without any problem.

It was another day before the runway could be cleared mainly with shovels and brooms. We made a two hour fifteen minute flight into Beirut with no more shocks on the way. However the ferry flight of the other Dove was a different matter. Gerrard and I had taken off from Tuayf on an overcast day and were flying at nine and a half thousand feet when we encountered icing conditions. We were about sixty miles south east of Damascus and I decided to drop down to a lower altitude because we had no de-icing equipment of any sort and the only solution was to keep in the lower, warmer levels or to return to Turayf which I was loath to do.

I called Damascus to explain the situation but did not receive any acknowledgement. The conditions were worsening and chunks of ice were now collecting on both propellers and breaking away to rattle along the side of the fuselage. Then two things happened together. Damascus came on the air with a course to steer and the curt instruction to climb immediately to fourteen thousand five hundred feet and to maintain this altitude until further notice, and Gerrard suddenly exclaimed in my ear "Paddy, bloody fighter on my side."

I looked past his head and sure enough there was a Syrian jet struggling to keep his speed down to ours. Gerrard had opened his window for a better view as the glass was completely iced over. The fighter pilot, his head just visible, was pointing violently upwards, indicating we should climb and the thought went through my head, "Or else!"

There appeared to be no inter-communication between us although I called continuously on the Damascus frequency. Gerrard indicated a downward movement with his hand that must have been seen by the jet. I reduced power to drop rapidly down and away from the jet, which, to our infinite relief, was not seen again. We broke through a scattered cloud base with ample air space above rugged mountainous terrain. We inched our way

256

through a gap in the range south of Baalbek to join the Beirut circuit with great relief. As Gerrard remarked when we were on the ground, "What is the fighter going to tell his boss about losing us?"

We tried another attempt with the Sikorskys. We installed a spare engine in the better of the two machines and switched main rotors. Log book entry for February 26th reads: '(My birfday 52) —WM blades fitted as best of bad lot — replacement engine fitted to G-APXF.'

It was safe enough to fly and I checked out a British pilot, Craig Anson, to fly the other machine on the assumption that another set of rotor blades could be found. This was not to be and it was rightly decided that unless it was possible to fly both machines in company, it was safer to truck them to Beirut. This was done just ahead of the civil war.

After the war I flew out to Beirut find them, but they had disappeared and Lloyds were unable to help. While I was there a massive bomb exploded in the University grounds uncomfortably close to my hotel.

It was off to Canada again in July 1974, with Mel O'Reilly, in another Alouette. We flew across from Calgary to Ontario to be based in a motel on the north side of Lake Shebandowan. We were fire fighting again. This was a huge conflagration in Quetico Provincial Park with many ground and aircrews involved. We flew in each day at dawn and returned at last light. We moved fire crews, pumps and all the associated equipment. All fires were numbered and ours was fifty-seven. Then another fire took us to southern areas of Ontario and yet another to a timber plantation near Thunder Bay. We were a long way from home.

On the homeward flight the radio went unserviceable and so it was not possible to contact any of the airports en route. We knew that Winnipeg airport would not let us refuel without radio contact but we also knew the Alouette would burn diesel fuel. In fact the fuel we were using then was JP4, which was basically diesel. We were following the Trans Canada highway west and when a convenient gas station appeared, we landed and to the astonishment of the female attendant we filled up with diesel.

After coffee and a snack we took off well satisfied with the turn of events and Mel was saying, "Lots of problems at Winnipeg. Even if we could get in without radio, they would probably not let us out without a lot of hassle." I was nodding when suddenly a bright red warning light lit up on the instrument panel indicating that the fuel line was blocked.

It was obvious that sooner rather than later the engine would suffer from fuel starvation and although fitted with a filter bypass, the engine might quit. So we put down on a piece of land which was obviously used for light aircraft. There was a Cessna and a wooden hangar but no people. Mel, good engineer that he was, had an adequate tool kit and we spent three hours draining the fuel and cleaning the supply pipes where a yellowish substance was building up. Mel said, "Just our bloody luck. It looks like this stuff has some sort of additive for diesel powered trucks, with piston engines." The substance was gummy and we had to use gasoline to clear it from the fuel pipes and parts of the engine. A local farmer drove us into Winnipeg where we bought a 45-gallon drum of the correct fuel. It was almost seven hours before Mel and I took off again.

"Do you know," said Mel "The sales distributors of these French designed helicopters have been heard to boast that their turbine engines can run on almost anything, including melted candle grease?"

Two chastened but wiser aircrew landed at Calgary.

By August I was flying a Bell 206 Jet Ranger moving men and equipment to the site of a new dam on a giant hydro-electric scheme for the production of electricity on a scale never before seen in Canada nor the United States. The whole operation was under the control of the *Societé d'Energie de la Baie James* based in Schefferville. For near enough five hundred miles west of Schefferville and over to Hudson Bay, the country was basically flat, with some low-lying scrub covered hills and without roads or means of surface communication of any kind. The engineer and I were based at Lac Brisay together with about twenty other crews and their helicopters. We all lived in tented accommodation. Another thirty or so helicopters were working off a smaller lake.

With deteriorating weather conditions, snow flurries, freezing rain and reduced visibility great care had to be taken to avoid the very real possibility of a collision. Unfortunately one of the local air traffic controllers refused to speak anything but French and for those of us who, like me, were not bi-lingual, very dangerous situations were to develop.

Winter had started early that year and when combined with the language problem it was something we could all do without. Logbook entry September 8th reads: 'Heavy snow unable go KA26 — return to camp visibility in very heavy snow down to quarter of a mile — language problem controller.' Again on September 12th: '06.45 off. Weather zero/zero at times en route drill site Lac Grande. Heavy snow and most unpleasant flight.'

It was with a feeling of relief that I left late in September in a passenger carriage attached to an iron ore train.

An offer came from a Gulf operating company in the Middle East to fly one of their Sikorsky 62 amphibians powered by a single General Electric 1200 horsepower gas turbine engine. This was to be another offshore oil operation based at Doha. It was more of an airline operation with rostered flights on a strict schedule and position reports to be made at various specified points. The maintenance was airline standard and excellent. Nevertheless, the age-old problems of sea fog, sand storms and limited visibility had not gone away.

With a load of nine passengers plus one in the co-pilot's seat we headed back from one of the offshore rigs. We were flying on a radio bearing and homing on an NDB, non-directional beacon, when an almost instant wall of fog blanked out the way ahead. We were three miles from the coast. As we neared the land, which was only intermittently visible, I was flying very slowly and just above the sea, maintaining some visual contact with the surface. Visibility was soon little more than two or three hundred yards and too risky to attempt to enter the docks area where there were a number of masted vessels and, at low level, a good chance of hitting one of them. I landed on the water to slowly taxi in, to hover off and land at the base. At the end of the contract I had flown three hundred and twenty hours bedevilled by fog a lot of the time. Logbook entry for January 23rd gives an indication:

'Doha — 'D' return flight dicey with 60 metres visibility in fog. Speed 10/15 knots at 5 feet on water with nil vis. Last five miles interesting!!' Rig to rig and into Doha was the pattern and deadly monotonous most of the time.

In the spring it was back to spraying phosphates on Forestry Commission pine tree plantations in Wales. To distribute the chemical, the Bell 47 was equipped with a large bucket mechanical spreader attached to the cargo hook under the machine. But because trees had often been planted on steeply sloped land which called for contour flying, the desired degree of accuracy was not always achieved. This was due in the main to the impractibility of marking the end of each run with balloons or with flags to allow a definite and accurate spacing between each pass.

Weather was the major hazard here also, strong winds in the higher mountainous sections created operational difficulties. The bucket-distributor with its six hundred pounds of fertilizer, was at its most efficient when flown over the canopy at about thirty feet but strong gusty winds made this both difficult and dangerous. Even at a speed of thirty miles per hour it was bad news if the bucket hit the treetops.

Nevertheless, weather permitting and the bucket behaving it was possible to move large tonnages in a day. Logbook entry for 10th May reads: 'Drop 18 tons super phosphate in three hours elapsed time.' At the end of that contract I left for Scotland and what I thought was a more mundane existence of pipeline patrol in the Edinburgh area.

The Bell 47 was a leased machine and, with a gas company official on board, we flew down the pipeline to check for gas leaks, vandalism or anything untoward. It was October and by evening we had checked many miles of pipeline and had refuelled at Prestwick Airport. We were on long approach for Edinburgh Airport when I detected a slight vibration. I landed, dropped off the observer and arranged our timetable for the next day. I had lifted off to fly the few hundred yards across the airfield to the normal parking point that was within a short walk to my hotel when, suddenly, at little more than a hundred feet, the vibration became severe and rapidly worsened. The machine became difficult to control and I quickly put down on the grass next to the taxiway. I shut off the engine and did a careful visual inspection of the machine and in particular the main rotor blades. I could find nothing wrong. In these circumstances there was no option but to send for an engineer from the leasing company.

Mid morning next day a very experienced engineer arrived whom I knew well. After a brief inspection he said, "You've been very lucky, Paddy. You've got a loose main rotor mast." He added, "How come you have no engineer on this job?" A good question, but this happened quite often. Constant expert preventative maintenance is absolutely essential for the safe operation of any rotary-wing aircraft and was often neglected in an effort to economise in the cutthroat business of getting lower than another company's bid to obtain the contract.

Gas pipeline patrol was generally flown at a height which seldom exceeded two hundred feet, and at a speed that varied between forty and sixty miles per hour. This height and speed permitting a reasonable scrutiny of the area directly above the buried pipe. In parts of England and Wales where there had been intensive coal mining, soil subsidence occurred and on one occasion was of such severity as to expose a section of pipe, requiring a repair crew immediately. I made a radio call and was told a crew would be on its way within the hour. We carried on along the line and the observer suddenly said, "What the hell are those people doing up there ahead?" Up ahead there were four or five figures who, as we approached, appeared to drop some tools and make off in the direction of the nearby village. We circled a large hole revealing a section of pipe with spades and tools scattered around. At that time such circumstances would have suggested IRA involvement.

The observer yelled excitedly, "Get the police out here, there's no company pipe work scheduled for this area." It took the police about twenty minutes to get there and as they drove their vehicle across the field to where we had landed the helicopter, five men were seen strolling back to the excavation. They gazed with astonishment at the helicopter and the police. It appeared they were pipeline workers who had finished one job earlier and simply moved on to the next job on their list and not told anybody. They were going off for a drink at the local pub when we saw them.

One day, following a major north-south pipeline which carried a pressure of one thousand pounds per square inch, we saw a recently constructed children's playground built over the top. Hard to credit but the local council was unaware of the pipe's existence and so, in effect had built the playground on top of a potential land mine. Pipes could and did fracture to blast the covering soil for hundreds of yards. The observer said, "They will have to rip all that out under our supervision. Someone on that council is due for a rocket." How could the council not know the pipeline was there? They must have given permission for the pipeline to be installed in the first place.

In April 1976 I was in Qatar, geological surveying in the super hot desert. In the autumn I was flying pipeline patrol in the Yorkshire Dales. We were flying along, minding our own business, when there was a tremendous 'swoosh' and in front and slightly below us a jet fighter was rapidly disappearing.

The observer was shouting in my ear, " Holy smoke, he went under us and could have hit us — we must report this to Civil Aviation!"

"No way," I retorted. "It was probably a NATO aircraft. It could have come from anywhere in Europe and was probably authorised for low flying. I'd be filling in forms for the next three months and nothing would happen."

I told him the best course of action was probably to invest in a rear view mirror, like fighter pilots did in the Battle of Britain — at their own expense.

It was more than likely that the fighter hadn't seen us. Nor would he know of our presence on a low level inspection. The military are a law unto themselves and always have been.

I went to Rhodesia in November 1976. It was governed by Ian Smith who headed a locally formed administration described by the British Government as an illegal regime. I had witnessed the transfer of twentieth century power by colonial governments to people with no idea of how to rule with efficiency and justice, but with easy access to a private Swiss bank account. It was a policy which had spawned corruption and barbarism on a grand scale.

Ethiopia has had self-rule for over a thousand years and still the population starves.

My business in Rhodesia kept me in Salisbury, now Harare, for a week. The country appeared to be well governed since Independence, but operating under very difficult conditions largely as a result of trade and other sanctions imposed by the UK. Rhodesia, being a land-locked country, even had a permanent British naval vessel on patrol off Beira, Mozambique to turn back any vessels suspected of carrying embargoed goods for onward carriage overland. All British registered aircraft and airlines were also forbidden to carry any such supplies in or out. However one owner/operator flew regular sanction-busting flights into Switzerland to collect essential articles of various kinds. These included air force blue material obtained from Poland. All transactions were in cash, carried on the outgoing flight.

Local people were beginning to carry side arms, very worried about the build up of troops and material, paid for by Russia and with Cuban personnel, within the adjacent Portuguese possession of Angola.

Many Rhodesians had come to England in the Second World War to help us against the Germans and here they were now, being cut off from everything they had helped to save. I had spent my life fighting against communist precepts in any shape or form and in November 1976 I was accepted for military combat duties flying helicopters at the Rhodesian Air Force Base of New Sarum with the rank of Flight Lieutenant. It was a strange experience putting on a uniform almost identical to that of the Royal Air Force which I had last worn over twenty years before. This time in a war against Soviet-backed so-called 'freedom fighters' determined to bring down a productive and orderly state, the so-called 'bread basket' of Africa.

The Queen's portrait still hung in the Officer's Mess and many of the older members had served in the British military. There were also a few Americans who had flown in Vietnam. Because of our ages we were known as 'The Retreads.'

I had been posted for conversion training to a twin-engined Dakota C47 Transport Squadron because the Commanding Officer of the helicopter unit had insisted that my age did not permit the skill required to pilot Alouette gunships and that a fixed-wing role of a more passive nature would be of more use to the Air Force.

This decision was not to my liking of course as my experience of heavy fixed-wing flying was extremely limited. However, I went solo in under seven hours. I had no wartime experience to draw on to fly wholly on instruments. As a helicopter pilot I was used to Arctic whiteout and desert sandstorm flying, but I always managed to achieve a visual landing. Now I had to learn to fly blind take-offs and landings. I flew a total of twenty-five hours including ten hours on instruments. At times I thought 'If I'm supposed to be too old to fly these peoples' helicopters, what sort of madness possessed me to be flying this?'

My involvement was not utilising my considerable experience as a rotary pilot. I flew a few flights as co-pilot including picking up Ian Smith and his wife from their farm to fly them into the Air Base. The Dakota's main role was split between food and provision supply to isolated field units and parachuting troops into critical operational areas. These aircraft were often hit by well-directed fire from the bush-covered ground. I had contacts in South Africa and knew that they were flying French manufactured equipment including Alouette and Pumas, and were having similar problems as the Rhodesians with Communist infiltrated armed terrorists.

Before committing myself to a course of action, my colleague in London contacted me. He had a Sikorsky 55, which had been in Rhodesia for about four years, hangared in a nearby civilian maintenance unit. Because of Mr Smith's UDI, the ownership of this or any other aircraft registered in the name of a British subject involved complex legal problems if it was desired to fly it out of the country and, in this case, to South Africa.

As an Irish citizen and as the registered owner, I could fly it out. He expressed me the ownership papers while I checked over the machine. He thought that Rhodesia had but a short time to survive and that political pressure would force Mr Smith out, to bring in a Communist sponsored native regime, which would 'liberate' any tangible foreign assets they came across. He was to be proved correct in both assumptions.

With help from one of the helicopter squadron's engineers, the big Wright Cyclone radial engine was made serviceable and the machine checked over thoroughly by a maintenance company on the airfield at Old Sarum.

Two days after my 55th birthday in February, we got the old Sikorsky into the air on its first test flight. I made numerous flights from that time to mid-March without any trouble. On St Patrick's Day I confess to a sadistic delight in putting on a display of helicopter aerobatics for the benefit of the Alouette Squadron on the other side of the airfield. I heard later that this was something of an eye-opener for the CO and his pilots. A visiting Group Captain from HQ was heard to say, "Is that the helicopter pilot we interviewed at Christmas? How did he end up in a Dakota Squadron when we are so desperately short of helicopter pilots?" This same officer was to send me my Rhodesian Air Force Commissioning scroll later.

An American pilot who was also leaving the Air Force and was to accompany me as co-pilot on the flight south, gleefully reported all this to me. He was a very experienced in aerial combat with a number of decorations earned in Vietnam. He had been given the run-around by some Rhodesian Officers who had resented his well-proven ability and some suggestions he had made for operational improvements may have been seen as criticism.

Our destination in South Africa was to be Grand Central, a small airfield midway between Johannesburg and Pretoria, which would involve a flight of about five hundred and seventy miles. In theory the Sikorsky was capable of completing the distance in a little over five hours plus the time required for a landing to refuel. I planned to keep the helicopter at tree top level until we crossed the South African border, thus by reducing line of sight, would afford only a momentary glimpse of the machine to gunners on the ground.

The machine was equipped with dual controls and we took turns either to fly or to sort out the navigation. At this height the maps were practically useless and, since we had no electronic navigational aids, this low level operation with only a magnetic compass for guidance was to have its moments.

Fort Victoria, one hundred and fifty miles south of Salisbury, was the first calling point for fuel. This engine was a thirsty brute consuming at least forty gallons an hour, giving us little more than three hours flying, allowing a safety margin. This leg had taken one hour fifty minutes, much longer than normal for the distance, due to strong headwinds. The next leg would take us to the customs entry airport of Messina in the Republic. This was an extremely unpleasant flight. The wind had increased and some of the terrain was very rugged with no friendly road to follow.

SAM heat-seeking missiles had been used against South African military aircraft operating along the border with Angola, almost certainly fired by Russian or Cuban 'volunteers'. Very low-flying aircraft were reasonably safe from this unwelcome attention but to ascend to anything more than eight hundred feet was potentially very dangerous. It was a turbulent two hours over the Limpopo river boundary to Beitbridge.

We called Messina on the radio but had no reply, and we discovered after we landed without speaking to anybody that the airfield was deserted. It was almost two hours before Customs and Immigration officials arrived. In the meanwhile Joe and I made a thorough inspection of the old Sikorsky and apart from a minor oil leak it was in good shape. For my part there was an immense relief that we had managed to get the machine out of the clutches of the rogue regime that would, undoubtedly, be installed in the country as its new rulers.

The customs man said, "We weren't expecting any flights today, but I see from the paperwork that this machine once belonged to the South African Air Force — welcome home." We topped up the tank and added a quantity of engine oil before lifting off for the next leg of one hundred and thirty-five miles to Potgietersrus. A distinctive ridge of mountains appeared ahead, marked on the map as the South Pan with a height of almost six thousand feet. To avoid the inconvenience of a climb to clear it we followed the railroad from Messina through a natural pass. After an hour and fifty minutes we landed at Potgietersrus, refuelled and took off to overfly Pretoria in the dark and finally landed at Grand Central. We had completed the whole flight in one day: seven hours and twenty minutes flying time.

On 5th April I carried the logbooks and documents relating to the helicopter into the London office. My intention was to immediately return to South Africa but I was offered one or two small immediate contracts. One was the delivery of an agricultural equipped Hughes 300 to Chartres and en route to check out the French pilot and endorse him on type. "Why me?" I asked, "Surely there is another pilot to do that?"

He replied, "Because the helicopter is on the French registry, and they need an experienced agricultural pilot to check out the French pilot. You are an obvious choice. Furthermore, it appears that because you trained in France and held a French licence, the authorities over there are prepared to accept you in this very temporary role. Nuff said?"

I grinned widely, remembering that the instructor who had checked me out all those years before could speak little English and I spoke even less French.

CHAPTER FIFTEEN

The S.A.A.F and After

THE SOUTH AFRICAN AIR FORCE COMMISSIONED ME IN the rank of Major, the appointment to be taken up in late July 1977. In the meantime I had a living to earn.

In June I went to Georgetown, Guyana to look at the possibility of buying a DC3 from a local airline. Shortly after my arrival I learned that a competitor had secured the best of the available machines but this disappointment was to have a profitable sequel. A visit to the local military air base revealed that the army was flying modern jet turbine machines including twin-engined Bell 212s, and it crossed my mind that we could perhaps get a contract to supply spares.

Talking to the Major in charge, we discussed business for a while and then when he found I was a helicopter pilot he said, "I don't suppose that you're interested but we have an old Bell 47 which was given to us by an international bank. Would you like to see it?" We went round the back of the hangar and there, partially covered by brambles and jungle growth, was the remains of a fairly late model Bell 47G5. The Perspex canopy was gone and the machine was covered in a mixture of grease and mud. The tail rotor assembly had been broken off and was lying on the ground below the tail boom. I asked where the rotors were and he pointed to the other side of the helicopter. There they were on the ground, stacked on top of each other. This model Bell was equipped with metal main rotor blades and apart from being very dirty, they did not appear to have suffered any discernable damage and might well be serviceable after professional checks for invisible damage such as internal corrosion.

My past experience in the field of salvaging aircraft helped me establish that there was no perceivable damage in the all important central basket or airframe which housed the engine, main rotor gearbox, the centrifugal clutch, free wheel unit and gearing for the tail rotor drive shaft and, of course, the vertical drive shaft to the main rotor. All of these items were seemingly in place.

Incredibly, since it had been built in Fort Worth its logbook had registered less than four hundred hours where one might have expected thousands. As an old engineering friend said, "Provided that you have a piece of tubing with the legal serial number of the helicopter stamped on it and the relevant log books, you have a helicopter." The bank was still the legal owner and it had repossessed it from a foreign consortium who had used it to fly out alluvial gold, dredged from rivers. The bank sold it to me for little more than scrap value which was considerably less than the cost of shipping it back to England on a Demerara sugar boat from Georgetown. It was rebuilt and put on the British registry and sprayed crops in Northamptonshire for at least four years.

Towards the end of July I had taken up my appointment and was stationed at Swartkop Air Force Base near Pretoria awaiting a conversion course onto the twin-engined, medium sized, troop carrier Puma. These were made under licence in South Africa. Shortly after arrival from Europe, Air HQ, to my astonishment, informed me that although part of my wartime aircrew service had been as a commissioned officer, it was in the capacity of an air gunner and not a pilot. Therefore it was required that the necessary military aviation training to be undertaken on the Base to qualify me for the award of South African Air Force Pilot's Wings. It came as a complete surprise that they should only tell me this now since they had been aware of these facts when I had been interviewed.

In Europe there was a lot of talk of non-South African volunteers being mercenaries but the pay, after tax, was less than five hundred and fifty pounds sterling per month, hardly a mercenary's motivation to fight. My own reason for being there had little to do with money but rather an increasingly old fashioned idea about the evil influence of Communism. I still had vivid memories of a red star on a khaki cap on a Malayan plantation so many years before.

Now in my 56th year it was necessary from the military point of view to attend, as a student, a course of flying instruction to 'wings standard' before becoming operational. Marty, the Officer

Commanding 17 Squadron remarked, "You'll be doing the training course on the Alouette. It may sound a bit crazy but that's what they want and how can you lose? The military system differs considerably from civilian practice and you'll find precision flying more exacting in an academic sense than anything you may have experienced in the more practical commercial flying world."

Marty proved to be prophetic. He was to be my instructor on several occasions and my dual cross country night flight to Rustoenburg and back had him on board. The discipline required to maintain exact altitudes with an allowed variation not exceeding twenty-five feet either way when flying the Swartkop landing circuit, took some acquiring along with the equally stringent rules applied to the consistency of airspeeds in practice engine-off auto rotations onto a runway.

Including the pilot, the Alouette 3 was capable of carrying six or seven people and was equipped with a larger turbine engine than its smaller sister, the Alouette 2. In an anti-terrorist operation, fitted with a 20 millimetre cannon, with fuel tanks and a considerable quantity of armour plate, it seldom carried more than the pilot and gunner/observer. In fact, on a hot day, up on the Angolan border, it was often a struggle to get off the ground even with this restricted loading.

Between the 3rd and 29th of August I had thirteen hours of dual instruction on the Alouette covering a variety of exercises. One of the instructors specialised in engine-off full autorotations, always landing at twenty-five miles an hour or more on smooth surfaced runways. One day, after another of these arrivals, I remarked, "If you have to do this for real in the bush, its surface will not be this kind and you're going to end up in a rolled up ball of metal!"

This comment evoked the response, "Well, Major, I'm sure that in that case I can get it to touch down with zero forward airspeed." There was an obvious reluctance to instruct zero ground speed autorotations, undoubtedly based on the fear of hitting the tail rotor on the ground in the required low level flare. There were many other exercises on this course, including loading and off-loading troops in a low hover, winching, confined area landings and simulated air to ground firing. I did a successful course termination test in mid September, officially recorded as an 'Alouette (3) Conversion Course'. The flying assessment on the certificate reads: 'General Flying: High Average and both Night Flying and Navigation: Proficient. Total Flying Time: 13,600 hours and ten minutes.'

Because of having to wait for this course I lost out on the Puma course and the next one wouldn't be before the following March at the earliest. No flying was permitted unless an airman or an NCO, frequently a qualified gunner, was a member of the crew. Their function, even when operating off a completely clear parade ground, was to lean out of the passenger compartment on the left of the machine to look back and check the tail rotor for sufficient ground or bush clearance, as applicable, before giving the pilot a hand signal that he was clear to land or lift-off.

My wings were pinned on my tunic by a General at Headquarters with the smiling comment, "We decided against the conventional presentation parade to avoid publicity and thereby discourage ex-air gunners and would-be pilots coming out here to join us." It was a proud moment.

There was a further delay in the Puma course and, as my original agreement centred around the flying of medium heavy, multi-engined helicopters, in weight similar to those flown on offshore operations, the postponement was a disappointment.

The Air Force was operating a number of Super Frelon heavy lift helicopters powered by three turbine engines. They were capable of transporting military vehicles and field guns which could be loaded up a ramp fitted aft. Number 15 Squadron, also based at Swartkop, flew these and it came to my notice that they were going to run a conversion course in the New Year. Accordingly I approached the Commandant with "What chance of getting on the Frelon course?" "Well," he retorted, "you are well acquainted with the OC of that squadron, you and he flew that old Sikorsky to the museum at Lanseria, but wait for the Puma course, we can use you on military ferry work in the meantime."

In retrospect, that would have been the thing to do but he'd got me listed for the Frelon course so it was now obvious that there was likely to be several weeks, at the best, of restricted flying activity ahead so I attended the military Afrikaans Language

271

Institute in Pretoria and, with a background of reasonable German, found it easy to learn.

My rank gave me seniority second only to the Commandant or the other Major who was deputy Squadron Leader. I still had no active service time, unlike most of the junior officers and this made me uncomfortable. I asked to be posted to Border country for active duty and got the usual reply, "Your age is against you for helicopter gunship activities in a war zone." I carried on doing air ambulance flights, troop deployments and stores movements.

In November, attired in brown army bush fatigues and floppy khaki hat, I took the army bus to Waterloof Military airfield where I boarded a C130 for the flight to Windhoek on the first leg to Caprivi Strip for active service. This was a two hundred and forty mile long narrow neck of land which had Angola and Zambia for its northern boundary and Botswana on the south. A thin wedge to the east touched the far north-western corner of Rhodesia and from this point it was about fifty miles to the Victoria Falls. The pilots of 17 Squadron did a tour of duty in this area on a roster basis. Some patrolled the strip while others patrolled the Angolan border. Their basic function was reconnaissance, working closely with army ground units in an attempt to eliminate the infiltration of heavily armed Russian or Cuban terrorists into the populous area of Windhoek.

All six Alouettes were protected by sheets of armour plate under the floor. The pilot had an additional piece fitted behind his backrest. The large jet exhaust was modified and deflected upwards to thwart SAM heat seeking missiles. We carried either a twenty millimetre cannon mounted by the left rear door or 0·5 Browning machine gun. The armour plate was to protect the occupants from the ground fire, encountered frequently in some areas, chiefly because of the altitudes at which we were required to fly. The most dangerous height was anything more than five hundred feet. SAM missiles were being fired from just inside the Angolan border and anything higher than five hundred feet gave them the necessary space to 'latch on'. With few landmarks, navigation at tree top height was difficult as we only had a magnetic compass and a radio.

I spent Christmas Day 1977 here, but to lighten the

atmosphere we entertained a female Army Captain to Christmas lunch. Fiona was extremely intelligent, very attractive, even in fatigues, and spoke six languages. Her high female voice could be heard above all the lower male tones in the Mess so she was called 'Hi Fi'. She was later to receive the Presidential Medal.

In January 1978 I was recalled to Pretoria to do the technical course on the Frelon. This had to be completed before any flying training could take place. This was delayed again and so I returned to Caprivi Strip until March. One dark wet night my mission was to airlift a very pregnant black lady from a distant village to the local hospital. The villagers lit a bonfire to guide me in. The return flight was a race against time and she gave birth less than five minutes after we landed in the hospital compound. It was a boy and was duly named Copter. On another occasion near the Botswana border, an old man had been gored by a buffalo. A passing military ground patrol radioed for us and we went to pick him up. Unfortunately he died before we reached hospital.

The helicopters flying at low level were extremely useful for following terrorist tracks through the bush. Working with ground troops we were able to direct them along trails that were only discernable from the air. In some instances two helicopters worked together as a team. One would fly very slowly and low over dense bush in order to spot and to follow any trail of disturbed undergrowth. Meanwhile the other Alouette, in constant radio communication, would be slowly circling about eight hundred feet up to provide top cover with its cannon.

Such operations were potentially dangerous of course as top cover flying invited the attention of SAM missiles.

The Super Frelon technical course occupied three weeks in April, covering the airframe, engines and performance specifications for this very large helicopter. There were five other regular Air Force Officers on this intake and I finished in a satisfying fourth place. It had been a long time since I had last done such intensive studying.

The Commandant of the Frelon Squadron that I knew had

been posted and his deputy had taken his place. He was one of the few Afrikaners who resented the presence of overseas volunteers in the Air Force and was not forthcoming with assistance or advice to guide me through what was, in effect a conversion course onto a new type. My exercise had commenced on 16th May and after a row with this officer terminated on 5th June with a total of twelve hours logged instruction. During this period of nineteen days, I had been subjected to veiled dumb insolence from this officer. I was not to graduate. It is of interest to note that in any event Air Force regulations would have required me to fly as co-pilot for twelve months before being promoted to a command. It could be argued that during such a prolonged period any alleged shortcomings could have been remedied. I understand that this officer was later severely criticised, but it was with much regret that I resigned my commission after barely a year of service.

I went back to Canada on a survey project flying an Alouette 2, based at Grand Prairie, Alberta. The work was interesting and varied covering geological mapping and marine drilling on behalf of a company which was primarily an operator of earth moving equipment. Although the flying was very intensive the field maintenance of the helicopter was almost non-existent. It was an oft-repeated story of a licensed engineer only being called in when there was a legal requirement to do so. It says much for the Alouette that it flew in excess of one hundred and eighty hours during a six-week period, most of the time without a mechanic.

This flying had included the rescue of a power boat crew which had run aground during a international boat race on a nearby river. We gave our assistance with two forest fires and undertook a flight on one hundred and forty miles to a downed Gazelle to pick up its two crew. We took a new fuel control unit with us to replace the faulty one, which had caused the Gazelle's turbine to flame out and the crew to make a safe autorotative landing.

In September I had fun flying a Piper Tripacer for joy rides round Blackpool Airport. I did five-minute flights from take-off into wind and returning to land downwind, with tower clearance. My logbook entry for one day notes twenty-two flights and sixty-six passengers. It was not all round Blackpool Tower. Some flights were up to Morecambe or Lancaster and afforded me the opportunity of working up sightseeing patter for the passengers.

I was contracted to revisit Guyana to look at an extensively damaged twin Bell 212. This machine was being operated by the military at the time of the crash and would have been one of the machines in the hangar when I bought the Bell 47, which the bank had owned. The accident had occurred on the edge of a river separating Guyana from Surinam and not the safest area to operate in. Both countries were in dispute and had fortified posts on both sides of the river. Our interest was in salvage and rebuild for onward sale. If our bid was successful the military would have to lift out the damaged machine with another Bell 212. They flew me from Georgetown one hundred and ninety-five miles south to the crash site, where, in a skilful manoeuvre the pilot landed me close by the damaged helicopter. It was a round trip of three hours fifty minutes over mosquito-ridden swamp. Not a pleasant flight.

Going back to my hotel that night a small party of Americans was being greeted by a local reception committee in the foyer. They were surrounded by a lot of professional cameramen and photographic equipment. I was told that they were some kind of religious group and that one was a US Senator or Congressman. The manager of the hotel told me this sect had a large commune of around a thousand people to the north of Georgetown, close to the border with Venezuela. There was a DH Otter out at the airport ready to fly the American group out to the commune the next day. The manager grinned at me and said, "You should be pleased — the commune is called Jonestown."

The next morning my usual driver was not available to take me to the airport, he was busy ferrying the Americans and as I got to the airport these people were boarding the twin Otter to fly to the commune. The next day the press was full of the unbelievably horrifying mass suicide or massacre of all of the commune's inhabitants: men, women and even children which had occurred there.

When I returned to Georgetown a week later my Canadian engineer told me a curious story. It appeared that two days after the killings the Air Force had sent one of their large helicopters out to the commune and Jim had gone along to keep a watching brief on the engines. At this stage it seemed that there was

275

considerable uncertainty as to what had actually happened. Jim said, "We flew at about one thousand feet and even a mile or so from the commune, the rancid decaying smell of death was everywhere." He went on to say that after landing it was discovered that quite a few of the corpses had been shot through the head and it certainly appeared that, at the last minute, many had refused to obey the order of their religious leader and take the poison.

He also said there was a rumour circulating that an armed party in military camouflage had been seen about this time, heading towards the border with Venezuela, a country violently opposed to the Marxist rule in Guyana. I had earlier been told in 1977 that a Venezuelan government delegation had visited Georgetown for discussions with Guyanan government officials and had been scheduled to remain for two weeks but left hurriedly after only forty-eight hours and without explanation.

To a large extent law and order had broken down in Guyana. Georgetown was an unsafe city to move around in, even during the day. It was unwise to wear anything that looked expensive or carry other than a very small amount of cash. As her taxi stopped at traffic lights on the way to the airport, one airline stewardess had her finger neatly removed with a knife by a thug. He had reached through the open window and failed to get the engagement ring off her finger so had removed both ring and finger together. Thefts from foreigners happened all of the time. An American lady standing outside the main door of the hotel waiting for a taxi had her necklace wrenched off by a passing youth.

Our bid for the crashed helicopter was rejected but it was bought by an American friend of mine. Barry told me that the military had refused to let him take the controls of their helicopter in the initial, extremely marginal manoeuvre required to lift the damaged machine vertically upward and out from the jungle. The ordinary army pilots were deemed too inexperienced for such a dangerous operation so their most senior pilot was flying their helicopter when, after a successful lift-off from the confined clearing, the underslung load began to oscillate violently as the machine gathered speed in forward flight. It seemed the pilot was unaware of the action he should take to combat the problem and, close to his machine becoming totally uncontrollable, he jettisoned Barry's newly acquired helicopter from one hundred and fifty feet to the jungle floor.

Barry said, "No sweat, I'd taken out insurance to cover this possibility," and the insurance people were no doubt completely satisfied with what, on paper, suggested a highly experienced senior military pilot carrying out a difficult job. Barry collected a very reasonable sum and followed this up by purchasing from the insurance company, for a pittance, what was now a very battered semblance of a helicopter and got most of it back to Georgetown from where it eventually went back to the States to be rebuilt.

I travelled on from Guyana to Uruguay to look at the possibility of purchasing surplus military equipment including a WWII Mustang fighter and in conversation with an Air Force officer the subject of cars came up. Many of the vehicles around Montevideo were Model T Fords and a car collector friend in London had asked me to look into the possibility of acquiring one. I found that although I could purchase one of them easily, to get it out of the country would be quite another matter.

The Air Force officer told me the following story; "About three years ago," he said, "an Englishmen went into the interior to locate a car called an Invecta, a very rare type of racing car of Great War vintage. He found the farm and a very elderly English lady answered the door. He introduced himself, and she told him the car had gone. Her late husband had sold it to another Englishman some years before. Then she added that she still had the aeroplane which her husband had been flying up to two weeks before he died. "He had brought it back from France after WWI when he was a pilot in the Royal Flying Corps."

He accompanied the old lady to a shed over an overgrown grass runway and inside the shed sat a Sopwith Camel. With great excitement he bought the machine from her and spent the next few days cleaning it up until he managed to start the engine. In the meantime local farm workers had cleared the runway.

The Camel with its Rhone Rotary engine was worth a King's Ransom had he cased it up and transported it out by road, but he attempted a take-off and halfway down the field it flipped over, caught fire and was destroyed. Fortunately he wasn't hurt. He was an experienced pilot but was not aware that this unusual and for its time, revolutionary engine with its radial cylinders literally turned with the aircraft's propeller and produced a torque effect strong enough — when applying full power for take-off — to toss the whole aircraft onto its back.

After that I was contracted on behalf of Queen Charlotte Helicopters in Canada to fly for their lumber company. The Queen Charlotte Islands are in the Pacific, fifty miles west of Prince Rupert, British Columbia. The town of Queen Charlotte lies across the inlet on Graham Island. Our base was at Sandspit, and that name describes it exactly. These densely forested islands have some of the largest and tallest trees in the world. It was not uncommon for them to attain heights in excess of two hundred and fifty feet. Most of the special wood used in the manufacture of Mosquito aircraft came from these islands.

The vast lumber operation included three jet turbine Bell 206s, a Hughes 500D and two DH Beaver float planes. Frank Beban, who looked like Hollywood's idea of a lumberjack, owned the company. I have never worked for a better company chairman. The Hughes was a pilot's machine; a joy to fly but cramped, noisy and uncomfortable for any passengers. The maintenance set-up was excellent. There was no hotel but Frank had one erected from prefabricated sections which arrived on a train of barges hauled from Vancouver Island by tugs.

Lyell Island, the principal source of lumber, lay due south of Sandspit. The island was interlaced with logging roads which were often wet and muddy, built on precipitous mountain contours. The predicable result was that massive and heavily laden vehicles slipped off the track. It was usually possible on this well equipped island with specialised lifting gear, to retrieve a vehicle but not its displaced cargo.

Lyell Island was normally a thirty-minute flight from Sandspit in the Jet Ranger. However, high ground on a direct route involving a flight at three thousand feet above sea level, often increased that time due to low cloud, which could force us to fly

278

along the coast and across a considerable area of very cold sea. The constant presence of often dense sea fog made for some very unpleasant flying.

Gold had once been discovered on Graham Island and more recently another similar find had been reported. This had the predictable effect of pulling in a lot of prospectors. We were put to use moving complete tent camps and their inhabitants from one rugged site to another and in assisting pegging claims by recently arrived prospectors.

In June, an urgent message was received at Sandspit. A seaman on the American *MV Philadelphia* had suffered a stroke and immediate hospitalisation was essential. The position of the vessel was given as ten miles north-west of Langara Island en route for Seattle. Because of my considerable experience of offshore flying it was agreed I would take the flight. The *Philadelphia* was a container ship and we sighted it with no trouble and radio contact confirmed that it had a helicopter-landing pad on which we promptly put down. But it was with considerable difficulty that the patient was hoisted up onto the flight deck from the living quarters two decks below. This took almost an hour and all the time the ship was drawing away from the land, making at least twenty knots. Although we had more than sufficient fuel for the return flight, my concern, as usual, was with the fast deteriorating weather and the banks of low thunder-clouds building up along the now distant shore. In the event, the return flight was without difficulty and the old man made a good recovery in hospital.

Although quantities of massive logs were rafted by the lumber company to various destinations, the majority were transported by specially equipped ships which anchored at the entrance to the inlets where there were small seas of floating logs and giant lifting gear to hoist them on board. These ships were crewed by men who flew up from Seattle twice a week on a chartered jet and our three helicopters stood by at the airport to take them out to the ship. The flight called for no particular skill, but landing on a vessel, often cluttered with cables, winches and derricks, called for a certain amount of 'know how', particularly in a rolling sea.

These crews had a distinct preference for the Bell Jet Rangers.

279

There was always a concerted rush to get aboard them rather than into the cramped passenger space on the faster Hughes 500. I used the 500 on timber cruising; a method of inspecting densely forested areas. With the observer beside me in the roomy 500 cockpit it was very comfortable but if you were a passenger squashed into a cramped space and deafened by a very noisy transmission system, it was a different matter altogether. Its four short-bladed articulated main rotor was an advantage when landing in very enclosed clearings and its vertical lifting ability with an underslung load was superior in all respects;

The machines used to be an attraction on the Vancouver, British Columbia, Hospital fête days. And I was told that I would be an attraction to the 'older gals'. I had no rejoinder to this slur but it was a successful day — my flight log records the uplift of 106 adults and 110 children on pleasure trips.

At the end of July 1979 I went by rail from Queen Charlotte up through Squamish to Whistler at the base of the Blackcombe Mountains. The skiing areas on Mount Whistler were poorly equipped and a very small village provided accommodation. I was to be substitute pilot for a week on an Alouette 2. The flying was a log removal operation in order to clear a downhill area for the first real commercial ski slope on the mountain. Two powerful heavy lift helicopters carried underslung great tree trunks from where they'd been felled down into the valley below.

The proposed starting point for the ski run was at around six thousand feet so the work these pilots were doing was not for the fainthearted. My job was merely to collect the rope 'chokers' from the dumped logs. I flew them back up to leave them close to the next log to be hoisted into the air, where ground handlers attached the long line from the high hovering helicopter to the log. At times other equipment had to be moved and because the slope was still covered in tree stumps, branches and up-ended massive roots, it could be very difficult to find a safe landing spot to off-load.

There was little time in the air because of the short distances involved but it was all very trying on the nervous system and I was more than delighted to hand over to the regular pilot. Sadly this helicopter crashed a week later. An eighteen-year-old ground handler lost a leg and one man was badly gashed. The pilot escaped unhurt. The police reported that the rugged terrain hampered rescue efforts.

As I was about to leave Vancouver for Calgary, the owner of a local helicopter company contacted me. He had been in touch with Calgary in an effort to find a pilot for a delivery flight and Calgary had given him my name. When we met we both realised that we had flown together before in Dawson Creek. Now he had a Jet Ranger with mechanical problems at the north end of Lake Winnipeg. He had the spares and an engineer ready to go in two days time and although I had my plane ticket booked for London, the chance of flying the helicopter a thousand miles across Canada was too good to pass up. "Where's the ultimate destination?" I asked, "Vancouver?" "No." he said, "Its our old sparring ground — Dawson Creek. No mud there these days. You can walk around without leaving your boots behind!" None of us who had flown on the Defence Line would ever forget the tenacity of the spring mud.

Mark, the engineer, and I subsequently flew up to Lake Winnipeg and into Norway House, a small settlement on the northern shore. We had the machine operational by the late afternoon and finished off some of the jobs which had not been done because of its unserviceability. We ferried fire hoses, portable fire pumps and other associated items back to the airfield from outlying bases. Many of the local Indians had been on the fire fighting crews and they helped me locate a large, very expensive water dropping bucket which had been lost in a swamp.

On August 13th we left on the first leg to Dawson Creek. This first leg was worrying because the one hundred and fifty miles into the settlement of The Pas was over mostly uninhabited swampy terrain, and great stretches of open water. Our radio was not functioning and a forced landing would be bad news. It need scarcely be mentioned that the helicopter was not equipped with flotation gear nor Mae West life jackets.

But we got to Edmonton without incident. We were both tired and hungry and made for the hotel where, we had been told we had reservations. None had been made. I had no intention of paying for my own accommodation and Mark, a company employee, eventually got through to the company owner, who complained we had got him out of bed. He asked waspishly, "Why doesn't the pilot use his credit card?" "Tell him I haven't got one," I replied. In the end the owner made arrangements to pay our hotel bill, but these things leave a nasty taste. It is one reason why I only ever carried cash when working. I was paid eventually for the flight but the company went into liquidation by the end of the year.

In August I had a business trip to Norway and another to Uganda. Entebbe's Lake Side Hotel, a model of its kind on the side of Lake Victoria had been looted and stripped of everything of any value. Vandalism on an immense scale was very obvious and those who had worked hard in that country had all been expelled.

CHAPTER SIXTEEN

Return to the Americas

I RETURNED TO CANADA IN MAY 1970 TO FLY THE LARGER model Bell 204B, which was similar to the 'Hughie' of the Vietnam War. We were employed by the Alberta Forest Service but before the contract started Howdy McPhail approached me and offered me five days flying, spraying a caterpillar infestation in a Cessna 188 Ag Wagon. My logbook entry reads: 'Wingman spraying beetles Meadow Lake Farms — two aircraft loose formation.'

Howdy was the other pilot. He has since died.

The Bell 204B was powered by a large single turbine and could accommodate eight passengers and lift close on four thousand pounds in a under slung 'water bombing' fire fighting bucket. This machine was one of several acquired from Thailand where they had been used on police security operations. Unfortunately the owner of the Canadian company which had imported these machines had been killed when flight-testing one of them. The cause was thought to be mechanical failure. My engineer was one of the best in Canada, Red MacKinnon, with whom I had previously worked in Ontario in 1968.

On May 15th, Red and another engineer, Gunther, flew with me on a fire fighting operation in the Lesser Slave Lake 'Provincial Park' of Northern Alberta and we landed at Inverness Camp to begin moving crews around what, on the map, is marked as a 'Park' but is in effect a wilderness. On the 17th we experienced rain showers, hail and lightning strikes which started numerous bush fires, some of which we extinguished by water bombing. My logbook reads: 'Water bomb fire, 25 trips, average load in bucket 3,500 pounds.'

Red usually came along on these forays, to guide me in the visual placement of the water bucket on the lake and, by dunking it in a low hover, effect a refill. This could be a tricky manoeuvre over a forested swamp hole or a clearing partially obscured by smoke and burning cinders.

All airborne forest fire fighting techniques, which must include large fixed-wing aircraft dropping water or fire retardent, are much the same across Canada or the States, but this small operation in Northern Alberta gave me cause for concern with the machine's maintenance.

The tail rotor transmission drive shaft started to throw out a considerable quantity of grease where it emerged from the main gearbox. This should have been a sealed bearing. Red repacked the bearing every time we came in and had ordered a new unit from base but this showed no sign of arriving. We had no idea how long we could carry on continually repacking the bearing before it seized. We now tried not to fly more than two hours before repacking it again.

This unhappy situation, disquieting at best, was to be compounded by other problems. My logbook records: '27th — low stratus cloud — crew moves — aircraft u/s again — engineer neglected to reconnect oil pipe and blew up air cooler.' Gunther was the culprit, but Red and I were to blame for not running a check after packing the defective bearing with yet more grease. By June 2nd, because of heavy rain, the fires were subdued and I handed over to a relief pilot while I flew to the Quebec—Labrador border to deal with work on the railroad. I showed my relief pilot around the machine, especially emphasising the bearing problem. He was a very experienced recently retired military man with around ten thousand hours to his credit.

On 15th June, Trans-Quebec helicopters at Seven Islands put me through a proficiency check on the Bell Jet Ranger and cleared me for a month's flying. Even though it was June, rain, snow and sleet with night temperatures below freezing were the norm. I aborted one flight because of slushy snow and sleet in the air inlet ducts. The engine was not fitted with deflector plates to prevent this lethal arctic mixture blocking the inlet and depriving the engine of air. For Canadian contracts, and in place of the not altogether efficient deflector plates, most turbine powered Bells were fitted with a centrifuge system designed to separate and eliminate cohesive particles of snow and sleet to permit adequate airflow.

On one trip we carried a large, flat radio aerial dish for thirty-eight miles as underslung cargo and deposited it on a mountain peak. The cargo tended to oscillate violently when we were flying at anything more than twenty-five miles an hour and it was a long, slow unpleasant journey. The next day a railway worker was badly injured by the robot iron ore train and we flew him to hospital in Seven Islands. Two days later we were charted to take a group of fishermen and their gear from a tourist camp to Magpie Lake east of Seven Islands. Nobody could ever say this job was boring.

I stopped for coffee at Magpie Lake and was served by a very attractive young lady. "You're Paddy Jones," she said and I thought my fame was assured, until she added, "I remember you from the fishery patrols when I was a little girl." That torpedoed my ego.

The company asked me to fly one of their Bells down to Montreal for a periodic overhaul. After six hours forty minutes of flying we arrived to devastating news. The Bell 204B I had been flying only five weeks earlier had crashed and burned out, killing Red McKinnon and my relief pilot. No reason was given for this awful tragedy.

I flew a Bell Jet Ranger equipped with float pontoons from Lake Engler in north-west Saskatchewan to Uranium City forty minutes away. The whole flight was over swampy, interconnected waterways mostly choked with weeds. Uranium City was a mushroom town which had sprung up overnight when vast deposits of uranium had been discovered. At its peak the community had been likened to that of Dawson City in the gold rush.

The helicopter company had its headquarters in New Brunswick, from where it sent spare parts and mail for Uranium City either by helicopter or by Athabasca Airways in a single-engined Otter. Throughout Canadian summers, floatplanes were very popular.

One pilot, followed by the inevitable swarm of mosquitoes, came into the eating tent and sagged onto a box which passed for a chair and said, "I've been flying since five this morning and won't be finished until after eleven tonight."

So much for the mandatory maximum flying and duty hours

enshrined in law. This blatant breach of the regulations which many employers demanded of us was very common in Northern Canada where, in summer, it's daylight for most of the twenty-four hours.

My helicopter engineer, George Brown, knew his job but we did not always see eye-to-eye with regard to field maintenance. The machine's Allison engine had problems which, unless more than the usual care was taken when restarting from hot, could result in severe destructive damage. Brown's company had suffered five compressor failures and one complete loss of a turbine in a comparatively short space of time during the season. My logbook for the 4th August reads: 'With an Alouette engine this would be a very good helicopter.'

To be fair to the Allison engine many of its problems lay in its over-sophistication and its use in the type of bush work which its more ruggedly constructed piston predecessors had pioneered.

We were pestered by harmless black bears but had seen grizzlies from the helicopter. One black bear was shot invading the cooking tent but it could not be buried because it was impossible to dig a hole deep enough in the permafrost. If it had been left where it had been killed the stench would soon have become unbearable, so we slung it under the helicopter and I flew it out well clear of the camp and dropped it in the bush. I have always found it infinitely sad to see a wild and basically harmless creature destroyed simply because its nose had indicated a nice change of diet. Realistically I suppose that although this type of bear was harmless unless it had cubs, it could be extremely destructive. Almost a year to the day later my logbook recorded: 'All day on fires at Lac Renault and Cedar Rapids caused by one bear knocking over a propane fridge and burning down the cabin.'

As George Brown and I flew into Uranium City on the last day of the contract my entry in the logbook says: 'Uranium City for pilot switch — whole area forest fires. About to evacuate town. Fire within one mile of town perimeter. Smoke problems on approach.'

The European winter saw me engaged on the commercial side

with visits to Norway, Finland, Sweden and Algeria. In Algeria I came across a Piper Cub which an American had flown from the East Coast of the States — an impressive achievement. In Algeria I tried to buy some old Hughes 269A helicopters which were supposedly for sale, but got nowhere, due to political problems. So it was with a sense of relief I went back to Saskatchewan to fly a Cessna 188 Ag Truck for Howdy McPhail. The first job was to spray scrub trees which were to be eradicated so that the land could be cleared and used for cereal growing. The herbicide was a mixture of 24D and 245T. 245T which has since been banned in Canada although the New Zealanders carried on using it for several more years. Most of the work was done in and around Regina. I used a wheat and barley farm airstrip as my base and stayed with Doug Ellis, the farmer and his family. We also sprayed large acreages of flax as well as cereals.

Some of the flights from Doug Ellis's property could involve ferry trips of twelve or more miles because the fields to be sprayed didn't have an airstrip. On several occasions, having taken off at first light, we encountered fog sitting over the crop to be sprayed, making the job impossible and we had to return to the Ellis farm with a fully loaded aircraft. Landing in an empty machine was no problem, but due to the short length and uneven surface of the farm airstrip it could become very tricky with a fully laden aircraft. On such aborted sprays we could be loaded with one hundred and thirty gallons or more of an expensive liquid cargo. Jettisoning it was not the way to make friends.

For a week in July I was required to fly a Hughes 500 again for the *Societe d'energe de la Baie James* to the west of Shefferville on the Hydro Electric project. Again, I had problems with one of the controllers who refused to speak English. Knowing my knowledge of the language was minimal, he insisted on giving potentially critical in-flight instructions in French. These controllers were all fully capable of giving instructions in English but a minority, on purely political grounds, were refusing to do so.

This infantile stupidity almost caused a collision between my machine and a Bell Jet Ranger, both of us coming in to deposit heavy underslung cargo loads on a common landing pad. I vented my anger by saying, "Please give your instructions in the international language which we all understand. You must be aware that we pilots are by no means all French Canadians." Several were from Europe including a Finn and three Germans.

The controller attempted to interrupt in French but I overrode him. "My friend," I said, "The generally accepted language is English and not a bastardised Quebec interpretation of French." As can be imagined this dialogue did not go down well. My log book records: 'Am told to transfer N BR2 due lack of French. Will probably tell 'em to stuff it!' Next morning I flew to the sub-base for a pilot and machine switch and as my logbook records: 'Self to Montreal FM. Yes I did!'

At the end of the month I flew a Hughes 500 on forest fires around Lac Renault and Cedar Rapids in Quebec. News of my language problems had preceded me but the French Canadian crews were easy to get along with and the Crew Chief, Pierre, greeted me with the comment, "Our boys speak French and English and if they can't, they do pretty well on sign language."

The base of operations was the main highway. Very tall trees lined both sides of the road and nearby forestry had been reduced to charred stumps. Lightning strikes had started a fire within half a mile of the camp, the smoke ascending hundreds of feet. It took the combined efforts of five twin-engined fixed-wing water-bombing aircraft to get it under some sort of control. Our helicopters landed hose reels, portable fire pumps and the crews to man them in a clearing with a creek running through it.

Two days later torrential rain assisted our labours and extinguished the fires and reduced the hazard of further conflagrations. The helicopter was now engaged in the retrieval of the equipment from the surrounding bush and bringing in small parties of isolated fire crews. Some of the equipment had to be underslung vertically out of small clearings often accompanied by clouds of ash and cinders creating temporary visibility problems.

By the end of the month the worst was over and I flew the Hughes from Matagami to the airport at Rouyn. Three days later I was sitting in a Bell 47 near Banbury in England, contracted to spray fertiliser on potatoes and Brussels sprouts around Hereford.

In October, 1981, I passed the Full Flight Instructor's Rating (Helicopters) with Norman Bailey Helicopters at Blackbushe. The ground school requirement of 'chalk and talk' directed at an imaginary student was to follow the same style and patter utilised in countless flying schools. My previous experience as a Flying Instructor was a great help. Every two years in the UK a CAA Examiner or a delegated representative gets to re-examine you to check you are still teaching correct procedures. In the States the same time period applies but a satisfactory continuous instructional record usually gives an automatic pass. I was told that the English authorities usually make a meal of it, which I was to find to my cost several years later.

1982 opened with more aerial top dressing in the west of England but this time the Bell 47 was equipped with an Allison Gas Turbine engine. The 'hybrid', named after its developer, Joe Soloy, was the first to be placed on the British Aircraft Registry as G-SOLOY. Although the initial flight testing and theoretical computations required of the machine by the CAA had been conducted by another pilot, I was the first to fly it on agricultural operations in England. The gas turbine engine was similar to that fitted in the Bell Jet Ranger and very much lighter than the piston version it had replaced. In theory it should have been capable of carrying a greatly increased load but there were transmission torque restrictions, which meant that, although more than ample power was available, vitally important moving parts in the transmission train were not stressed for anything much in excess of the specification for the lower powered piston engine version.

According to the logbook summary for March, the helicopter never carried more than six hundred and seventy pounds of pellet fertiliser plus the weight of a hydraulically driven underslung bucket. Nevertheless it was very much a 'pilot's machine' and a dream to fly. On cross-country ferry flights it slid through the air with a smoothness and speed difficult to describe.

Howdy McPhail had come over from Canada and we flew a delivery flight to the first farm for nitrate treatment. All he was interested in were the economics of this new engine. He was already assessing the cost of a replacement turbine engine for its piston counterpart. My logbook records that we plastered a field of young barley with liquid seaweed. It was also my sixtieth birthday. We continued the work until the end of April. Around sixty hours of flying time on the Soloy had been completed without anything other than minor problems. The contract for this machine had expired and it was replaced by a piston engined Bell until the end of May. Then I was asked to fly a Jet Ranger for Norman Bailey as an air chauffeur for Derby Day at Epsom.

There were five outward trips, with four passengers, each from London in the morning and returning with the same passengers after the race meeting. The first flight had Britt Eckland in the front next to me. A friend told me she had said, "Yes, I flew both ways in the same helicopter with a really gorgeous pilot sitting right next to me!" I confess that made my day.

Then it was out yet again to Uganda to test two ex-Police Air Wing helicopters, one, a Bell 47, the other a Jet Ranger. Both required a lot of maintenance before earning a legal permit to fly.

Jock Jackson was an American fixed-wing pilot and a licensed engineer. When he discovered I also had a fixed-wing licence he asked me if I would like to help out with a delivery flight across Kenya in a Piper Aztec. It looked very old and tired but mechanically it was reasonably safe for the three-hour flight to Nairobi. There it would be completely overhauled. He had liked the regime under Idi Amin because Amin liked to fly. Now he had gone, the local engineers and pilots were not trained properly and were useless.

After a quick conversion course at Entebbe airport, Jock and I headed out for Kenya on September 5th and we passed through some very rough mountainous country. We had a worrying twenty minutes when the starboard engine intermittently lost power. However, we landed safely after three hours and fifteen minutes.

Back in England once more. there were several minor projects including delivery of a very old model Bell 47J2 where the pilot sat up in the nose with a bench for three passengers behind him. My next flying contract was to be my first in America. This was to spray against gypsy moth; a foliage eating insect which had infested large tracts of forestry in Pennsylvania. The helicopter was a three place Hillier 12E similar in performance to the Bell 47. Various companies had come together to take on this contract and my machine was owned by Barry Pruss who I had last met in Guyana. He had phoned me in England to offer me the job and explained that it involved flying very low over high trees in mountainous terrain for long periods. How could I refuse?

The helicopter was airborne out of Harrison, Ohio on May 12th 1983 and flying via Columbus, Wheeling and Washington, we night stopped at Bedford and next day flew on via Chambersburg to Gettysburg. The latter part of the journey was over hilly country and abundant pine forests. My logbook entry for the forty-minute flight between Bedford and Chambersburg has a terse but descriptive entry: 'Friday 13th begad — over high hills and heavy forestry!'

The engineer who had driven our supply truck from Harrison met me to tell me the operation was stood down until Monday. The small town of Gettysburg was full of tourists and we were lucky to get motel rooms. I was hoping to run the London Marathon in 1984 and took every opportunity to get in some training. This weekend was no different and I spent hours running over the Civil War battlefields.

The spraying was completed over a three-week period with most of it spent near the centre of the state. It was organised by the Department of the Environmental Resources for the Bureau of Forestry at Renovo, a small town on the impressive Susquehana River, surrounded on all sides by vast tracts of state forest with nowhere to go in the event of engine failure. The weather was a problem and high winds and torrential rain near the northern tip of the Appalachian Mountains forced me to put down on a forestry gravel road in the middle of nowhere one day.

The Moshannon State Forest to the southwest of Renovo was sprayed together with sections of badly infested trees near Tamarack. Here were the largest underground gas storage caverns in the world. There were a few days when the Hiller covered a thousand or more acres over a period of five hours flying time. The tanks carried around ninety gallons of a diluted insecticide with a low application rate of one and a half gallons per acre.

Some of these great forests were bordered by swiftly flowing rivers interlaced by more minor creeks and many, due to the rains, were raging torrents. None the less they were often the only

291

avenue of escape, albeit a very wet one, in the event of a power failure. The swathe distance between runs had to be judged by eye as there was no method we could employ over such an impenetrable wilderness of high trees. Much of this operation was both difficult and stressful with severe turbulence hitting us without warning caused by the combination of high winds and mountainous terrain.

The Chief Forester complimented us on a good job adding, "See you all again next year." But I had already decided that enough was enough. The return trip to Harrison was beset by bad weather and high adverse winds which necessitated a landing in the grounds of a farmhouse near Wilmington, Ohio, because I was low on fuel. A full jerrican of fuel had been secured in the cabin for just such an emergency and it was enough to get us to a small airfield at Clinton, which had a refuelling facility. Logbook entry reads: 'Land in hail and heavy rain — refuel — torrential rain — unpleasant! I landed at Harrison with a huge sigh of relief.

Soon it was back to Hereford for June, flying a Bell 47. I was working for Mike Davis, boss of MD Helicopters. We had been friends for a long time and he reminded me of the last time I had worked there. I had been spraying until it was late evening and the light failing to the point where I could not see the two men marking a large fifty-acre field of potatoes. They were supplied with boxes of matches and instructions to strike one or more as soon as they could see the helicopter coming towards them. The sudden striking of an old fashioned match lit up the field marker, otherwise invisible against a dark hedge.

I went back to Ohio for the summer, doing spraying work there and also in Indiana and Kentucky. We sprayed crops of soybean, sweet corn, pumpkins, melons and a small acreage of tobacco. It was one of the hottest summers on record and day temperatures were in the upper nineties. Although an air-filtering mask was worn and both of the Perspex side doors had been removed, the intense heat combined with chemical fumes on landing to refuel the spray hoppers, contributed in no small way to a miserable summer. The job was also blessed with vile ground organisation.

For this, the owner of the aircraft was in no way to blame. The machine was rented out to a local corn and seed merchant, a man who had no idea how to conduct a safe and efficient aerial spraying operation. We were applying insecticides and herbicides, some of which possessed selective weed control properties. Due to the hot, dry weather, on a number of occasions, I had advised the contractor not to apply the chemical as serious damage to some neighbouring crops was likely to occur. Later an insurance claim came in from a soybean farmer who claimed that the whole of his crop had been written off. But I was only a helicopter pilot, what did I know? The entire seasonal spray operation was abysmally organised from beginning to end. Water tankers were not positioned correctly and all too often errors were made in booking areas to be sprayed. Landing sites had not been pre-arranged and, to economise on moving a tanker, the contractor tried to get me to land illegally on the verge of a main highway.

There was a notable exception to this otherwise dreadful operation. An ex-helicopter spray pilot called 'Corky', who was paralysed from the waist down as the result of a flying accident, showed how to organise a spraying operation. This was near Indianapolis. He had arranged an adequate water supply, made sketches in considerable detail giving obstructions such as telephone wires or power cables and noted which chemicals were to be used and application rates for each field.

The last operation was near Harrisburg on an experimental farm. The logbook entry reads: 'Ferry to experimental farm, Purdue University for test flying various insecticides on soybean. Weather very hot. 21 flights with following insecticides against Mexican bean beetle — Testing residue life of compounds — Ambush — Lannate — Nudrin — Pydrin — Payoff — Cython and unnamed compounds. Temp. 1500hrs 104 deg F Total 18 plots. Deadly heat.' On a personal note I lost my Swiss Army knife, a Christmas present from the South African Air Force.

During this contract I had been staying in a Hotel at Lawrenceburg next door to a small automobile spare parts store, whose owner, an elderly man, had been an apprentice at Ford's, Dagenham many years before. I spent some evenings with him as he like to talk about Dagenham and things English. One evening he asked me if I drank cocktails. A bit bemused I said, "Yes, why?" He had seen some bottles being sold off at a market and had bought them. He opened the fridge and took out two grey earthenware bottles each sealed with a wire cap. We opened them — mine seemed to be mostly gin and it tasted fine. We had several and I left him and retired to bed.

I was wakened in the middle of the night by the local police banging on my door. Was I the pilot out of Harrison? Had I been with the old man last night? "Come with us," they said. They marched me down to the automotive store where the body of the old man lay on the floor, obviously dead. The police, now very officious, asked me if this was the man I had been drinking with the previous evening. The only answer was 'Yes.' "We have been into the store and found a few of these empty bottles right next to the ice box and it looks like there are more inside. Looks like he had been drinking them. Did you have any?"

I looked at the bottles and with a queasy feeling in my stomach replied that I'd had two or three drinks. I explained briefly what I knew of the origin of the bottles and a doctor was called who eventually determined that my friend had died of a heart attack and that there was nothing more sinister in the bottles than really strong cocktails.

Nonetheless I had lost all interest in going back to sleep and spent the rest of the night in the company of a bottle of Scotch and the radio. No, I didn't fly the next day.

CHAPTER SEVENTEEN

Flight Instructor

LATE IN MARCH 1977, I HAD FLOWN AN OLD SIKORSKY 55 helicopter owned by Autair out of Rhodesia and into South Africa, there to be placed in safe storage at a small airport known as Grand Central, halfway between the cities of Pretoria and Johannesburg. Shortly after this I joined the South African Air Force with the rank of Major and, later, whilst flying Alouette 3 gunships, I got permission to have the Sikorsky stored at the South African Airforce Museum at Lanseria and flew it there, with my Commanding Officer, Commandant Frane, in the co-pilot's seat. This old Sikorsky had been the very first helicopter to enter military service with the SAAF many years before and, not surprisingly, the Airforce was interested in possibly actually acquiring it as a permanent exhibit in its museum.

In the event, Autair, the machine's owners in London, were more interested in selling it commercially, but were not successful in doing so and, consequently, a few years later, it was transferred by road to be stored in a hangar on the small airfield known as Wonderboom, near Pretoria. There it stayed for many years until some kind of agreement was finally reached between Autair and the SAAF and I was asked to fly it to my old Service Base at Swartzkop. It was rumoured the SAAF had swapped an old Harvard for it, of the type I'd once flown in sky writing.

The story of the Sikorsky should have ended there in a safe and honourable retirement. But it didn't. To my disgust and that of Warrant Officer Stein, the Sikorsky expert who'd been my engineer/gunner when I'd flown patrols along the Angola border on the lookout for Cuban and Russian insurgents, it was crashed by a pilot attempting an impossible landing at a nearby military museum. This fine old machine was a total write-off.

Since 1981 I had held a Full Instructor's Rating on helicopters which I had renewed every two years with no problems. It was now November 1987 and a renewal was due again. It was arranged for it to take place at Cranfield. In addition to other operations of an instructional nature, much of them overseas on both fixed-wing and helicopter; something like nine hundred hours had been logged in England. Although my licence was endorsed to instruct on several types of helicopter the majority had been on the Robinson 22. This machine has been subjected to a lot of criticism recently, but I had five hundred accident free hours as an Instructor on this type. The majority of my students gained their licences on this machine.

I took a Robinson up to Cranfield. The Examiner was employed as a senior instructor at a large flying training school on the airfield. During the flying test I had a difference of opinion with him concerning the suitability of the weather for the test. This may have had some bearing on his subsequent actions. On several occasions he made it known that my flying technique was not up to scratch. I could see the way the wind was blowing.

Not wishing to waste time and money, I promptly terminated the exercise and put down onto the airfield to fast taxi back to the Control Tower. He yelled, "You're taxiing too fast!" Knowing it to be a no win situation I retorted, "If you don't like it, you can get out and walk."

There was a further unpleasant sequence of events in de-briefing and of course he did not renew my rating. As I was leaving I reminded him that two years earlier he'd had no problems at all in renewing my rating and so, what price the on-going efficiency of the fifty or so students who had passed through my hands? As I walked out the door I heard him mutter that what had happened in the past was unimportant.

I later discovered that, before moving to Cranfield, this examiner had been based at an airfield in the south-east where, through lack of attention to the critical engine temperature gauge when starting up, he had allowed two Allison Jet Turbines to dangerously overheat. On both occasions the engines were a total loss and on both occasions he'd had students on board. Consequently he had left the south-east airfield in something of a hurry and had turned up at Cranfield. A few weeks later, conducting an instructional exercise involving slope landings with a borrowed Robinson 22, and with a student under instruction on board, he lost control to roll the machine over. Another complete write-off. Fortunately both he and the student were unhurt. But such was the gentleman that the CAA had designated to carry out examinations!

Hot starts were a very dangerous phenomena and could occur when the starting batteries were low on power, but there were other reasons. There was a simple and efficient drill to be employed if the temperature gauge showed signs of a faster than normal increase in temperature: it merely involved closing the throttle. Any competent pilot would know that and this man was an 'examiner'.

The only bad time I had with a Robinson 22 was near High Wycombe in 1987. I had a lady student on board for a trial instructional flight. This type of exercise was a fairly normal procedure for those who might decide after the completion of the short flight that they'd like to take flying lessons. In order to add a little variety to these excursions and to afford a break for the student, it was common to momentarily land and immediately to take off again from a small farm near a village called Stokenchurch. Apart from breaking the possible monotony of flying over the relatively open countryside, it demonstrated, for the benefit of the student, that the helicopter did not require a long runway. The farm was owned by an old friend who did not mind me using one of his fields occasionally. The flight had taken thirty minutes and the lady was delighted with it saying she would be back for lessons.

I was in the flight office filling in the paperwork for the next training sortie when the pupil returned hurriedly saying, "Paddy. I think there's a hole in one of the rotor blades." We walked out to the machine and sure enough near the trailing edge on one of the two main rotors was what appeared to be a well-defined bullet hole right through the blade. The police were brought in and I took one of them up with me to show him the track of our flight, but nothing was ever resolved. I expect that sort of thing in Malaya or Angola but Buckinghamshire?

In November 1986, Ira Curtiss, the owner of the one and only Robinson 22 in Chile and who had received flying instruction from me, met me in Santiago. A London company was interested in acquiring two helicopters, one known to be in Paraguay, the other thought to be in Chile. Ira had been a fixed-wing aerobatic pilot and had only recently taken up rotary-wing flight. It was hoped that his Robinson would be the first of many in Chile. The military had shown an interest in its potential for flying training.

Ira introduced me to the second-in-command and Director of Operations of the Chilean Air Force, Lieutenant General Ramon Vega Hidalgo. Could I put on a demonstration for his officers? Of course. So that afternoon, the Robinson, an Alpha model with full instrumentation, was put through its paces for forty-five minutes. Several full engine-off autorotations were demonstrated down to the grass and these together with other manoeuvres, spectacular but serving little practical purpose, were displayed to the assembled military.

There was a second flight at the request of the General, who, saying, "I'd like to make a flight with you," had climbed aboard. I flew him over the foothills of the Andes at six thousand feet and he seemed very impressed. Whether any order was ever placed I don't know.

I flew a Cessna 140 to Quintero on the Pacific coast over some magnificent mountain scenery but with considerable turbulence. I had been told of a large cache of spare parts for the Bell 47. They were there sure enough, in a large storehouse, and I have yet to see so many spares in one place. Unfortunately they were useless to us because there was no documentation of any kind with them and so legally we could not acquire them.

I also took the opportunity before I left for home to fly with Ira in his Stinson 108. It certainly brought back early memories of my time in Australia.

Returning to England I tried once more to renew my Instructors Rating but with no success. I had done a refresher course at Fairoaks with Captain Summers. He said, "You'll have no problem. The flying was fine and the board work is just as they want it."

I briefed the Examiner and flew with him in the Bell. He said, "If you can satisfy me with the result of the written test and a verbal quiz, the most I can award you is an Assistant Instructor's rating." He continued with, "Have you flown a Bell before?"

I gave up and told him that an Assistants rating was no use to me and would place me in the position of having to ask a fully rated instructor to check my student before I could send him solo.

After the failure to get my Instructor Rating back I went on a contract to Fort McMurray in Alberta to fly a Bell Jet Ranger for the Syncrude Oil Sands Complex. It was a long time since I had flown out of there, which was when it was known as Site 800 on the Canada Defence Line.

Much of the country on both sides of the Athabasca River was muskeg swamp. Torrential rain had stopped the use of trucks and severely restricted the tracked vehicles like the Bombadier. So both of the company's helicopters were employed flying dawn to dusk moving men and equipment over gravel roads that were really covered in mud, sometimes as much as four feet deep. I flew in excess of forty hours in five days, logging twelve hours forty-five minutes on one day. It rained continuously accompanied by high winds. It was demanding and dangerous work.

It stopped raining and we went back to normal working hours. I took two passengers up to a scrubby and relatively dry clearing in the centre of a swamp of vast proportions. The two men returned to the helicopter after twenty minutes wanting to go to Kearl Lake, a short distance north-west. I gave them the thermos while I checked the machine, then with the three of us aboard and doors shut I applied the starting procedure. There was no response. I spent an hour checking the battery and anything else I could think of but the engine was dead. Because we were on the ground our limited radio equipment was incapable of contacting the base in order to enlist help or technical advice. It was a bad situation and someone had to walk out to the nearest road several miles away. As I was in current running practice having just done the London Marathon, I was nominated. Fortunately Peter Stevens insisted on coming with me, leaving Rod Hoffman in the helicopter in case anyone came looking for us.

It took just over five hours to reach the Kearl Lake road. At times we were up to our waists in ice-cold water and on occasion both of us fell into weed-clogged creeks. In sight of the road I got cramp and had it not been for Peter who supported me over the last four hundred metres I don't think I would have made it. After I had recovered, we walked for another hour and a half before a forestry truck picked us up to take us to Mildred Lake. Later that evening I flew back with an engineer to the patiently waiting Rod. The engine fault turned out to be a stuck solenoid and very simple to fix had I located the problem.

In August in England I was demonstrating a Robinson 22 when a gentleman who looked vaguely familiar approached me. He was a Greek businessman I had worked for several years earlier spraying olive groves in Kefallinia and Rhodes. This time he was looking for two helicopters and crews to spray locusts in Algeria.

My London colleague had provided machines and crews for Greeks before but was not keen to do so again. The financial arrangements had not always been honoured. Nevertheless, I took a chance and worked out an arrangement for two Bell Jet Rangers with spraying gear and crews to be leased from a British company and I would take operational control in Algeria. Both machines were air freighted to Algiers at the beginning of October.

We reassembled the machines outside the hangar in appalling heat. Temperatures rarely dropped below 100 degrees Fahrenheit during the day. In spite of the fact that we were in Algeria to combat what had been forecast to be an invasion of crop eating locusts on a totally unprecedented scale, no assistance of any kind was forthcoming from any Algerian official in his air-conditioned office. However, the ordinary engineers in the hangar did help when their bosses were absent. We eventually readied the machines for air checks and, having been flown and assessed fit for operation, there was no indication of any kind that they were other than completely serviceable.

Civil unrest was now rife. One day travelling to the hotel, our vehicle was stopped at an illegal roadblock near the city centre. A ragged gang of youths ordered us out of the car and then threw our personal belongings into the road. One of them was pouring gasoline over the vehicle prior to torching it when, to our immense relief, a tank and a number of soldiers rumbled up behind us and the would-be saboteurs took to their heels.

The police were polite and generally helpful. We were told, "When your two helicopters leave here for the operational area, it is unsafe to land anywhere other than at a military installation or protected airport. We are having a lot of trouble in the countryside." The machines were bearing the Arabic insignia of the Algerian Government but the policeman told us that this would probably work against us.

We gave a lift to two Eastern bloc engineers who had been left behind in Algiers when their aircraft had moved south. We flew in loose formation on a southerly heading through high rugged mountains and experienced periods of extreme turbulence. We stopped overnight at the well-guarded airport at Tiaret. The logbook blandly states: '2 hrs 5 mins turbulence — adventurous flight.'

Next morning we set out on the long desert crossing to the military base at Mecheria and were following the railroad when a red light suddenly appeared on the instrument panel. It was telling us that metal substances were being picked up on an internally fitted magnetic plug. The normal procedure would have been to land, take out the plug and inspect the metal to see what was happening. A large quantity of metal could indicate that the engine was breaking up. We found a spot to land far away from any villages. Tim looked at the plug but was not certain what it showed. He cleaned the plug and as we got airborne he pointed at a mass of people racing towards us with sticks and cudgels. Whether this was a friendly greeting or not could be open to debate, but we did not stay around to find out.

An hour and forty minutes later we were approaching Mecharia. We skirted a large half moon shaped mountain called Djebel Antar and saw large groups of people collecting in what we assumed to be the town square. Bearing in mind the police advice we flew into the local military base to be greeted with smiles from the Commandant.

Tim got out his toolkit and removed the plug. There were particles of metal attached but it was very difficult to determine where they had come from. Metal particles do find their way into engines from contaminated fuel and oil. We knew this engine had been recently overhauled by a facility near Oxford. It was possible

301

that small slivers of metal in the working parts had not all been completely removed prior to the engine being topped up with oil. If this was the case then there was no problem because, either with usage or with draining the oil, the engine would remedy itself. We were now five hours flying time from Algiers. We did not have a replacement engine and if this one was about to become unserviceable another had to be obtained from England and because of the time delay, we could lose the contract for both machines.

I made the decision to carry on to our destination, El Abiodh, a completely isolated village with a small airfield. We arrived over it mentally congratulating ourselves, when the red light came on again. We put down and dropped off the two long-suffering Yugoslav engineers whose many fixed-wing aircraft were lined up on the strip. Inspection revealed more metal on the magnetic plug. So now it was obvious, a replacement engine was necessary. Fortunately, the locusts had not yet made an appearance and HQ at Algiers decided to bring us back because large swarms were on the Tunisian/Algerian border. Again I took a calculated risk to fly back to Algiers, with the other helicopter flying with us keeping a watching brief and acting as insurance.

Both aircraft landed back at Algiers without any unexpected problems. The red light came on from time to time and Andy would circle the spot while I put down and Tim cleared the plug. All he said was, "It's getting much worse." After flying over the formidable range of mountains into Algiers my logbook tersely records: 'Very hard on the nerves.' That was an understatement.

We were posted to Bou Saada, two hours flying time away on the edge of the Sahara. In the meanwhile Tim and I had quietly arranged to have an exchange engine air freighted from England and delivered by truck. Before leaving, Tim and I had a long discussion regarding the durability of our engine. "I don't know," said Tim, "It should have quit by now but if you're game for another two hours flying over the mountains into Bou Saada, I'll hack it."

The logbook makes interesting reading: 'Engine chip light on 8 mins out of Algiers. Most unpleasant flight through initial mountain range — extremely rugged — very windy. Ran into sand storm 60 knot wind — land work's compound — stones thrown at both aircraft — police arrived and assailants ran away — cleaned magnetic plug engine — took off from Dirah at dusk with restricted visibility. Chip light on again 15 mins before landing Bou Saada in dark. Tim and I very relieved. Most unpleasant 5 days.'

The owner of the aircraft had come out from England and with his help Tim, Andy and myself rigged up a wooden tripod. The place was in the open desert on the edge of the sand airstrip. There were no buildings or facilities at all, just the very long emergency runway. The engine arrived that evening and we set to work. We also fitted low volume spray equipment and finished off with the calibration tests.

At last both aircraft were ready to combat the locust hordes when they moved in. Believe it or not, they never did!

Obtaining turbine fuel was a major problem. It was the responsibility of the Algerian Government to place fuel drums at various locations. These were usually outside towns or villages or, wherever possible, on local airstrips being used by the Eastern bloc fixed-wing spray crews. All too often we would arrive to find no sign of fuel so we adopted the habit of carrying an emergency supply in two jerricans in the passenger cabin.

The Eastern bloc aircraft used normal aviation gasoline in their piston engines but we, with jet turbines, had to burn JP4, a type of diesel. Their pilots often came across and helped us with the hand pumping into our hungry fuel tank. Some were Russians, some from Bulgaria, Hungary and Rumania, all flying Russian machines including the massive single radial engined Antinov. Their cruising speed was little better than 90 miles per hour and they had flown at this speed from Eastern Europe to Algeria.

Locusts were in short supply so we were directed to fly further afield hunting swarms and all the time public unrest was building. Disturbances then started to spread into the areas where we were swarm hunting and we were informed by Military Intelligence that some of these insurrectionist groups were in possession of ground to air missiles. At this time we were based at Bechar near the Moroccan border and we had a Major attached to our unit for a day or so. He was a helicopter pilot who had trained in Russia and knew the area well and how to avoid the most dangerous areas. One of our flights took us along the sluggish Zousfana River to an oasis called Tarhit where we saw what is reputed to be the highest sand dune in the world, towering several hundred feet above the desert. At a local airstrip we stopped to refuel and there were dead locusts everywhere. Vehicle wheel tracks suggested that they had been sprayed from the ground.

At an agricultural project one day, we heard the sound of gunfire. We rapidly took cover under a scrub bush and within minutes a light tank and an armoured car came screaming up to disgorge heavily armed militia who headed past at a run towards the source of what was now heavy firing. We sprinted back to our machine and executed the fastest take-off in history. The local police came to see us later and said, "You were lucky, Captain. One of my men was badly injured but we got seven of them!"

The contract ended near the end of November. My logbook entry for the 27th reads: 'Flight check — Bulgarian pilot as passenger — Engineer on board — Weather very wet — cold, temp 45 F.' This sort of weather in Algeria is described as arctic.

Getting my money out of the Greek businessman was another long story. Only after much hassle and many months later did I get a payment but not all that was due to me by any means. This time I did learn from experience.

The suspension of the British Helicopter Flight Instructors Rating had not been forgotten. Accordingly and, I confess, to make a point, I completed ground and flight school instruction in the United States for a Commercial Flight Instructor addition to my FAA Licence. Having passed the written tests, I took the flying examination in a Hiller in Quakertown, Pennsylvania and passed. My Examiner, an ex-USAF Colonel, complimented me with, "If all of my applicants were up to your standard my job would be a deal easier!"

It was 17th May 1989 and I was sixty-seven years old.

304